Manipulating Globalization

ASIA-PACIFIC RESEARCH CENTER

Studies of the Walter H. Shorenstein Asia-Pacific Research Center

Andrew G. Walder, General Editor

The Walter H. Shorenstein Asia-Pacific Research Center in the Freeman Spogli Institute for International Studies at Stanford University sponsors interdisciplinary research on the politics, economies, and societies of contemporary Asia. This monograph series features academic and policy-oriented research by Stanford faculty and other scholars associated with the Center.

Manipulating Globalization

THE INFLUENCE OF BUREAUCRATS ON BUSINESS IN CHINA

Ling Chen

Stanford University Press
Stanford, California

Stanford University Press
Stanford, California

Printed and bound by CPI Group (UK) Ltd, Croydon, CR0 4YY

Library of Congress Cataloging-in-Publication Data

Names: Chen, Ling, 198– author.
Title: Manipulating globalization : the influence of bureaucrats on business in China / Ling Chen.
Other titles: Studies of the Walter H. Shorenstein Asia-Pacific Research Center.
Description: Stanford, California : Stanford University Press, 2018. | Series: Studies of the Walter H. Shorenstein Asia-Pacific Research Center | Includes bibliographical references and index.
Identifiers: LCCN 2017038610 | ISBN 9781503604797 (cloth : alk. paper) | ISBN 9781503605695 (epub)
Subjects: LCSH: China—Economic policy—2000– | Industrial policy—China. | Local government—China. | Bureaucracy—Economic aspects—China. | Globalization—Economic aspects—China.
Classification: LCC HC427.95 .C433414 2018 | DDC 338.0951—dc23
LC record available at https://lccn.loc.gov/2017038610

Typeset by Thompson Type in 11/14 Adobe Garamond

For Sophie

Contents

List of Illustrations

Figures

Tables

Acknowledgments

Writing this book turned out to be a longer journey than I originally thought. It took me five research trips in China throughout 2008, 2009–2010, 2011, 2014, and 2017. The process involved a total of 18 months of intense fieldwork across approximately 10 cities and discussions with 272 interviewees, such as local bureaucrats, firm managers, and scholars. These trips were not only to collect adequate qualitative and quantitative data; they also served the purpose of keeping the research updated as much as possible. As many correctly observed, "China is a moving target." Catching this target means constantly staying on top of what has happened, is happening, and will likely happen with government officials, foreign investors, and domestic businesses on the ground. Equally challenging is making sense of the extremely complicated relations through a social-scientific lens and communicating to readers without inducing boredom. Paradoxically, what I ended up demonstrating toward the end of this book is that many elements remain firmly entrenched. The varieties of local capitalism that started to take shape more than 100 years ago in China have set regions on different paths of development in the globalized era today.

It is absolutely impossible to accomplish such a task alone. I am grateful for so many people who have helped me along this journey, and I ask for forgiveness if I leave anyone out. First of all, sincere thanks go to Kellee Tsai and Mark Blyth. They are my academic parents. Kellee has been one of the most amazing scholars that anyone could possibly have the luck to work with. I thank her for her continuous guidance, patience, and critiques over the past 11 years. I have learned a tremendous amount from her, not only on how to produce academic work but also how to be a respectable scholar. It also would not have been possible for me to make it this far without Mark Blyth. I truly appreciate the incredible amount of support from him along the way, both when he was at Johns Hopkins and after he moved to Brown. His encouragement has been crucial for me to get through the toughest times in my academic life.

Special thanks go to Peter Evans for being generous with his time. Peter carefully read and provided insightful comments on various chapters of the project at different stages. It was a privilege for me to work under his guidance, and his work has always inspired my own. I also thank Erin Chung, Ho-fung Hung, and Margaret Keck for reading and commenting on my work and for constructive suggestions that significantly improved the project. In addition, I thank Brown University for hosting me as a visiting research fellow. I am grateful for helpful discussions with Melani Cammett, Patrick Heller, and Richard Snyder.

I have been very fortunate to benefit from two postdoctoral positions, at Stanford and at Harvard Kennedy School. As a Shorenstein Postdoctoral Fellow at Stanford, I received valuable feedback from participants in the China Social Science Workshop led by Jean Oi, Andrew Walder, and Xueguang Zhou. I thank them for sharpening my perspectives through challenging questions, which propelled me to thoroughly revise and rewrite the manuscript. At Harvard Kennedy School, I benefited substantially from various workshops and events at the Ash Center directed by Anthony Saich. I thank all the participants in the Rajawali workshop for their insightful questions and feedback.

The final part of the book manuscript was completed after I joined the Johns Hopkins School of Advanced International Studies (SAIS) as an assistant professor. I have been surrounded by wonderful colleagues with sharp perspectives and an eagerness to help. The book was substantially improved and became more cohesive due to comments and suggestions from Deborah Brautigam, Andrew Cheon, Charles Doran, Carla Freeman, Dan Honig, Pravin Krishna, Mike Lampton, Matthias Mattijs, Jonas Nahm, David Steinberg, Pavithra Suryanarayan, Heiwai Tang, and many others. For superb research assistance, I thank Yuanchen Cai, Dario Sidhu, Hao Zhang, and Yujin Zhang.

Margaret Pearson and Meg Rithmire deserve special mention for their extremely careful reading of every page of the manuscript and their detailed and remarkably insightful comments both on paper and in person. The book would have been in much rougher shape without their input. Many other scholars have read and commented on the project at various stages. I am grateful for insightful feedback from Loren Brandt, David Bulman, Xun Cao, Bruce Dickson, Gary Gereffi, Xian Huang, Kyle Jaros, Lizhi Liu, Eddy Malesky, Melanie Manion, Andrew Mertha, Victor Shih, Susan Shirk, Juan Wang, Yuhua Wang, Joe Wong, Dali Yang, Jin Zeng, and Lu Zhang. I also thank participants in the "New Faces in China Studies" Conference in the Department of Political Science at Duke University and the China Speaker Series at the University of California San Diego. My heartfelt thanks go to Yue Hou, Xiaojun Li, Adam Liu, and Fei Yan for providing me spiritual as well as academic support. They are not only rising stars in our field but also incredibly sincere friends whom I am blessed to have.

Research on this book was made possible by support from multiple sources of institutional support received at different times, including the Social Science Research Council, the Andrew Mellon Foundation, the Shorenstein Postdoctoral Fellowship at Stanford University, the Chiang Ching-Kuo Foundation Junior Scholar Grant, the OYCF–1990 Institute Joint Research Fellowship, and the Nicole Suveges Research Fellowship.

Perhaps those who deserve the most thanks for the book itself are the numerous local officials, businessmen, and development zone managers in China that I interviewed and conducted semistructured surveys with, although I was able to mention only some of them in the book. I have learned tremendously from them, and I thank them for correcting my naïve views about Chinese political economy from time to time. I appreciate the generous help offered by Chen Guangjin, Jin Xinyi, Li Jianjun, Yuan Ruijun, Zhao Shukai, and Zhang Changdong. Without these scholars, I would not have been able to carry out even the initial field research in many of the Chinese cities, not to mention conducting semistructured interviews, implementing surveys, or collecting quantitative data from hundreds of thousands of firms. I also want to reserve special thanks to Zhu Tianbiao for introducing me to the field of political economy while I was an undergraduate student at Peking University. He certainly caused a critical turning point in my life. After taking his classes, I decided to pursue an academic career rather than working as a consultant for a foreign firm in China.

Last but certainly not the least, I owe the most gratitude to my family. I want to give sincere thanks to my husband Jeff. In addition to being an excellent scholar himself, he has always made time to support me as much as he possibly can. He is always the first reader of every piece of my academic writing and provides detailed, constructive feedback. He has been very patient with my working habits. I am also very grateful to my parents, who have worked hard to provide me unconditional support throughout my life. Without them I would not have been able to make it nearly as far as I am today. My daughter Sophie was born at the final stage of completing the manuscript. She brings light to my world, and I dedicate this book to her with love.

Ling Chen
Washington, DC

Major Abbreviations

BIP	Bureau of Investment Promotion
BST	Bureau of Science and Technology
CCP	Chinese Communist Party
CRT	Cathode ray tube
EIC	Economic and Information Commission
ETDZ	Economic and Technology Development Zones
FDI	Foreign direct investment
FETB	Foreign Economic and Trade Bureau
FIE	Foreign invested enterprises
HLM	Hierarchical linear modeling
HTDZ	High-Technology Development Zone
IC	Integrated circuit
ICT	Information communication technology
ISI	Important substitution industrialization
IT	Information technology
JV	Joint venture
LCD	Liquid crystal displays
MNC	Multinational corporation
MOC	Ministry of Commerce

MOST	Ministry of Science and Technology
NDRC	National Development and Reform Commission
ODM	Original design manufacturer
OECD	Organization for Economic Cooperation and Development
OEM	Original equipment manufacturer
SDPC	State Development and Planning Commission
SETC	State Economic and Trade Commission
SEZ	Special economic zone
SPC	State Planning Commission
SSTC	State Science and Technology Commission
TVE	Township and village enterprise
UNCTAD	United Nations Conference on Trade and Development
WFOE	Wholly foreign-owned enterprise
WTO	World Trade Organization

Manipulating Globalization

CHAPTER 1

Bureaucrats, Businesses, and Economic Policies in a Globalized China

In 2005, China's then Minister of Commerce, Bo Xilai, tried to convince Organization for Economic Cooperation and Development (OECD) representatives in a Paris conference that China did not pose a real threat to manufacturing industries in other countries. "China must export 800 million shirts in exchange for the value of only one Boeing A380 aircraft," he said. The comment was intended to relieve the worry of conference representatives from industrialized countries in light of China's large trade surplus. When the statement was later released in the media, however, it aroused strong sentiments from the Chinese public. "China is absolutely miserable," lamented one web commentator. "China cannot be the permanent factory for the world," wrote a Yale-educated Chinese intellectual, who later turned his comment into a book (Xue 2006). Many voices questioned the sustainability of relying on cheap labor and razor-thin profit margins, calling instead for fundamental changes in the manufacturing industry.

To get the story straight, the challenge for China—and for other emerging economies throughout Asia, Latin America, and Africa today—is not simply a matter of switching from making shirts and shoes to producing computers and airplanes.[1] In fact, China's largest manufacturing industries have already changed from textiles to computers and mobile phones.[2] Between 1995 and 2006, China's share of the world's high-tech exports has increased almost eightfold; since 2006, the country has become the world's largest high-tech exporter, surpassing Japan, the United States, and the European Union (Meri 2009). Globalization has undoubtedly contributed to the ascendance of China as the world's manufacturing titan. The problem, rather, is "high technology but low (or no) innovation." The fragmentation of the manufacturing process allows the country to engage in the mass production of high-tech goods with little innovation and much reliance on the low cost of labor. With labor and material costs sharply rising, strikes increasing, export markets shrinking, and currency appreciating, policy makers have started to realize that the economy has hit a turning point that needs to go beyond the "middle income trap."

The Chinese state, to its credit, is actively trying to address the problem. Just as they created preferential policy packages to attract foreign direct investment (FDI) decades ago, the Chinese state has recently launched a big transition. The central state issued a combination of government funding, taxation, land and utilities reduction, and tariff exemption, among others, to promote innovation by their own industrial firms, 93 percent of which are domestic private businesses. The government ranked development zones, assigned and evaluated policy targets, and admonished firms that they ought to exit the "race to the bottom" competition, invest in innovation, and move up the value chain. Indeed, Chinese officials constantly cite Japan and South Korea of the 1960s as role models, where a developmental and authoritarian state used industrial policies as carrots and sticks to push firms to develop global competitiveness.

The success of such state-led transformation is based on two assumptions: that local officials have the incentive to implement such policies and that these policies, when implemented, will work. These assumptions, surprisingly, are also often suggested by many studies of industrial and development policies. In reality, however, when policies are implemented, they produced a highly mixed and confusing picture, causing intensive debate among scholars and policy observers. There were pessimists who showed considerable doubt about China's ability to build its indigenous competitiveness beyond just being the world's workshop, optimists who saw Chinese firms as an ultimate beneficiary of global production with or without state support, and alarmists who took the state's plan seriously and expressed deep concern about the implications of the state-sponsored plan for the market economy (Arayama and Mourdoukoutas 1999; Chan and Ross 2003; Steinfeld 2004, 2010; Gilboy 2004; Branstetter and Lardy 2006; Breznitz and Murphee 2011; Herrigel, Wittke, and Voskamp 2013; Brandt and Thun 2010; McGregor 2010; Miles 2011; Dean, Browne, and Oster 2010; Bradsher 2010).

The goal of this book is not to side with any of these groups but to actually *explain* the source of the confusion. It explores the roots of substantial variation in implementing economic policies across this continent-sized economy. Even within the same industry and at similar levels of economic conditions, heterogeneity persists throughout main manufacturing cities. Among other contributions, this study unpacks the ways in which local bureaucrats interpret state upgrading policies, fight for resources, and form coalitions within a globalized context where foreign and domestic businesses coexist. It also unfolds in detail why well-intended, seemingly unified national policies end up producing heterogeneous and often counterproductive outcomes. Whereas, in some cities, government advocates for reforms were able to seize the initiative to introduce a matrix of new policies and garner resources, the same initiative was retarded by the vested interests and bureaucratic competition in other cities. Although government support in funding and tax cuts succeeded in nurturing motivation for upgrading among local private businesses in some localities, it dampened their incentives to invest in learning and innovation in other localities, deprived them of developmental spaces, and left firms in a continuous, desperate race to the bottom competition.

Such variation needs to be understood in light of China's two stages of transformation, the attraction of FDI in the first stage and the push for local upgrading in the second stage. The strong bias in favor of foreign firms throughout the 1990s and early 2000s has made China the largest recipient of FDI among developing countries. With inward FDI to China reaching an annual record of US$105.7 billion and foreign invested enterprises (FIEs) producing 88 percent of China's $282 billion high-tech exports, global firms have become part of daily economic life (National Bureau of Statistics [NBS] 2007, 2011; Ministry of Commerce [MOC] 2008). For this reason, China presents a new generation of "globalized" economies—notably Brazil, Russia, India, China (BRIC)—in which FDI played a much more essential role in comparison to the last generation of East Asian developers (notably Japan, South Korea, and Taiwan) (Hsueh 2011; Tsai and Pekkanen 2006).

In the mid- to late 2000s, however, the central state gradually phased out preferential policies for FIEs and used similar policies in government funding and tax breaks to promote indigenous technology competitiveness, especially among domestic private enterprises. Yet instead of replacing the previous pro-FIE policies, the old and new initiative coexisted with tension in localities, creating competition for shifting resources among government–business coalitions who saw themselves benefiting from different policy paradigms. This book finds that the type of alliances that local officials formed with FIEs in the earlier stage shaped the interpretation of policies, the patterns of bureaucratic competition, the dynamics of resource allocation, and local development trajectories in the later period. That is, even if one could argue that foreign capital is not as important as it was in the 1990s, the potential strength of vested interests that it cultivated among the local bureaucrats and the incentive structure it built for domestic businesses remain path dependent in the 2000s.

The influence of globalization on policy outcomes, however, was made possible only through local bureaucratic agents. In an authoritarian country where businesses do not have direct channels to influence the party state, local state officials are the direct agents who conduct economic policies and advance the interests of their business clients.[3] This book finds that local bureaucrats who are employed in the Chinese state apparatus—reaching 14 million people in 2010—developed their own ways of attracting global capital and seeking domestic upgrading by adapting and tailoring state policies.[4] Their interests, policy preferences, and developmental strategies were deeply embedded in the norms and institutions of local capitalism that had been developing for more than a century. During different periods of time, these local forms of capitalism drove bureaucrats to define their business clients; to advocate, resist, or revise the emerging policies of upgrading; and to coordinate the production relations between foreign and domestic firms.

The influx of foreign capital *conditioned* local transformation, but such a transformation is *enabled* by local bureaucrats. The interaction of the two generated profound consequences. In the process of creating local policy, the role of foreign capital in exports and the concentration of large foreign firms intensified or mitigated the struggles among government departments over resources, providing far more obstacles in some cities than others for the allocation of budget for technology upgrading. In the process of policy implementation, the offshoring strategies of foreign firms and the government officials' active embracing of strategies shaped the configuration and sequence of industrial development in a city, which facilitated or dampened the effectiveness of development policies at the firm level.

As such, state-led development is not best understood as Beijing using policies to directly influence local firms, at least for the majority of manufacturing industries.[5] Rather, the process of creating and implementing state-led policies involves introducing new dynamics to complicated contexts where persistent local conditions and varied degrees of globalization mutually accommodate each other. This book examines precisely how the logic of globalization was incorporated into fragmented forms of local political economy and how the ambitious state-led development agenda was also interfered with and altered by foreign capital at the local level. As such, seemingly well-intended state policies may generate unexpected outcomes in localities where local government institutions and production relations were mismatched with the task of the industrial transformation at hand. The project, thus, calls for new ways of understanding globalization, state-led development, and comparative capitalism.

State-Led Development with Complicated Implementation

The first major goal of this book is to unravel the politics of economic policy implementation in authoritarian multilevel countries. The finding that "economic policies are political" (Alt and Crystal 1983: 33) has long been acknowledged but with few analytical frameworks developed for authoritarian regimes, where the state is not submitted to the electoral pressure of societal groups. When such topics are discussed in the context of the authoritarian developmental states of Japan, South Korea, and Taiwan in the 1970s, the assumption is often that the state can enforce its strategies once policies are formed by an autonomous and capable bureaucracy under the guidance of a pilot development agent. This assumption is premised on the coherence of the state, a relatively clear goal of national development, and domestic ownership of businesses (Johnson 1982; Amsden 1989; Wade 1990; Evans 1995). As such, the issue of "policy implementation" by local government agencies is largely neglected. To the extent that it is discussed in the context of embeddedness and networks of the state with businesses, the assumption is often that the policy processes run directly from the national government to businesses.[6]

This book challenges these assumptions and draws attention to the myriad of strategies that local government agents have employed to manipulate national economic policies in China, where national initiatives are implemented as mandates through a province–prefecture (city)–county–township–village hierarchy. Many studies have recognized local governments in China as important units of analysis for economic outcomes and the wide regional variation when carrying out central policies (Oi 1999; Whiting 2001; Ong 2012; Rithmire 2014, 2015; Shen and Tsai 2016). They argue that in an environment lacking the rule of law and protection of private property rights, local governments assume a crucial role through orchestrating market production, selectively providing subsidies, and coordinating relations among enterprises (White 1988; Oi 1999; Walder 1995; Blecher and Shue 1996; Blecher 1991; Duckett 1998). Even within the same region, one often finds conflicting stories of local states being development promoting and development thwarting at the same time (Unger and Chan 1999; Sargeson and Zhang 1999; Segal and Thun 2001).

This book resonates with the emphasis on the local state, but it further opens up the black box of local politics and goes beyond demonstrating local variation. It contributes to the understanding of the sources and mechanisms of local policy variation. Studies of industrial, economic, and technology policies typically focus on showing how such policies vary across several locales in China (Breznitz and Murphree 2011; Steinfeld 2010; Thun 2006; Brandt and Thun 2016). Although these studies touch on a number of the sources of variation, such as Maoist legacies in the economic structure or the localities' relationship with the central government, they often do not systematically articulate the mechanisms through which these factors affect investment and economic policies. In particular, the issue of local governments' decision making and implementation (that is, why they choose to embrace or resist certain policies and why they distort policies toward one direction rather than others) are underinvestigated. This lacuna is especially surprising, given the widely observed phenomenon of policy adaptation and selective implementation (Tsai 2006; O'Brien and Li 1999).

Once the issue of complicated implementation is brought into studies of state-led development, as this book does at China's prefecture city level, one finds that the willingness of government to devote resources to technology upgrading and innovation is an outcome of bureaucratic competition based on the fragmented interests of the department agencies and their long-established business clients. That is, whether local advocates for new state initiatives were able to garner resources and build institutions cannot be taken for granted. It is a process requiring careful scrutiny against the institutions of cadre evaluation and structure of "fragmented authoritarianism" governing bureaucratic politics in local China before one is able to confidently discuss implementation at the industrial and firm level (Chen 2017).

Globalization, FDI, and Local Coalitions

The breaking down of the assumption on a coherent and single-level state is an important step in understanding the complication in implementing industrial policies and development policies in general. What further complicates the case, however, is the systematic influx of FDI. Unlike the previous generation of catch-up economies in East Asia that limited the entrance of foreign capital (despite promoting exports and trade), China has become an exemplar case of the "globalized" generation of countries including, among others, Brazil, Russia, Malaysia, and India.

These countries have seen an increase in FDI since the 1990s. The rise of global value chains and production networks has fragmented the production process and created manufacturing opportunities through outsourcing and offshoring (Whittaker et al. 2010; Chen 2014). The active attraction of FDI by national and local government officials and development zones also contributed to the globalized context. When globalization became not only a context but a "constitutive element" of the economy, regulating and coordinating the relationship between foreign and domestic firms became a key challenge for local governments (Hsueh 2011; Ye 2014; Yeung 2009).[7]

Policy and scholarly debates have ensued. Although not widely noticed in Western scholarship, the debate in light of earlier dependency theory and the so-called Latin Americanization of China reached its zenith among Chinese scholars and observers in the 1990s. The concern they expressed was that China's overwhelming reliance on attracting FDI would produce a series of negative consequences, including trapping domestic producers in maquiladora-style sweatshops and increasing levels of inequality (Gilboy and Heginbotham 2004). This was certainly going against the broad trend of returning to a neoliberal globalist ideology at the time, which cast FDI in positive light (Williamson 1989; Little 1982; Myint 1987; Bauer 1981; Krueger et al. 1983; Bhagwati 2004). At the same time in Western academics, a spate of "second image reversed" works has started to examine how economic openness influences domestic coalitions and politics, among which a growing body of literature has emphasized FDI.[8] Some have investigated the general economic influence of FDI on domestic growth and development. Others have looked at the political influence of foreign investors in facilitating liberal-oriented reforms and practices, curbing (or increasing) corruption, shifting national debates, and challenging central state authority (Frieden 1991; Zweig 2002; Huang 2003; Gallagher 2005; Pearson 1991; Malesky, Gueorguiev, and Jensen 2014; Sheng 2010; Wang 2014; Pinto 2013; Zhu 2017; Long, Yang, and Zhang 2015).

Regardless of the explanatory objectives of previous works, many of them make their argument based on observations of an overall structural variable, often the value of FDI as a percentage of gross domestic product (GDP) in a locale.[9] When explaining the outcome of domestic upgrading policies, however, one finds that FDI, as a general structural factor, cannot account for local differences in a universal and linear manner. In fact, it will be shown that cities with similar levels of FDI dependence (and a similar level of economic development) often end up with contrasting degrees of support for new policies. This is a clear case in which we need to unravel the in-depth mechanisms through which FDI is exerting the influence.

Rather than assuming the direct influence of all foreign firms by inferring backwardly through statistical results, this book finds, through intensive field research as well as quantitative evidence, that the majority of foreign firms do not have direct access to city decision making or the possibility of using money to buy votes for their favored politicians (Wang 2014). Instead, they exert their influences *through* local bureaucrats, the real decision makers in local economic policies. The local state still matters in the new wave of globalization. Given the relatively weak role of industrial associations in aggregating and representing business interests, businesses tend to form patron–client relations with the bureaucrats who regulate them. At the city level, the influence of foreign firms is indirect and significant only when they are able to contribute to cohesive and strong vested interest coalitions among the city bureaucrats. At the firm level, the influence of offshoring strategies on the effectiveness of policies and domestic private firms also clearly differs between the large and small foreign firms. Their impact is uneven, and whether they "crowd out" or "crowd in" domestic businesses varies.

As such, similar to the need to break down the state, one should also disaggregate FDI. The influence that globalization and foreign capital have on state-led development cannot be simply captured by a sweeping claim. Instead of assuming that foreign capital completely dominates the local development agenda as classical dependency theory would predict or dismantling the state power as a neoliberal force, this book illustrates the more nuanced way in which various facets of globalization interact with the local state in shaping coalitional politics behind China's upgrading policies.

The Argument

The major argument of this book is that the campaign of FDI attraction in the 1990s was a critical juncture for the subsequent campaign of industrial upgrading in the 2000s, as the type of foreign firms with which the local governments forged alliances shaped the coalitional politics of decision making at the city level and laid the structural foundation for policy implementation at the firm level. When other factors are controlled, cities that initially focused on attracting large top-ranked global firms were surprisingly less able to garner resources and effectively implement policies in comparison to those started with smaller firms at the lower position of the value chain.

The first important influence of FDI attraction lies in the policy-making process in response to the rise of a paradigm for domestic competitiveness. Potentially, this paradigm could be—and has been—viewed as a de facto change of government-supportive policies (such as government funding and tax breaks) from foreign firms to domestically owned firms. Foreign influence on domestic policies is most significant when it sharpens bureaucratic struggles between winners and losers, and such influence is most powerful when it has political value to local elites. The new initiative in upgrading is most likely to be seen as a threat by a vested-interest coalition among city government bureaucrats in charge of international commerce to fight against policy implemented by the newly emerged domestic technology department. The international commerce bureaucrats are more likely to form a cohesive coalition when foreign firms overlap with exporters in a city. At the same time, such a coalition is more likely to win the competition for resources controlled by top leaders when foreign firm production in the city is concentrated in large firms. Combined, these two conditions contribute to *cohesive* and *strong* vested interests. In cities that started by attracting smaller foreign firms and with more domestic producers participating in production, the configuration mitigated the cohesiveness and strength of vested interests. Bureaucratic competition over resources was kept within the issue area of domestic technology, which allows advocates for reforms to make progress.

The second crucial role of FDI attraction lies in the implementation of policies at the firm level. In cities where the local government prioritized the attraction of large foreign firms at the top of the value chain, they settled on a group offshoring strategy. This strategy created a hierarchical segregation between foreign and domestic enterprises, deprived the latter of developmental space, and trapped them in a continued race to the bottom competition. The structure of production drastically reduced the effectiveness of government upgrading policies (including funding and tax cuts) at the firm level, dampening the incentives of firms to upgrade. By contrast, in cities where local government predominately attracted small "guerilla investors" at the bottom of the value chain, the major production strategy connecting foreign and domestic firms was subcontracting. This strategy broke the hierarchical segregation and enhanced the effectiveness of the upgrading policies by strengthening the incentives of domestic firms to move up the value chain. The processes of policy making and policy implementation were mutually reinforcing.

The interaction of global capital and local political economy has therefore produced four crucial dimensions that have influenced development trajectories, which are fleshed out by four subarguments of the book. First, the increase in inward FDI gave rise to investment-seeking states across China, which created beneficiaries among local bureaucrats. Second, the export share of FDI and the concentration of foreign firms affected the varied responses of bureaucrats to the rise of domestic upgrading and cultivated competing government–business coalitions within the city bureaucracy.[10] These coalitions shaped the amount of resources that a city was willing to invest in domestic technology. Third, the type of foreign firms a city attracted also influenced the effectiveness of implementing upgrading policies at the firm level, as well as local firms' upgrading capacity, which largely reinforced decision making at the city level. Finally, when placing regional development trajectories in a much longer historical context beyond the contemporary era, I find the ways in which government–business relations took shape and their development priorities to be deeply embedded in varieties of local capitalism.

GLOBALIZATION AND THE RISE OF INVESTMENT-SEEKING STATES

Although the year 1978 marked China's opening to foreign investment, it was not until the 1990s that China had a systematic influx of FDI throughout the country. As soon as the central state gave the green light to local authorities for approving FDI, Chinese officials throughout the country launched a zealous campaign of FDI attraction. Using measures such as land discounts, aggressive tax cuts, government funding, and bank credits, local officials went out of their way and competed to bring in foreign investors as a way both to establish political achievements under the cadre evaluation system and to promote local growth. During this period, China saw the rise of international commerce departments in most of the city governments, as these bureaucrats controlled most of the "resources-bearing" policies that they are able to grant to FIEs. At the same time, these bureaucrats also became the major beneficiary of the FDI-attraction paradigm.

The type of investments that local officials prioritize, however, diverged across major cities. In some cities, such as Suzhou in the Yangtze River Delta, officials prioritized the attraction of large-scale multinational corporations (MNCs) at the top of global value chains. In some other cities, such as Shenzhen in the Pearl River Delta, officials brokered informal contracts with many small foreign firms established by "guerilla investors." The time period of FDI attraction in the 1990s indeed laid the industrial basis for local manufacturing industries over the next decade. However, more important and often unnoticed was the way in which a city government's global allies affect coalitional politics and the implementation of policies. The distinct types of FIEs and their export activities in a city affected the patterns of bureaucratic competition within the fragmented bureaucracy for the period promoting domestic competitiveness. Furthermore, the rising offshore or subcontracting strategies and the configuration of production interfered with the effective implementation of policies at the firm level further down the road.

GLOBALIZATION AND BUREAUCRATIC COALITIONS

The feature of "fragmented authoritarianism" and the pressure of the cadre evaluation system in Chinese bureaucracy led to rampant competition among bureaucrats (Manion 1985; O'Brien and Li 1999; Li and Zhou 2005; Liu and Tao 2007; Landry 2008; Shih, Adolph, and Liu 2012; Lieberthal and Oksenberg 1988; Lampton 2013; Mertha 2006, 2009; Ang 2016). This book builds on previous works by showing how bureaucrats compete over power, policies, and resources, but it goes further to explore what difference this competition makes and how exposure to globalization complicates the policy process. China's transformation from an FDI-centered development approach to domestic competiveness involves two major government agencies in a city, the international commerce departments who may see themselves as potential losers and the domestic technology departments who are potential winners. The features of foreign firms that bureaucrats attracted in a city shaped both the alignment of interests and the strength of coalitions behind the new policies.

Although the rise of the domestic competitiveness paradigm is often viewed as harmful to foreign firm interests, it is not necessarily perceived as being detrimental to international commerce bureaucrats because their function is to regulate FIEs and exporters, which can be domestic businesses. The policy is viewed as uncontroversially detrimental only when the entire realm of international commerce perceives their interests as being tied with foreign firms and rallies together as a vested interested group. When FIEs and exporting firms overlap in a city, international commerce bureaucrats become the primary regulators for foreign firms; hence, they see foreign firms as their long-term business clients. The rise of new policies hurts their interests and arouses a coherent voice of opposition. In contrast, even when a city has many FIEs, if it has less overlap between foreign firms and exporters, international commerce bureaucrats can have clients that are domestic exporters as well as foreign firms. This is a situation that mitigates the foreign–domestic struggle, which builds bridges rather than walls. In this case, most bureaucratic competition has been kept within departments in charge of domestic technology and the implementing agencies of the new policy, which essentially facilitate the carrying out of policies.

In addition to FIE–exporter overlap, when FIE production in a city is concentrated in a few large global firms, vested-interest groups are found to have more bargaining power—and are, therefore, more likely to be strong—compared to those in which output is shared among small and medium foreign firms. City party secretaries and mayors have tended to favor and develop close relationships with bureaucrats who are able to help significantly and rapidly boost city indicators. In economic decisions over budget and resource allocation, the vested-interest group is able to use the existence of large foreign firms and wield more persuasive power with top city leaders. Such a strong competitor diverts resources toward other policy goals and marginalizes bureaucratic reformers who were the "institutional builders" for domestic private firms. This circumstance prevents the domestic technology coalition from increasing resources for science and technology upgrading that they can use to establish local funds, industrial parks, or innovation platforms.

As such, foreign firms became a valuable resource on which bureaucrats draw to interpret policies, boost policy targets, and fight for resources that are favorable to their own coalition. This book, at the same time, avoids a deterministic approach and elucidates the way in which the features of domestic bureaucratic politics are internalized and channel the impacts of foreign capital, making bureaucratic competition an obstacle to policies in some cities more than others.

GLOBALIZATION AND THE EFFECTIVENESS OF POLICIES FOR LOCAL FIRMS

In addition to local coalitional politics in city policy making, foreign firms that were attracted to a locality also interfere with the process of policy implementation at the firm level. Although the most heightened period of FDI attraction took place in the 1990s, once FIEs came in, they shaped the local configuration of production throughout the 2000s. That was why government policies that use funding and tax cuts to encourage local firms to engage in technology upgrading did not always translate into results. Even when controlling other features, government funding and tax cuts are much less likely to generate upgrading incentives in cities that are dominated by large-scale FIEs compared to those with smaller guerilla FIEs. This gap is found to be quite significant, even among coastal cities with similar levels of economic development.

More specifically, taking China's largest manufacturing industry (that is, electronics) as an example, the book found that, when a city government allied with large global firms, the emerging supply gap between global and domestic firms encouraged both the government and MNCs to promote a group-offshoring strategy, which co-outsourced foreign suppliers to the same region, based on the leading firms' connections with global suppliers and the deliberate planning of bureaucrats in the international commerce. This strategy ended up occupying the middle and lower levels of the production chain with foreign firms, which amplified the power disparity between global and local firms, squeezed and segregated the latter into the bottom of the value chain, and forced them to compete for cheap labor and limited production opportunities. Under such circumstances, even when domestic technology officials used government funding and tax breaks to encourage upgrading behavior, such as investment in research and development (R&D) and patent applications, they still could generate hardly any incentives and behavior among domestic firms.

By contrast, smaller FIEs were situated at the bottom of the global value chain and did not have the organizational resources to initiate group outsourcing. Over time, they found local subcontracting to be a more attractive option. This allowed the local government to use the subcontracting needs of smaller global firms to help build local capabilities. This upgrading strategy broke the hierarchical segregation between global and local firms, undermined the power disparity in local production, and reserved more developmental and upgrading space for local producers. At the same time, the strategy of starting from the bottom broadened grassroots state business developmental coalitions that resisted the predesignation of business winners. Domestic producers demonstrated a much higher level of ambition to invest in learning, and the same policies of government funding and tax cuts were found to be much more effective to generate firm-level upgrading incentives. The firm-level outcomes, in turn, reinforced either a narrow vested interest benefiting from hierarchical segregation of foreign and domestic firms or a broader coalition that bridges interdepartmental competition in the process of budget allocation at the city level.

GLOBALIZATION AND VARIETIES OF LOCAL CAPITALISM

Placed in a comparative context over long stretches of time, the book traces the divergent paths of local economic transformation to historically entrenched patterns of local capitalism, a process in which the formation of bureaucratic preferences is essential. As such, it uncovers the nature of capitalism in authoritarian yet globalized China. Globalization has generated important influences on local development in the contemporary period, as previously mentioned. However, from a longer time horizon spanning the past century, it is the local form of capitalism that selectively incorporated globalization into its own logic by interest-driven bureaucrats.

The perspective advanced here draws on the "varieties of capitalism" approach used to study advanced industrialized countries and, increasingly, East Asia and Latin America (Hall and Soskice 2001; Vogel 2006; Schneider 2013). I apply the varieties of capitalism approach to the subnational level and show the historical origins of such capitalism prior to the contemporary period (pre-1978). On this point, I build on other works that have long noticed the persistent patterns of local economic orders, such as Locke (1995) on Italy and Herrigel (1996) on Germany.[11] Furthermore, in contrast to the varieties of capitalism approach, I emphasize local bureaucrats' preferences and their reaction to centrally driven policies in shaping local capitalism, rather than firm-level institutions in finance, employment, and coordination, as such institutions were still fairly weak in China during the periods of the 1990s and 2000s. Although localities dominated by top-down modes of capitalism bear certain similarities with Schneider's (2013) argument of "hierarchical capitalism," my emphasis has been on the state's deliberate selection of such business alliances and the subsequent consequences of the development strategies on domestic bureaucratic decisions and domestic businesses.

In the much-heated debate over Chinese capitalism, some scholars see China's development trajectories as relying on bottom-up processes involving grassroots-level private businesses, whereas others focus on the rise of top-down state capitalism based on public ownership. A third group noticed China's transition from one to the other and has discussed the complicated relations between the two.[12] This book shows that capitalism has taken a variety of forms, top down or bottom up, at the local level within the same country. I argue that the preferences of local bureaucrats emerged from varied degrees of political mobilization and different levels of responsiveness to upper-level political signals during the state-building process. It is these bureaucratic preferences, rather than economic structures measured by enterprise ownership, that ultimately define local bureaucrats' choices of businesses allies, their relationship with the major businesses, and their strategies of promoting local development.[13]

As such, my argument also goes beyond the conventional market versus state dichotomy and the active versus dormant state distinction. Rather, it shows that local state officials have been actively involved in the economy throughout China but that they can generate very different policies and state–business relations that are embedded in bottom-up, as well as top-down, modes of capitalism.

Using the Jiangsu and Guangdong regions as important examples, I trace the emergence, survival, and reinforcement of bureaucratic interests and the sticky patterns of government–business relations through comparative historical analysis across four periods, including the late Qing and early republican period (1895–1920), the Mao era (1949–1978), the post-Mao period (1978–1990), and the globalized era (1990–present). I found that, in each period, the degrees of political mobilization for development shaped the goals that bureaucrats prioritized, the policy tools used to achieve developmental goals, and the breadth of state–business coalitions. In Jiangsu, where bureaucrats were historically motivated by political promotion, they sought narrow alliances with big business at the top of the hierarchy and habitually launched top-down campaigns to accomplish central policy mandates. In Guangdong, where bureaucrats were historically driven by practical economic gains, they protected small businesses with diverse flexible measures that often circumvented central policies. The rise of top-down and bottom-up modes of capitalism in the two regions produced rewards that, in turn, reinforced the distinctive local state preferences embedded in the local form of capitalism.

These historically entrenched patterns of state interests and state–business relations survived during the Maoist period of state building and were carried into the contemporary period, which conditioned and contextualized the different global business allies that local governments choose and their subsequent response to domestic upgrading in the twenty-first century. Along the line of historical institutional perspective, preferences, institutions, and development certainly reinforce each other (Thelen and Steinmo 1992; Mahoney 2000; Pierson 2004). However, even the emergence of the critical juncture in the current period (that is, localities' different priorities, with FDI attraction following China's embrace of globalization) still reflects the continuity (although not the complete stagnation) of local legacies.

Thus, what I argue in the book is quite different from a scenario where local forms of capitalism are either homogenized by forces of globalization or demonstrate permanent resistance to globalization (Andrews 1994; Hall and Soskice 2001). Rather, I show how local capitalism is able to *incorporate* globalization into its own trajectories by helping to advance the interests of bureaucrats. As regions with different foreign capital responded to the upgrading initiative by devoting more or fewer resources to the upgrading initiative, and as the logic of global production interacted with local upgrading policies, the produced feedback loop that justified city-level policy making in the short run reinforced bureaucratic preferences in the long run.

Such alliances between local bureaucrats and global firms, however, generate unintended consequences on policies and often distort the incentives of domestic producers in a way that is not anticipated by the central state. In particular, although regions with a top-down developmental approach were able to produce stunning industrialization before the globalized era (such as within the Sunan area), they fell into the pitfall of cultivating narrow developmental coalitions due to bureaucratic competition from the vested interest department and the group-offshoring strategies of leading global firms. In contrast, the fortunes reversed for regions that are embedded in the bottom-up mode of capitalism, as they were faced with more favorable patterns of bureaucratic competition and subcontracting strategies that were more conducive to cultivating upgrading incentives among local producers. The local state, in other words, implemented industrial upgrading policies in response to the call of the central state, but the success of such policies was determined by the long-term local institutional environments, which were created by the local state itself over long stretches of time and were not entirely anticipated by the upgrading policies themselves.

The insight generated from this study, however, is not restricted to the uniqueness of the Chinese context. It sheds light on East Asian and Latin American countries as well. The advantages of a particular type of local capitalism for developing local competitiveness are not permanent and have undergone changes with shifts in the global context. During the previous wave of globalization (between the 1970s and the 1990s), promoting the exports of domestic firms was the major way of integrating into the global economy, and the penetration of FDI was highly restricted. The Northeast Asian developers, including Japan, South Korea, and Taiwan, created miracles through institutions that supported major domestic winners at the top of the production hierarchy. The rise of FDI and global outsourcing from the 1990s onward, however, unleashed FDI and exports at the same time without a period that focused exclusively on exports. The entrance of global capital altered the microfoundation of state intervention in developing economies such as China, Vietnam, Singapore, Thailand, and Malaysia in Asia and Brazil, Chile, and Mexico in Latin America. The globalized context within each economy has made the top-down pattern of capitalism much harder to mobilize the upgrading incentives of domestic firms. Among other factors, the state's intention to promote upgrading has been largely complicated by the problems of coordinating foreign–domestic firm relations and at the same time struggling to exit the "middle-income traps" (Doner and Schneider 2016). There are, in short, no one-size-fits-all types of comparative institutional advantages for effectively implementing a local economic transformation.[14]

The Research Design and Methodology

To explore how the penetration of global capital influenced policy making at the city level and policy implementation among firms in the city, I use a mixed-methods approach. I develop my theory from qualitative data and comparative case studies before testing the argument across hundreds of cities and thousands of firms. This book uses the prefecture city level as the major unit of analysis, as the local variation of policy implementation is most significantly manifested at this level. The province level is simply too broad to capture the vast variation among cities, as will be shown. The county level, in contrast, often does not possess the decision-making power for many of the industrial policies concerning government funding and tax breaks for domestic technology, as Chapter 4 will elaborate.

I develop the theoretical arguments through controlled comparative case studies among cities with similar levels of economic development before testing arguments with quantitative data. The case studies are based on more than 270 in-depth interviews with local government officials and business managers (typically one to two hours long) in 18 months of field research throughout 2008 and 2011. To explore government–business alliances and patterns of bureaucratic competition behind the city-level decision making, I coded and analyzed the texts of 118 of the semistructured interviews with officials in the international commerce and domestic technology departments in the cities of Suzhou, Wuxi, Ningbo, and Shenzhen. Then the argument was tested by using newly constructed datasets that cover the jurisdiction of 300 prefecture-level cities (where statistical data exist) over the course of multiple years.

To investigate the effectiveness of upgrading policies among firms in a city, I similarly generated arguments through paired comparisons of cities throughout different stages of development, restricting the comparison to the electronics industry. The comparison draws on both in-depth interviews as well as an original survey of 200 firms.[15] This was followed by a construction of unique measures of effectiveness for government funding and tax breaks and the testing of argument through a multilevel dataset that includes 159 cities (which are the ones that have the electronics industry) and 6,740 domestic private electronics firms. Finally, in tracing the historical roots of local variation and placing Chinese localities in a comparative historical context, I consulted a collection of local gazetteers, archives, and historical studies.

Plan of the Book

Chapter 2 examines the rise of the FDI-attraction paradigm at the national level and the emergence of local investment-seeking states in the 1990s. It explores in detail the varied strategies that city governments employed to attract foreign investors to launch the campaign of FDI attraction, ranging from tax cuts and land and utility discounts to industrial zone establishments. At one end of the strategic continuum are local governments that prioritized large leading multinationals that have been playing the role of the "dragon's head" at the top of the global value chain whereas, on the other end, are cities where bureaucrats brokered deals with small-scale foreign firms established by "guerilla investors" at the bottom of the value chain through flexible arrangements.

Chapter 3 traces the relative decline of the previous FDI attraction paradigm and the emerging paradigm of domestic technology competitiveness, drawing on government documents, media text analysis, and interviews. The chapter then introduces the actors, the arguments, and the matrix of supporting institutions and policy tools underpinning the two policy paradigms. It draws attention to the coexistence of the two paradigms at the

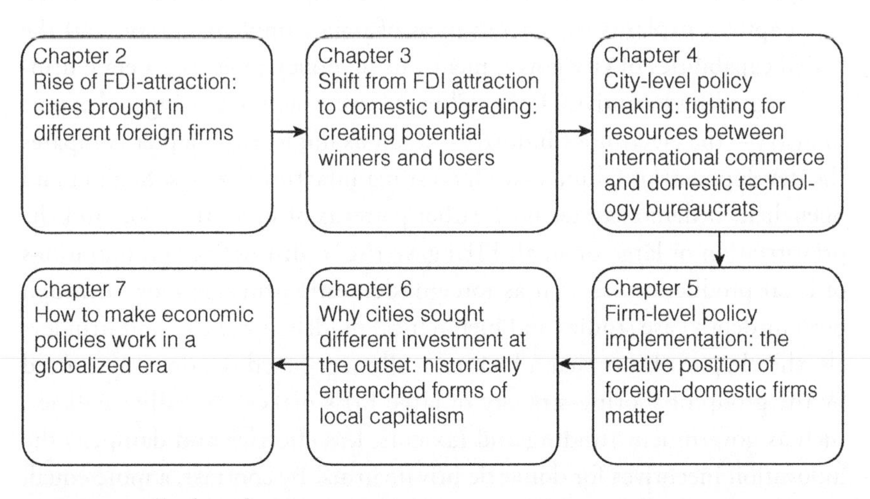

FIGURE 1.1. Book road map.

local level, where policies and institutions of FDI attraction profoundly affect the government's response to domestic upgrading and their choice of development strategies.

Chapter 4 delves into the coalitional politics of policy making and resource allocation by investigating the response of city government officials to the rise of domestic technology in competition with the FDI-attraction paradigm. The chapter examines the patterns of bureaucratic competition between international commerce departments and newly emerged domestic technology departments and their respective business clients, including foreign and domestic firms. I explain the influence of FDI attraction on domestic politics by showing (1) how the overlap between FIEs and exporters shaped the degree of perceived threat and the cohesiveness of the vested interests in international commerce under the rule of fragmented bureaucratic competition and (2) how the existence of large FIEs strengthened the bargaining power of the vested interest bureaucrats against allocating resources to the domestic technology coalition. The direction and the magnitude of foreign influence, therefore, are filtered and channeled through local bureaucracy, giving rise to either deadlocked struggles between different departments or productive competition within the same issue area that facilitates the budget allocation for various forms of government funding, service platforms, and cost rebates for enterprise technology activities. The chapter develops a two-by-two matrix framework through comparative case studies and text analysis of interviews before testing the hypothesis using quantitative data across more than 200 prefecture-level cities in China.

Chapter 5 explains the effectiveness of policy implementation and the varied capabilities of city governments, using policy tools to generate firm-level upgrading incentives. Using China's largest manufacturing and export industry—the electronics industry—as an example, the chapter compares the development of China's two largest manufacturing cities, Suzhou and Shenzhen. It demonstrates how earlier patterns of FDI attraction and the prioritization of large or small FIEs gave rise to distinctive configurations of local production, as well as foreign–domestic firm relations. Through both in-depth case studies and hierarchical models at the city and firm levels, the chapter shows that a hierarchically segregated relationship started by the group offshoring strategy of large FIEs makes upgrading policies, such as government funding and tax cuts, less effective and dampens the innovation incentives for domestic private firms. By contrast, a more equal, broadly connected relationship started by the subcontracting strategy of small FIEs makes upgrading policies more likely to generate firm-level innovation behavior and contributes to the competitiveness of domestic private firms.

Chapter 6 traces the historical roots of local variation by chronologically and cross-sectionally placing China in a comparative historical perspective. It compares varieties of local capitalism in China across four periods, including the late Qing and early republican period (1895–1920), the Mao era (1949–1978), the post-Mao period (1978–1990), and the globalized era (1990–present). The chapter explores how the historically entrenched top-down and bottom-up modes of capitalism have conditioned local government preferences, as well as their reaction to centrally driven development initiatives, leading them to attract large or small foreign firms in the globalized era. The narrowly selective development strategies based on top-down capitalism were more effective in the industrial transformation during the preglobalized era before the 1990s. The influx of FDI since then, however, has unleashed new complexity so that cultivating bottom-up, broadly supportive networks with small firms was more likely to provide an institutional environment for the competitiveness of domestic private businesses.

Chapter 7 summarizes the findings of the book and highlights the implications of this study, both theoretically and practically, for the political economy of development in emerging economies. Starting with a story of Japan in the 1960s, the chapter shows the different ways that the Chinese economy integrated into the world economy. The chapter draws attention to how global production fragmented or integrated state agencies and businesses, shaped the ways they perceived their interests, and ultimately affected the political environments for domestic private firms. The chapter also discusses prospects and constraints for change for local capitalism. The chapter then broadens out to map major Asian economies in Northeast and Southeast Asia in a comparative picture. It finds that the earlier generation of developers was able to participate in global production by shielding the penetration of FDI to local settings. They were, therefore, far less sensitive to developmental coalition problems, compared with the current generation of developers that experienced high levels of localized global capital during their major growth periods.

CHAPTER 2

Chasing Foreign Capital

In 1979 and 1980, when the first group of FIEs was established in China, only five cities on the southeast coast were open to foreign investment. Today, a local government official would feel ashamed if he or she could not come up with a list of locally registered FIEs that are among the Fortune Global 500, such as GE, Nokia, Samsung, Siemens, and Foxconn. Between 1980 and 2010, inward FDI in China increased from US$57 million to US$105.735 billion while exports of merchandise grew from US$18 billion to US$1.578 trillion, making the country the largest recipient of FDI among developing countries and the largest exporter in the world (Figure 2.1). As of 2009, 52 percent of FDI and 95 percent of exports have come from manufacturing industries, of which the electronics industry accounts for 19 percent and 35 percent, respectively (National Bureau of Statistics 2010). This rapid speed of integration into the world economy has been unparalleled among other developing countries as well as among East Asian newly industrialized countries during their catch-up stage.

Beneath China's continuous integration into the global economy is not simple liberalization of the country's economic system but the formation of distinctive local economies and the ways that the local government regulated and interacted with businesses. In many ways, the penetration of foreign capital has been uneven, with different types of foreign invested firms established in localities with their outsourcing and offshoring activities. The emerging composition of foreign and domestic firms and the relations of production have generated profound impacts, both on the local coalitions of the city governments and on the ways in which they allocate government

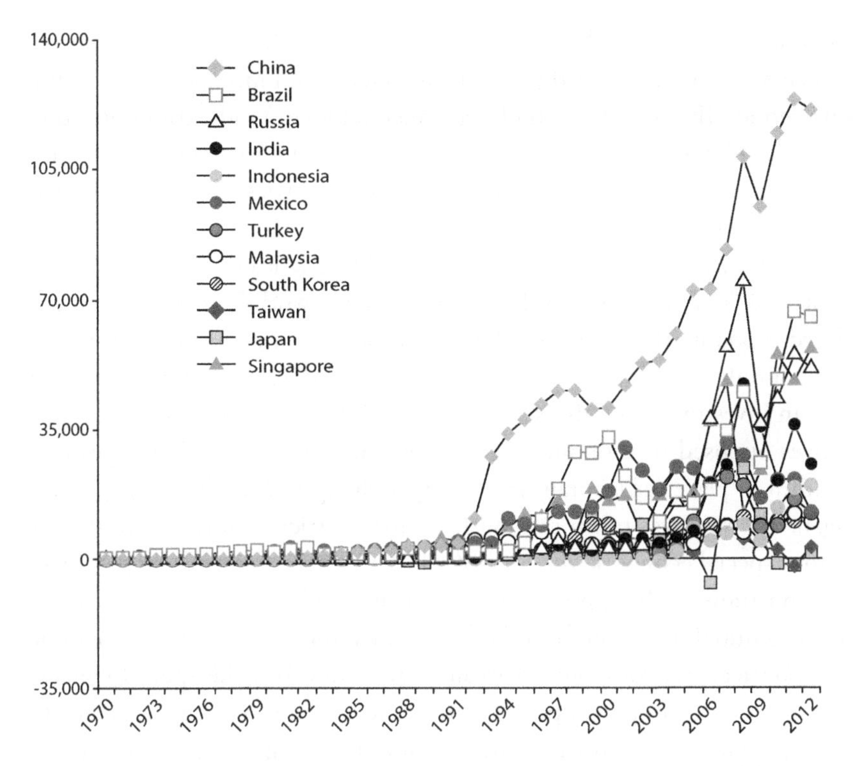

FIGURE 2.1. Inward FDI in top developing country recipients, 1970–2010 (The order of countries in the graph is ranked by inward FDI in 2012, as listed on the right).

SOURCE: United Nations Conference on Trade and Development (UNCTAD) (various years).

support among firms. This chapter starts with the initiative at the national level before examining local strategies of investment attractions.

The Rise of the Pro-FDI Agenda in Post-Mao China

Since its establishment in 1949 and before its reform and opening in 1978, China has mainly relied on import substitution industrialization (ISI) as a catch-up strategy typically seen in many other developing countries in the earlier stages of development. The central state provided subsidies and protection for capital-intensive and technology-intensive industries such as steel, chemistry, electronics, and machinery. Instead of directly importing these goods from developed countries, state-owned firms manufactured these goods by themselves based on the import of machinery and technology from abroad (often the Soviet Union). The electronics industry was largely oriented toward the national defense and military needs during this period. The computer and integrated circuit (IC) industries were good examples of where the state provided heavy subsidies in an effort to reduce the technology gap between China and other countries, albeit with limited success (Pecht 2007: 71–72).

In a dramatic shift in foreign policy, the Dengist leadership initiated the reform of "opening China's door to the outside world" in 1978 to an enclosed economy that had been dominated by central planning. This initiative not only aimed to boost domestic economic development by attracting foreign investment but also served as a political strategy to counter conservatives opposed to economic reforms by launching gradual changes in a handful of places as laboratories for larger changes (Naughton 1995; Shirk 1993). The step was taken cautiously at first, restricting foreign investment to four special economic zones (SEZs) in Fujian and Guangdong provinces and constraining the approval of investment mainly to joint ventures. There was also initial suspicion from the foreign investors about China's economic and political environment (Pearson 1991). However, the special concessionary tax and financial policies provided by the central government to these policies increased the credibility for attracting foreign investments, especially from Hong Kong and Taiwan (that is, the China circle firms). It was in SEZs that the earliest form of foreign investment—contractual alliances—started to emerge between foreign firms and domestic partners. Foreign firms provided original materials, original samples, and original components together with capital and machinery whereas domestic firms engaged in processing and assembly before the final products were handed to foreign firms for reexport. Although the 1979 Chinese–Foreign Joint Venture Law mentioned the need to introduce technology, the major emphasis in attracting foreign investment during this period was to promote exports and increase foreign exchange reserves.

The development experience of SEZs provided the initial soil for the growth of the pro-FDI agenda and the subsequent rise of the Economic and Technology Development Zones (ETDZs). Contrary to common belief, the original intention of the central state in launching ETDZs did not lie in simply replicating SEZs in a larger geographical area. Deng Xiaoping and Zhao Ziyang did publicly endorse the achievement of SEZs before they pushed for the expansion of coastal development strategies, yet it became much clearer later that both the amount and the quality of foreign investment in SEZs was deemed far from satisfactory by central leaders, as these investments were mainly comprised of labor-intensive processing exports that involved little transfer of technology and considerable high cost (Pearson 1991: 151). The ETDZ plan thus was intended as a reformulation of SEZs that went beyond simple trade promotion (Pi and Wang 2004: 38; Naughton 1997: 92; Naughton 2007: 407). In 1984, the Central Committee of the Chinese Communist Party (CCP) and the State Council jointly started the initiative in 14 coastal cities, with Dalian being the first ETDZ. The primary goals of developing ETDZs, according to the major conference document, were to "break a new era by taking advantage of foreign investment and introducing advanced technology" (The Central Committee of CCP and the State Council 1984). In the following initiated policy, ETDZs were required to "arrange every aspect of work around the central task of exploring technology and carefully select the foreign investment projects" (The Central Committee of CCP and the State Council 1985). The 14 zones were granted similar beneficial policies as SEZs but were intended by the State Council to have a "higher starting point" so that they could better recognize the function of four windows, that is, the windows of technology, of management, of knowledge, and of foreign policies (S. Li 2008: 76).

THE FIRST STAGE: FORMING JOINT VENTURES

It was within such contexts that the idea of "exchanging market for technology" gradually rose to the top of the national economic policy. The term originated from China's automobile industry in the early 1980s and was later widely used as the central tenet in support of policies for encouraging inward foreign investment in most manufacturing industries, both at the central state and local levels.[1] The main argument was that by allowing foreign investment to enter the domestic market, China could use its huge domestic market as a powerful bargaining chip for the introduction of advanced technology. *Market* in the initial stage referred to the sale of international products in domestic markets but later was broadly used as a term to mean the entrance of FIEs into mainland China, even though they may mainly focus on export. In terms of the type of technology that was needed, the China Joint Venture Law stipulated that such technology and machinery should be advanced and "appropriate to China's needs" and that when foreign investors intended to cheat the Chinese partner with "backward" technology and machinery, the Chinese partner should be compensated (National People's Congress 1979; State Council 1986). The 1986 "Decision of the State Council to Encourage Foreign Investment" further specified the preferential policies for the technologically advanced enterprises in which the "foreign investors provide advanced technology, engage in development of new products, or upgrade the existing products." These enterprises were provided with lower charges of basic utilities, priority loans from the bank, and a wide range of tax exemption policies (State Council 1986).

There were two underlying assumptions of the argument of "trading market access for technology." First, foreign investors were willing to pay for the cost of entrance by transferring part of their advanced technology. Second, the Chinese side could gain bargaining leverage over foreign investors by approving their entrance to the domestic market. These assumptions, however, were severely challenged in the two actual stages of joint venture formation. The earlier stage was marked by controlling FDI entrance and forming strategic joint ventures (JVs) in several selected industries. Although intended to be modeled after Japan, South Korea, and Taiwan, the selective JV stage that relied on foreign capital for transfer of technology turned out to be significantly different from the developmental states, which relied on reverse engineering and self-learning for technological catch-up (Kim 1997; Leng 2005). Largely but not entirely, the controlled JV stage gave place to a new process in the 1990s, which saw the influx of FDI on a much larger scale to local development zones across the country.

In the JV period, the state poured a massive amount of capital into forming a selective few JVs in the cathode ray tube (CRT) industry and the IC industry. The Ministry of Electronics wanted to limit the entrance of foreign capital and technology to a few large capital-intensive firms so as to create national champions similar to *chaebols* in Korea (Huchet 1997: 271). Given the large amount of resources that the state invested in each firm, only a few domestic state-owned firms gained permission for production and enjoyed the "benefit" of becoming joint-venture partners. In the CRT industry, the state bank invested US$20 billion to establish several major JVs in the 1980s and early 1990s, including Beijing Panasonic, Shenzhen SEG Samsung, Shenzhen SEG-Hitachi, Thomson Foshan, Changsha LG Philips, Nanjing Huafei (Huadian-Philips), and Shanghai Novel. In the IC industry, with effort from the State Council leadership group (*lingdao xiaozu*) and the Ministry of Electronics, Shougang NEC, Shanghai Belling, and Shanghai Philips were formed in the 1980s.[2] This was followed by two huge investment projects in the 1990s: the more than 2 billion yuan "908 project" that created Huajing (which later turned into a JV) and the almost 5 billion yuan "909 project" that gave birth to Huahong NEC. Despite receiving a substantial amount of subsidies during the creation and production process, most of the JVs failed to master the core technology and suffered from substantial losses. All initial JVs in the CRT industry eventually went out of business as foreign partners withdrew investment from CRT and marched into liquid crystal displays (LCDs), leaving the Chinese partners who lacked capability in LCD to close down. It was much more costly for the JVs in the IC industry to quit production, even after Huajing and Huahong lost billions of RMB. These JVs were eventually transferred into processing firms, which gave up the original goal of leading the IC industry with independent product development (Gao 2003; Q. Hu 2006).[3] As a result, an increasing amount of these electronics products in China—85 percent of IC products and almost 100 percent of flat screen products—still had to rely on imports (Zhang 2008).[4]

The reasons for the failed marriage between Chinese and FIEs ranged from cultural differences to conflicts in enterprise management.[5] However, more than anything else, the JV experiment revealed that transferring technology through JV was just wishful thinking.[6] Despite the Chinese government's claimed intention to promote knowledge transfer and the creation of policies to encourage acquirement of technology, there was a lack of incentives from both the supply and the demand sides. On the supply side, once the JV was created, it immediately became part of FIE's global outsourcing strategy. The parent companies in OECD countries, which controlled the China branch, had no plans to conduct product development, design, or research and development (R&D) in China. Consideration to preserve core technologies and the lack of property rights protection in China further restrained the transfer of technologies. For example, the major goal for Huahong's collaboration with NEC from Japan was to upgrade its technology capability in producing 6-inch chips, yet NEC firmly restricted the transferring of technology at every step. Instead, NEC's goal was to gain low-cost memory cards from Huahong and resell them at higher prices in the international market. Production lines only involved directly introduced and applied designs that were already developed in parent companies (Q. Hu 2006; Luo unpublished).[7] Thus, in many aspects, the JVs did not depart too far from the early forms of contractual alliances in SEZs in terms of degree of technology sharing, albeit on a larger scale and in more technologically advanced industries.

On the demand side, the R&D department of the JV became a rubber stamp where the Chinese staff were discouraged from carrying out any independent R&D, which would both run counter to the global strategy of the FIE and increase the likelihood of direct competition with the foreign brand products. For example, in both SEG Samsung and SEG-Hitachi, R&D staff from the China side predicted the change of technology and proposed conducting independent research that went beyond the CRT technology. However, this effort was turned down by the company, and technicians sent from Japan. As a result, the Chinese R&D staff, who were most likely to have demand for technology, either remained idle or later flew to other companies (Lu 2011; Xu 2007). The Chinese managers of the JV, who were usually not adequately trained in understanding technology and were pressed by other concerns such as total production and employees' welfare, ended up not having strong incentives to facilitate learning and allow foreign partners to monitor and supervise the production process, as long as the share of the profit for the Chinese side was guaranteed.[8] There was no denying that certain technology had to be purchased to complete the production that complied with the standards of quality, yet most of these purchases tended to be direct imports of machinery and product lines rather than the actual learning of technology. Over time, the dependence on foreign partners for technology and management deepened (Pearson 1991: 177–182).

Hence, there was a growing discrepancy between the central government's claimed intention in attracting FDI and the actual results produced at the firm level. Although the government recognized the importance of acquiring advanced technology and at times did bargain for the goal, it ignored the feasibility of forcing foreign investors to transfer technology and the fact that such a strategy ran directly counter to the logic of a hierarchical global production order, which the JV was subject to. It also neglected to implement incentives for managers and technicians from the Chinese part. The assumption that foreign firms would be willing to trade technologies with their entrance was directly contradicted in the JV stage. Such failure caused two major consequences in the electronics industry. First, regardless of whether the state intervention was indeed the cause of the failure, the approach of central government-led effort in developing the high-tech industry was largely delegitimized, and, for a long time, the state moved away from any centralized industrial policy (Naughton 2007: 26). Second, an increasing number of FIEs, such as Panasonic and Samsung, shifted their outsourcing strategy from JV to wholly foreign-owned enterprises or increased their share to more than 70 percent (Luo unpublished; Naughton 2007). The failure, surprisingly, did not delegitimize the pro-FDI agenda. Rather, a new process of attracting FDI enabled proponents of the agenda to reinterpret and thus gradually modify the meaning of "exchanging market for technology" toward the direction that justified foreign investment on an even larger scale.

THE SECOND STAGE: COMPETING FOR FDI ACROSS THE COUNTRY

Acknowledging the overly ambitious plan of introducing advanced technology through FDI, the central government started to move away from the centrally controlled bilateral mode of creating JVs between a selective few firms. The national conference of ETDZs was held at Tianjin in 1987 and Shanghai in 1989. These conferences marked important turning points. Based on the experience of the previous period, the Special Economic Zone Office proposed "three major focuses" (*san weizhu*) to be the primary goals of ETDZs in place of the previously assigned function of "four windows." The ETDZs "mainly focus on attracting foreign investment, on industrial development, and on creating foreign reserves through exports." The policy initiative, along with the delegation to local governments of the power to approve foreign investments, provided legitimate grounds for ETDZs to attract FDI in a bold manner (Tao 2006). Many officials in the ETDZs viewed this switch as a welcome change that was more practical and realistic than the previous period (Pi and Wang 2004). Starting with the 14 ETDZs and later spreading into thousands of development zones across the country, local governments sought opportunities for attracting FDI through every possible means. The early 1990s thus began a stage in which the central government loosened control on both the number of FIEs that sought to enter China and the number of localities that sought to attract FDI.

At the global level, it was during the same period that the antenna of global production networks in automobile, electronics, and information technology (IT) began to reach into developing countries in a systematic way, not only for gaining access to the domestic market but also for taking advantage of low-cost labor. Rather than trading and competing with final products that include every single step of branding, design, marketing, component manufacturing, assembly, and distribution, firms and economies (national or local) increasingly specialized in specific stages of production, albeit with varying degrees of modularization and fragmentation (Gereffi, Humphrey, and Sturgeon 2005; Herrigel, Wittke, and Voskamp 2013). Thus, it was not surprising to see FDI pouring into China during this period given the needs from both the foreign and domestic sides.

With local governments gaining increasing authority to approve FDI projects (any project within US$30 million) in the late 1980s, the 1990s brought a massive proliferation of zones across the country (Yin et al. 2007). Among them, 32 were granted the title of state-recognized ETDZs, but hundreds and thousands emerged from various other levels. The "zone fever" brought fierce competition in attracting foreign investment through various packages of preferential policies. In addition to the tax exemption and other policies stipulated at the state level, local governments also provided other preferential policies, ranging from tax breaks for both national and local taxes to tariff reduction for import of raw materials, components and machineries, tariff exemption, low-to-zero land price, and discounts on office rental price.[9]

The rising number of ETDZs and the increasing proportion of FDI in China's GDP also empowered government agencies that regulated foreign investment and trade. The Ministry of Foreign Trade and Economic Cooperation (MFTEC) (MFET before 1993) was the main agency that made and implemented FDI-related policies. In 1999, the MFTEC formally gained the authority to approve and regulate all the ETDZs, taking over the function from the Special Economic Zone Office. The Economic and Trade Commission (ETC) also gained significant power during the two decades of opening, but at a less rapid speed, as the key function of regulating FDI and ETDZs was in the hands of the MFTEC.

The ETDZ phase of the FDI attraction, however, was not simply a localized and expanded version of the JV period. Although officials still talked about "trading market access for technology" in the 1990s, the main proponents of FDI attraction tweaked it into an argument that allowed FIEs to come in so that domestic firms would benefit from the "spillover effects" in technology and the opportunities to learn management skills from foreign firms (Gallagher 2005). Thus, direct influence of FIEs through forming JVs with Chinese partners was no longer the focus; the key was the general demonstration and the competition it created for the region. The priorities of localities became "taking advantage of" (*liyong*) FDI in boosting local industrial and economic development.

Choosing Global Allies: Varieties of Investment-Seeking Local States

Although the initial open-door period of China took place in the 1980s, it was not until the 1990s, well after Deng Xiaoping's southern tour and when China entered the stage of local competition for FDI, that China experienced a systematic influx of FDI. In explaining how China became the top country in foreign investment attraction, scholars have focused on a wide range of reasons, ranging from using FDI as a channel of financing for domestic private businesses to the rise of outsourcing activities from global firms and the spread of development zones (Huang 2003; Steinfeld 2010; Zheng 2014). What these works did not give adequate attention to were the crucial roles of local government officials during this period of time, who actively took the opportunities presented in globalization by offering aggressive preferential policies to foreign investors and who crafted the institutions of the development zones. Local officials' FDI attraction strategies are not only important for understanding the rise of investment-seeking states in the 1990s. These strategies, as will be discussed in later chapters, also laid the very foundation for bureaucratic coalitions during the industrial transformation to local competitiveness in the 2000s.

The role of local officials needs to be understood against the backdrop of the Chinese local economy. In the 1980s, the success of the Chinese economy largely resulted from public enterprises (both state owned and collectively owned) in local China, which were then dependent on the soft credit that the state provided. In the 1990s, however, the implementation of a tax-sharing system squeezed the local share of budgetary revenue, and the reform of the banking system posed hard budget constraints on these publicly owned enterprises by reducing their access to soft credit. Many of these enterprises experienced losses and substantial debts and became economic burdens for local governments (Whiting 2001: 265–290; Ong 2012). As these enterprises were reformed, privatized, or sold, local governments started to search for new ways to build political achievements and increase economic revenue (Tao and Yang 2008; Zhao 2009). The ascendance of the FDI-attraction initiative paired with the rise of outsourcing and offshore production of global capital provided opportunities and incentives for local governments to shift their role from direct owners of enterprises to investment seekers in fulfilling their developmental goals. Inviting business and attracting investment, widely expressed in the Chinese term *zhao shang yin zi*, became the key to these goals.

Politically, the hierarchical cadre evaluation system instilled strong political incentives for local bureaucrats to accomplish policy mandates and build political achievements through economic and industrial performance. The fall of the local publicly owned enterprises resulted in the attraction of outside investment as a necessary condition to boost the key performance indicators in GDP, industrial output and fiscal revenue. In addition to these basic economic targets, the goals of the two paradigms—attracting FDI and promoting high-tech industries—also began to be directly built into the evaluation system for the leading group cadres and for various state agencies and government-administered development zones, especially in the relatively developed cities on the east coast and the capital cities of various provinces in the hinterland. Examples include the number of FDI projects and the amount and speed of FDI attraction, as well as the number of high-tech enterprises and the proportion of output from high-tech industries (Gao 2015; Zuo 2015). Economically, the 1994 fiscal reform drastically increased the proportion of the central state's share of income and value-added taxes. Local governments thus competed to offer investors generous tax reductions or exemptions justified in the "beneficial policies" of the two paradigms. Adding to the benefit package were also state funds, reductions in land prices, and bank credit.

These beneficial policies became "resource-bearing" policies that local governments used to seek business investment as well as to build patronage connections. The rise of local investment-seeking states thus led to the formation of a strong alliance between governments and businesses in post-Mao China. Central to the maintenance of such alliances was the exchange relationship between bureaucrats and businesses based on the offering of beneficial policies. Bureaucrats provided businesses with beneficial policies in tax, land, and state funding, businesses, in return, helped build up political achievement indicators and generate local economic resources.

Although the evolution of post-Mao political and economic institutions crafted incentives for investment-seeking states across the country, bureaucrats did not respond to these institutions with equal degrees of enthusiasm. Rather, they tended to prioritize different goals in their in-

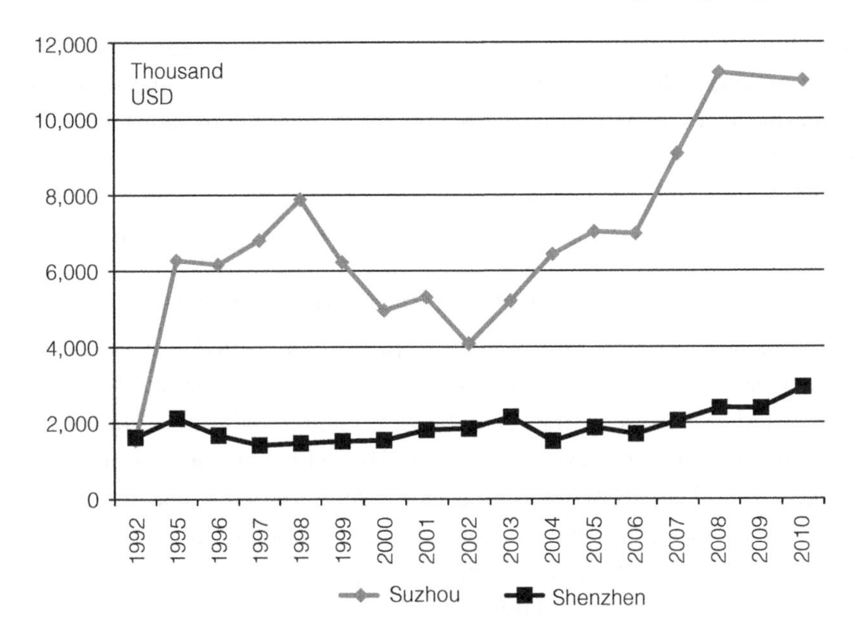

FIGURE 2.2. Average size of FDI projects in Suzhou and Shenzhen.

SOURCE: *Suzhou Statistical Yearbook; Shenzhen Statistical Yearbook* (various years).

vestment seeking. Bureaucrats in some localities (the Yangtze River Delta represented by Jiangsu) tended to seek allies from large, well-known multinational corporations (MNCs) that occupied the top positions of the production hierarchy so as to generate local indicators quickly. By contrast, their counterparts in other cities (the Pearl River Delta and Guangdong) put predominant focuses on nurturing state–business connections so as to generate immediate, practical economic benefits for the localities. Figure 2.2 shows the average size of FDI project attracted in Suzhou and Shenzhen between 1992 and 2010, in the two core manufacturing cities of Jiangsu and Guangdong, respectively. One can observe a persistent pattern of focusing on different types of FDI.

Although it could be argued that geographical proximity to Hong Kong may have contributed to the small size of the FDI projects in Shenzhen, this is far from the only cause. My field research in these two cities suggests that when Chinese ethnic firms (mostly from Taiwan and Hong Kong) sought to invest in these two regions, managers from smaller firms were typically rejected in the Suzhou area instead of the Shenzhen area.[10] I will demonstrate in the next two sections that the distinctive priorities of the local bureaucrats were clearly reflected in their different strategies of investment seeking, which shaped their later responses at the turning point to domestic firm competitiveness. Because these two regions pioneered the major strategies of local upgrading that were widely copied and practiced in other localities in China, they became highly influential in understanding regional trajectories of development. We will examine them in turn.

INDICATORS, ACHIEVEMENT, AND THE ALLIANCE WITH THE DRAGON'S HEAD

In the Jiangsu province, a major manufacturing base located in the Yangtze River Delta near Shanghai, investment seeking was clearly embraced as the most rapid and efficient strategy to boost economic indicators. Not every investment project, however, was equally favored by government officials. Large top-ranked MNCs stood out as the most favorable business allies for officials during the beginning of the 1990s. From the perspective of local bureaucrats, the essence of winning the political competition was not only realizing certain policy targets but also excelling at achieving them (or overachieving them) by accomplishing more and at a faster speed than peer competitors in other cities or counties.[11] The method used for score calculation in Jiangsu's cadre evaluation system can help to better understand the intensity of competition.[12] The score that city officials receive in cadre evaluation for a policy target is calculated as:

$$40 \times (X_i - \min(X)) / (\max(X_i) - \min(X)) + 60$$

In the formula, X_i is the actual value achieved for the policy goal, and $\max(X_i)$ and $\min(X)$ represent, respectively, the highest value and the lowest value of the indicators produced among all localities in Jiangsu.[13] The higher the value that a city achieved relative to other localities, the higher the score that city bureaucrats would receive. The system thus instilled strong downward pressure for higher-level bureaucrats to press lower-level bureaucrats within their jurisdiction for increasing indicators so as not to fall behind. At the same time, the institution also created upward pressure for lower-level bureaucrats to win over their peers for tenure and promotion.[14] The frequent news and media exposure of various rankings among different cities and counties further exacerbated the degree of competition. To excel at these competitions, bureaucrats had to search for, and often invent, the most efficient strategies for building up key indicators.

The Suzhou municipality/Kunshan city region was an excellent example of success in this respect. Suzhou, along with Wuxi and Changzhou, constituted the Sunan (southern Jiangsu) area, which was the wealthiest region and the earliest place for rural industrial development during the post-Mao era. Geographically, Suzhou includes seven city districts and five county-level cities (Changshu, Zhangjiagang, Kunshan, Wujiang, and Taicang). Central to the Sunan model was a strong involvement of the local government in publicly owned enterprises, including SOEs (state-owned enterprises) in the urban area and collectively owned township and village enterprises (TVEs) in the rural area (Oi 1999; Shen and Tsai 2016).

Although the role of TVEs and local developmental states in the 1980s captured most of the attention from scholars studying this period, these enterprises withered in part due to increasing debt issues in the face of soft budgets, and they were exacerbated by fiscal recentralization in 1994 (Ong 2012; Whiting 2001). Many important events took place in the critical juncture of the late 1980s and early 1990s, such as the Tiananmen crackdown in 1989, the beginning of the privatization of TVEs in the 1990s, the State Council's decision to open up the Pudong district in 1990, and the Southern Tour of Deng Xiaoping in 1992. At the same time, another process started to unfold. This process started with an initial FDI wave in Kunshan, spread across numerous other localities, and eventually washed away the TVE period by launching a new era in the 1990s. Not only did TVEs decline in the 1990s, but bureaus in charge of TVEs were also abolished. FIEs became the major development allies with local governments.

In the mid- to late 1980s, Kunshan became the region's pioneer advocate of the pro-FDI paradigm and established China's earliest locally funded ETDZ in 1985. Although the Singapore-Suzhou Industrial Park established in 1994 was the most widely known, Kunshan in fact had developed their own FDI zone almost a decade earlier. In 1987, Zhao Ziyang, the general secretary of the CCP, praised Kunshan's success during his visit and criticized Jiang Zemin, who was then the mayor of Shanghai, for dragging his feet in developing Shanghai ETDZ.[15] During the 1990s, numerous tours were organized for officials from other localities to study Kunshan's experience. By the end of the 1990s, the Kunshan model had been widely copied by localities within and without Suzhou. Not only did localities within Suzhou (such as Suzhou urban district, Wujiang, Zhangjiagang, Changshu, and Taicang) model their ETDZs after the Kunshan model, but other Jiangsu cities (such as Wuxi, Nanjing, Nantong, and Changzhou) all tacitly copied the same model, making Jiangsu one of the largest engines for inward FDI in China. A Wuxi city official, Mr. Liu, recalled that when he made his first trip to Kunshan ETDZ in the early to mid-1990s, he was simply amazed by the speed with which Kunshan attracted FDI. This was in sharp contrast to the TVE period, when Kunshan lagged far behind Wuxi. Mr. Liu thus immediately started pushing for the development of the Wuxi ETDZ after his return to Wuxi.[16]

What distinguished the region and contributed to its rapid rise was that only a few years after the establishment of the first FIE, local bureaucrats started to show clear "selectivity" in their preferences and strong "ambition" to attract large-scale, high-end (*gaoduan*) MNCs. Following Chinese General Secretary Zhao Ziyang's visit in 1987 and the subsequent state recognition of the zone, the provincial and municipality leaders immediately called for a "faster pace," "bold manner," and "higher starting point" in FDI attraction. In 1991, the Kunshan government responded by issuing its official decision to prioritize projects with "larger scale and higher technology."[17] Suzhou ETDZ, which was established after Kunshan ETDZ, did not even experience a few years of lead time with smaller FIEs before it directly leapt to a start by attracting top-tier electronics MNCs such as Samsung, Philips, Panasonic, and Logitech in 1994, with an average investment volume of US$100 million (Fan 1996: 23). Bureaucrats at various levels and in various departments were highly aligned in competing for and serving the interests of large MNCs, despite the fact that they fulfilled different functions in such investment-seeking processes (Bao 2006).

Large MNCs were chosen by local bureaucrats as developmental allies because they provided a shortcut for achieving political ambitions and building up economic and technology indicators, at a speed incomparable with small FIEs. Technology giants such as Samsung, Fujitsu, Foxconn, Compal, Intel, LG, Sharp, Philips, and Panasonic were simultaneously the major contributors to GDP, FDI, fiscal revenue, high-tech industrial output, and high-tech exports—all indicators that occupied the top position in the cadre evaluation system. These firms were regarded as the "dragon's head" enterprises (*longtou qiye*) that played a particularly crucial role in achieving rapid industrialization and economic development. Between 1986 and 1996, for example, industrial output in Kunshan ETDZ increased 58 times, exports 139 times, and total FDI 180 times. Suzhou soon rose to the top among Jiangsu cities in terms of all crucial economic indicators and has become the largest FDI recipient in China since 2001 (Zhong and Zhang 2009: 220; He 2002). The municipality leapt forward rapidly from a textile-production city to the largest global producer of IT products and one of the world's nine emergent new-tech cities (Rogers et al. 2001).

On the other hand, local governments, especially those in the international commerce department, often lacked the patience for and showed clear discrimination against small FIEs—which were viewed as "useless" to officials—by either turning them away or moving them out of the major investment zones (Xiao 2004; Guo 2006). An official in Suzhou ETDZ disclosed that the zone officials would basically not bother with any investment projects below US$30 million, which was the typical threshold for large projects in Jiangsu. Another Jiangsu official also admitted that he would not respond to any request for investment if they were small-sized FIEs.[18] In urban areas especially, small FIEs had a hard time getting land for their investment and were often squeezed by policies that favored large MNCs. Some small FIEs that entered the major development zones at the very early stage of the reform period were able to stay, but they had little bargaining power over local economic policies and felt the pressure of being kicked out of the zone at any time (Keng 2010: 253). In fact, Jiangsu bureaucrats tended to be especially proud of the Yangtze River Delta for its large-size, high-end investment, while showing disdain for the small-size, low-end investments in the Pearl River Delta.

Increasingly, the strategy of attracting large MNCs became in itself the target for local competition and ossified into a stable policy preference. The average size of investments in Jiangsu development zones expanded from US$3 million in the mid-1990s to more than US$10 million in Kunshan ETDZs and US$30 million in Suzhou ETDZs in the mid-2000s. By the end of 2003, 400 of the Fortune Global 500 MNCs had invested in the Yangtze River Delta, of which 91 poured more than US$8 billion into Suzhou, a record surpassing Nanjing and Wuxi (which had 37 and 58 of these firms, respectively) (Chen 2006: 67; Liu 2004). By 2006, 113 of the Global 500 had entered Suzhou by establishing 349 FIEs. Of the FIEs, 1,273 increased their investment volume, and 85.3 percent of FDI came from projects that were US$10 million or larger (Jiangsu Statistical Bureau 2008). The number of Fortune Global 500 firms a locality attracted also became a policy goal that cities in Jiangsu competed for as this not only boosted major economic indicators but was in itself a source of pride to glorify the image of the city in major media, statistical bureau rankings, and the annual reports submitted to the provincial and central government.

Nothing could be taken for granted in getting investment from large MNCs. The rise of Suzhou and the Yangtze River Delta rested on the adoption, adaptation, or invention of strategies that specifically prioritized large MNCs in exchange for impressive economic indicators and political achievement. The first important policy invention was to adapt the central government's requirement for the government's shareholding in joint ventures by directly attracting large wholly foreign-owned enterprises (WFOEs). As already mentioned, to accomplish or supersede the "hard targets" in FDI attraction and other economic areas, bringing in large-scale MNCs was the best choice. However, if local governments had adhered to the practice of setting up JVs in the 1980s and 1990s, the available fiscal income in their coffers—only 70 to 80 million yuan in the mid-1980s in Kunshan, for example—would allow them to participate in only small-sized JVs. This would accomplish policy targets at a much slower speed. With careful calculation of cost and benefit, local bureaucrats boldly decided to give up any profit shares in JVs and experiment with directly bringing in large WFOEs. The practice, which could be traced back to the mid-1980s, was first to register these enterprises as JVs on paper, then immediately change them into de facto WFOEs by transferring all government shares to the foreign side (Zhong and Zhang 2009: 53–54). Without taking the risk, recalled a top local leader, "It would not be possible for large MNCs to come in, and we would not be able to have the economic and industrial achievement that we have today."[19] Even the provincial government, which preferred the cautious approach of forming JVs in the 1980s, started to overtly praise the "unbeatable advantage" of attracting large WFOEs to Suzhou in 1993 (Gao 1993).

The second important policy weapon was to launch a campaign among all levels of bureaucrats to lure MNCs with aggressive beneficial policies. This was where one could see Mao's "invisible hand" in campaign politics (Heilmann and Perry 2011). Just as cadres were assigned the task of filling certain quotas in identifying "counterrevolutionaries" during the Mao era, each level of bureaucrats was now assigned a task of attracting a specific number of large-scale projects (Zhou 1995: 28; Lu 2003; Bao 2006).

Taxation was an especially useful tool, and tax reduction was as generous as a "five-ten" schedule, which meant tax exemptions for the first five years and 7.5 percent for the next ten years, in contrast to 33 percent for domestic firms. Although both Jiangsu and Guangdong offered tax reduction, their practices *after* the taxation period were substantially different.

Because Jiangsu officials prioritized performance indicators, one of which was revenue performance, they adopted the policy of tax collection followed by tax return (*xian zheng hou fan*). This means that city tax agencies first "collected" or "borrowed" taxes from large businesses. Then, they would refund or return the taxes to enterprises after their annual report to the provincial level so as to both guarantee high local indicators of tax revenue and provide an actual tax break for enterprises.[20] As will be shown in the next section, this was in direct contrast to the policies adopted in Guangdong for retaining the revenue at the local level.

Discounts in land prices were another source of attraction. The cost of developing land was 200,000 yuan per mu in 2005, but local governments in Jiangsu—especially Suzhou, Kunshan, and Wujiang—were willing to reduce the price to between 50,000 and 60,000 yuan per mu, or, at the county level, even offer free land for projects that exceeded 100 million yuan. In addition to the benefit packages, free factory buildings, discounts in utility rates, and government-designated banks for easy-access loans were made available (Yuan 2006; Sun 2007). A manager of a Japanese electronics MNC branch in Suzhou regarded many of these beneficial policies as simply hard to believe because they were not seen in any other developing countries.[21] Local officials who waited at the international airport and scrambled for investment opportunities were aware of the downside of such a "race to the bottom" competition, but, given the intensity of competition, they would rather not lose the game to other localities.[22]

The efficiency of local governments in the entire Jiangsu region was unprecedented. They went out of their way to ensure these FIEs a business-friendly environment, often at all costs. They provided and negotiated favorable conditions for FIEs with upper-level governments, just as they promoted collective enterprises in the 1980s. In the early 1990s, Taiwan Compal, the second-largest global manufacturer of notebook computers, planned to outsource to Shanghai, and it had the Shanghai government build 150,000 square meters of factory for the company. The Kunshan government immediately competed for this opportunity by offering even better tax and land policies, and relocated 80 households of peasants within 30 days to vacate the land to build the Compal factory (Zhang 1997; Zhong and Zhang 2009: 49). Similarly, Taiwan Jean Optoelectronics marveled at the speed of the Wujiang government, as it took the officials merely 97 days to have a 15-acre factory building constructed and turn in the key (Jin 2005). In fact, building an environment that "befriends the business, ensures the business, and enriches the business" became the slogan for local governments to serve foreign businesses and was formally published as government policy in cities such as Kunshan and Wujiang (Li and Zhao 2006).[23] Both ETDZs and High Technology Development Zones (HTDZs) established a package of services that simplified bureaucratic procedures for foreign businesses. Kunshan ETDZ also formalized these packages of services into rules entitled "The 28 Codes for Serving Foreign Business" so as to channel the behavior of bureaucrats.

Furthermore, to build up indictors as fast as possible, officials tended to focus on using generous beneficial policies to gain contract signatures from large MNC projects ahead of other localities. This tendency often led officials to risk signing contracts that were too ambitious to materialize or to create fake contracts for the purpose of accomplishing investment-seeking targets. Once the contract was signed, the actual implementation of the contract often took much longer due to the large size of the project (Wang 2006). This tendency was reflected in the relatively low ratio between actually used FDI and contracted FDI (also called utilization rate) in Jiangsu, which was on average 25 percent in the 1990s, much lower than the 42.3 percent in Guangdong during the same period. Even in 2001, when Suzhou rose to the top of all cities in terms of the volume of contracted FDI, its utilization rate in FDI was 42 percent, much lower than the 95 percent in Shenzhen (Zhou 1995: 27–29; He 2002: 18; Yang 1998).[24] The low FDI utilization rates certainly could cause wasted resources and corruption by using government beneficial resources to lure foreign investors. However, this method of FDI attraction nevertheless helped maintain Suzhou's position as the largest FDI recipient in China.

The efforts of Jiangsu's officials seemed to pay off. The impressive and rapid economic achievement earned them numerous political rewards. Jiangsu bureaucrats maintained their historical reputation for success in political promotion tracing back to the Qing dynasty. The political promotion of Suzhou and Kunshan bureaucrats was particularly eye catching. Kunshan city was widely regarded as the best "launch pad" for the successful takeoff of one's political career, and Suzhou became the "cradle of provincial governors" (J. Chen 2008: 75; Li 2004). Since the 1990s, five of the CCP secretaries from Kunshan were promoted from the county level to positions at the *ting* level or higher, including two provincial-level leaders and three prefectural-level municipality leaders. Three of the CCP secretaries of Suzhou, Liang Boahua, Chen Deming, and Wang Min, were, respectively, promoted to provincial CCP party secretaries and minister of commerce. On the one hand, the accomplishment of attracting investment brought political promotion, whereas on the other hand, political career success also reinforced the tendency to seek investment to build political achievement.

FLEXIBILITY, ECONOMIC GAINS, AND THE ALLIANCE WITH GUERILLA INVESTORS

Manufacturing localities in the Pearl River Delta represented by Shenzhen continued their tradition of being "petty capitalists" and took a practical approach by attracting small-sized FIEs; they were often referred to as "guerilla investors." The notion of "guerrilla investors" is borrowed from You-tien Hsing (1998: 4–5) and refers to small-scale investments negotiated with individual officials at the grassroots level that are highly flexible in terms of property rights arrangements and investment conditions. With the active help of local bureaucrats, these investors penetrated cities, counties, townships, and villages with small-scale investments that were highly flexible in terms of property rights arrangement. Instead of boasting target indicators and advertising their long list of large top-ranked MNCs as bureaucrats in Jiangsu tended to do, officials in Guangdong protected and hid these investment projects, especially during the initial years of China's opening to foreign investment.

Central to the attraction of guerilla investors was the practice of signing an "informal contract" brokered by local bureaucrats. Although the contract was nominally signed between a foreign investor and a local Chinese firm on paper, the latter often existed in name only due to the weak industrial basis of the Pearl River Delta. The local government was the de facto representative of the Chinese side. These enterprises were called *san lai yi bu* firms, which engaged in processing and assembly based on the supply of materials, sample design, components, and imported machinery from foreign investors. The Chinese side provided land, factories, and labor. After completing the final products, the foreign investor would submit an annual processing fee (*gong jiao fei*) to the local government. The contract was informal because the enterprise created out of the contract was not an independent corporation and did not have a formal legal status. Instead, it only had "special permits for production" issued by the local Industry and Commerce Bureau and was registered under a collective enterprise owned by the local government, usually under the name "Economic Development Company of X Township/County."

The first such informal contract in Shenzhen, for example, was signed in the late 1970s between Hong Kong Electrical and Electronics and Shangwu Brigade Processing Factory in Bao'an County, Shiyan Commune. The Shangwu village CCP branch was the actual representative of the Chinese side. The firm created by the contract, the Yigao Electrical Loop Firm, was set up on the second floor of the Shangwu village party branch office building as a disguised FIE wearing a collective hat (Zhou 2005: 48–49; *Southern Metropolis Daily* 2007). To use a common metaphor from local entrepreneurs, *san lai yi bu* could be seen as "a foreign-domestic marriage without a marriage certificate" (Lu and Xu 2009).[25]

Most official statistical data (except from the city of Dongguan) do not treat these firms as a distinct category, but it is estimated that, between 1979 and 2000, of the 12,000 Taiwanese-invested firms in Guangdong, more than 8,000 first established firms through informal contracting. Even as late as 1998, 660 of 850 FIEs attracted to Shenzhen's Longgang and Baoan districts that year initially took the form of informally contracted enterprises. In the electronics industry, at least 980 such enterprises were established between 1980 and 2000 (Zhou 2005: 49; Wang and Chen 2000; Wei, Zhang, and Guo 2010: 22). Compared to the "dragon's head" MNCs in the Yangtze River Delta that occupied the top of the value chain, "guerilla investors" in the Pearl River Delta engaged in components manufacturing and assembly and were mostly situated at the bottom of the value chain. These projects brought in new industries, such as the electronics and IT industries, but they were small in size and developed along the "old" mode of "petty" capitalism.

Local bureaucrats played a crucial role in creating, supporting, and legitimizing the "uncertified marriages" through flexible practices, and by doing so they increased ties with numerous small-scale foreign investors, especially overseas investors from the China circle of Hong Kong and Taiwan. Foreign investors could directly avoid paying taxes due to their lack of legal status, and they found the procedure of signing informal contracts with local bureaucrats in a week much more appealing than taking two months to formally register a foreign enterprise.[26] For local officials, informal contracting provided them quick access to the benefits of foreign investment—local industrialization and employment—while circumventing the cautious regulation of foreign capital by the central state. By protecting these enterprises under the "collective" umbrella, in a similar way to the protection provided during the Mao years, bureaucrats were able to preserve the image of a "socialist" country on the surface but gain the benefits of capitalist investment in reality.

Moreover, contracted projects provided local governments with revenue through the payment of the processing fee. In the Longgang district of Shenzhen, for example, after various taxes and bank fees were deducted, the enterprise kept 75 percent of the processing fee, and the remaining 25 percent was shared among district, township, and village governments. The exact division among the three varied according to the level of government that set up the project and signed the contract (Zhan 2007). A district government could gain 20 percent of the fee from a district-level enterprise but only 11 percent from a township or village enterprise. A township government received no share of the fee from a district-level enterprise but was entitled to 9 percent from a township enterprise and 8 percent from a village enterprise. This was in addition to the land-leasing fees that each level of government collected.

As such, bureaucrats at each level went out of their way to broker deals between foreign investors and nominally Chinese enterprises. They boldly promoted the practice of informal contracting, investing in infrastructure, leasing out collectively owned land for factory buildings, providing startup capital, and offering generous tax holidays in negotiating with investors, among other measures. In some localities, such as Jingsha township in Shenzhen's Baoan district and the Shahe township of Guangzhou's Tianhe district, where local revenue was initially not enough to cover the cost of factory buildings and utilities to attract foreign investors, local cadres experimented with raising money by issuing bonds and stocks to individual villagers and later turning the entire brigade into a shareholding company. Local residents increased their income not only through direct employment but also by holding these highly profitable bonds (Huang 1993; Guangzhou 2005). In other localities, bureaucrats provided land and allured foreign investors to provide the initial capital for building factories but under the name of local Chinese enterprises (Zhan 2007). The negotiation process between bureaucrats and investors was typically individualized and the conditions of investment tailored to the needs of the bureaucrat and the firm.

Like the Jiangsu cadres, Guangdong bureaucrats adapted central policies and invented the institution of informal contracting to attract FDI. Also similar to the Jiangsu bureaucrats, they used various beneficial policies to compete for investment. However, in contrast to the Jiangsu cadres, Guangdong officials were not primarily aiming to build up local indicators for political achievement, and they did not mind "hiding" the projects within their jurisdiction whenever necessary or underreporting the investment.[27] And, unlike their Jiangsu counterparts, which specifically concentrated on projects that were "high, large, and new" instead of projects that were "short, small, and quick," the Guangdong cadres held the latter as exactly the key for local development.

A crucial difference in taxation practices from Jiangsu and especially Suzhou was that instead of adopting taxation followed by return (*xian zheng hou fan*) policies, officials in Guangdong in effect implemented policies of exemption followed by taxation (*xian mian hou zheng*). This means that local city governments would first offer tax reductions and exemptions to enterprises. After the enterprises were established, local governments would then charge post hoc levies and fees and turn them into extra budgetary revenue (Fu 2000: 174–180).[28] Therefore, local governments in effect *increased* locally retained funds and local revenue bases at the cost of the revenue to the center. Although the central state attempted to rein in the local behavior of arbitrarily granting concessionary treatments, the beneficial policies generated by the two central policy paradigms provided a crucial justification for the practice whenever these treatments were approved or inspected by the upper-level government or corresponding agencies (Zhou 2005; Zhang 2012).

The focus of Guangdong was to bring investment in and establish FIEs in the easiest, fastest, and most flexible way. In this regard, local cadres' pursuit of pragmatism certainly demonstrated Deng Xiaoping's well-known saying that "it doesn't matter whether a cat is white or black, as long as it catches mice." The Suzhou strategy of ranking projects in a hierarchy and selectively providing support to those situated at the top was neither desirable nor feasible in the Pearl River Delta context. Instead of employing a top-down campaign-style mobilization in which all cadres collectively targeted the same large MNCs, individual bureaucrats brought in small-scale FIEs at the level of their personal capability in a much more dispersed manner. There was much less focus on large MNCs and far less discrimination against small FIEs. Furthermore, because the incentives for attracting FDIs were far more economic than political, Guangdong bureaucrats also did not need to risk signing hard-to-implement contracts or even fake contracts just for the purpose of acquiring signatures from large "dragon's head" MNCs and surpassing the policy targets in a fierce political competition.

Crucial to the process of attracting foreign investors through informal contracts was the fact that it gradually gave birth to domestic suppliers that gained orders from foreign producers. This means that informal contracting (*san lai yi bu*) firms gradually evolved to include two types of enterprises. The first type has already been mentioned: foreign-invested and foreign-controlled firms, most of which directly reregistered as FIEs during the 1990s (Wells 1983). The second type was firms run by domestic parties—publicly owned and privately established—that received orders from foreign companies. Due to their initial focus on processing and assembling based on imported materials, these firms were also widely referred to as "*san lai yi bu*" firms. However, they were independent domestic enterprises that were controlled and managed by Chinese managers rather than foreign firms wearing Chinese hats. They developed as some investors from Hong Kong and Taiwan no longer directly set up firms in Guangdong (or physically commuted there to guide the production) but felt more confident placing their orders with local producers that had already gained manufacturing experience. Among the foreign-invested firms that had already set up manufacturing in Guangdong, an increasing number also began to purchase locally rather than outsourcing to other producers in their supply chains, precisely due to their small size and limited capital and organizational resources. These foreign firms were responsible for providing materials and equipment, inspecting the products, paying the processing fees, and selling the final products but hardly intervened in the hiring of personnel or the daily management of production. The contracts between two parties were thus closer to compensation trades than joint ventures (Zhou 2005: 48). Most firms chose to engage in processing trade in the initial stage to accumulate capital, and over time the Chinese producers went beyond producing for a single customer and gained the rights to accept orders from other parties as well as to manufacture their own products.

With the rise of the pro-FDI paradigm and the stabilization of the FDI environment in the 1990s, not only did the first type of firms begin to register (or reregister) as FIEs, but an increasing number among the second type started to wear a foreign hat. The latter happened in the format of round-trip FDI, when a domestic entrepreneur set up a firm overseas (often in Hong Kong) and reinvested in the Pearl River Delta to enjoy the beneficial policies for FIEs. Skyworth Group, for instance, was established by a domestic entrepreneur, Huang Hongsheng, who returned to

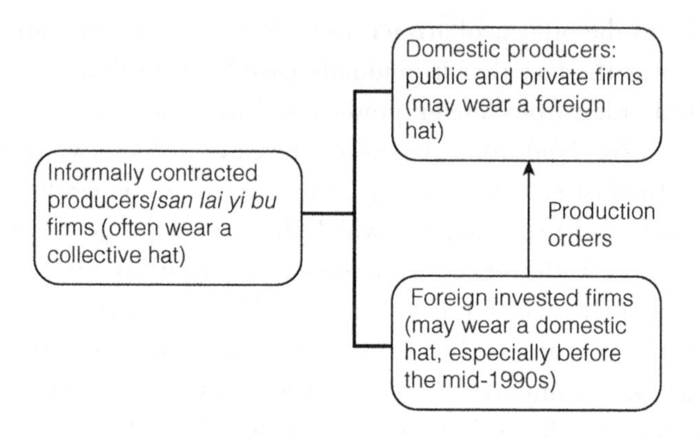

FIGURE 2.3. The emergence of foreign and domestic firms.

Guangdong from Hong Kong as a foreign investor. The enterprise was initially registered as a FIE and was changed to a domestic private enterprise only after it gained stable support from the local government.[29] The boundary between the two categories of firms—the ones invested by China circle entrepreneurs and the ones invested by domestic entrepreneurs— was thus increasingly murky. It is not exaggerating to argue that the small- and medium-sized guerilla investors from the China circle area laid the foundation for the emergence of independent domestic suppliers in Shenzhen, as illustrated by Figure 2.3.

The relationship between foreign and domestic firms in Shenzhen was very different from the one in Suzhou, although such an important difference might have been hard to notice at the beginning of the post-Mao era. Whereas the entrance of MNCs disrupted the development process of domestic firms, the guerilla foreign investors contributed to the growth of domestic producers. Such positive impacts of FDI can be traced to the pattern and sequence in which the local government intervened in the economy. Local bureaucrats adopted a broad-based strategy that encouraged a variety of sources, foreign and domestic, public and private, to set up firms and experiment with the production of electronics components or end products.

The Consequence of an Investment-Seeking State

The rise of distinctive FDI-attraction activities among governments during the 1990s and early 2000s generated important consequences for the adoption of distinctive strategies and development trajectories in the later phases of local industrial transformation. First, the type of foreign invested firms attracted to a locality influences the willingness of city governments to invest in resources to upgrade domestic technology, with the rise of the new paradigm to promote domestic technology competitiveness. As Chapter 4 will show, in cities where top-ranked MNCs were attracted, foreign firms and exporters largely overlap with each other, as domestic firms hardly control the channel of exports. These cities are far more likely to experience a cohesive, vested-interest coalition consisting of international commerce bureaucrats who fight the rise of domestic technology. These bureaucrats regard foreign firms as their clients (due to the overlap of foreign firms and exporters), and they viewed the shift in policy as a political threat. Furthermore, the production of foreign firms also tends to be concentrated in large firms with the presence of top-ranked MNCs. This feature increases the bargaining power of the vested-interest group and its likelihood of winning. Subsequently, bureaucrats of domestic technology also experienced more obstacles in pushing for an increase in science and technology funding and other resources.

Second, as Chapter 5 will show, the type of foreign firms that each government attracted also generated quite different incentives for domestic firms to invest in any upgrading, innovation, or higher-value-added activities. This feature has made some types of government support more effective in producing firm-level results than others. Cities dominated by MNCs at the top of the value chain tend to shrink the development space and quash the incentives for firms to engage in upgrading. On the contrary, counterpart cities with lower-ranked FIEs located at the lower segment of the value chain nurture the interest among domestic firms to upgrade. This means that regions are further trapped into the patterns and paths of development. These profound and long-lasting influences of China's engagement in globalization will be therefore unfolded in the rest of the book.

CHAPTER 3

From FDI Attraction to Domestic Competitiveness

> Despite the new situations we are facing, the strategy of "exchanging market for technology" remains effective.
>
> Guangming Daily, *December 4, 2004*[1]

> Some industries faced the embarrassing situation where "little technology has been acquired, and much market has been lost." Especially, China's entry into the World Trade Organization (WTO) and its commitment to further open the domestic market left little room for "exchanging market for technology."
>
> People's Daily, *March 30, 2011*

> Indigenous innovation is the core competitiveness of a country, is the vital choice that our country made in meeting future challenges, and is the fundamental path to realize the goal of building an innovation-oriented country.
>
> *Hu Jintao, Former President of China, 2006*

The rise of FDI-attraction strategies in China has aroused an increasing number of problems, ranging from deterioration of labor conditions to unrealistic competition for concessionary policies among local governments and rising environmental challenges. At the heart of the criticism of FDI, however, are whether China benefits from attracting FDI and the fundamental concerns regarding the lack of competeiveness of indigenous firms. The criticism emerges at both central and local levels, but the ultimate signal for industrial transformation was marked by the rise of central state discourse and preferential policy packages associated with indigenous innovation and domestic upgrading. This chapter traces the initiation of the transformation and the rise of new discourse within the central state. It then lays out the policy goals and matrix of institutions, supporting development zones (ETDZs and HTDZs) and policy tools within each paradigm, including government funding, tax breaks, and land allocation. The rise of the domestic upgrading paradigm, in competition with the previous pro-FDI paradigm, has created new pockets of resources but also instilled new incentives for political competition in local China.

The Rise of the "Indigenous Innovation" Paradigm and China's High-Tech Dream

The second policy paradigm originated in the late 1980s, a decade after the pro-FDI paradigm.[2] The emphasis on independent technological catch-up is not new. The idea can be traced back to the Mao era, but, before the late 1980s, policies involving this aspect had limited influence over government agencies that were not mainly concerned with science and technology. The division of labor during that time was such that the State Science and Technology Commission (SSTC) and its local subsidiaries were mainly responsible for science and technology policies at research institutions and the development of a select few high-tech, defense-related industries, such as nuclear weapons, aerospace, and mainframe computers. To put it more straightforwardly, these agencies were in charge of, and therefore mainly interacted with, scientists and technicians rather than enterprises. Thus, despite the fact that policies such as subsidizing science and technological research as well as rewarding technology progress always existed, they were mainly circumscribed to the science and technology (S&T) circle without major influences over the national economic agenda. Due to the dominance of the first policy paradigm in the 1980s, the main concern of S&T policies at the enterprise level was facilitating the "introduction" and "transfer" of technology from abroad. In fact, the "15-Year Science and Technology Development Plan" drafted in 1982 specifically mentioned that "the major technology needed for national economic development should be primarily based upon introduction of advanced technology from abroad," and should "move away from the full process of independent R&D" (State Planning Commission and State Science and Technology Commission 1982).

Starting in the mid- to late 1980s, however, a type of technonationalism advocating the promotion of high-tech industries started to rise in response to the first policy paradigm. Although it is hard to find documented records on the direct opposition to "exchanging market for technology" in the 1980s, partly due to the growing power of the pro-FDI camp, more recent reports suggest that there were widespread reservations against this strategy among bureaucrats and scientists within the S&T circle. Concerns about the relationship between introducing foreign technology and conducting independent research also sparked serious debates among policy makers (Zhu 1984). In March 1986, four scientists from the China Science Academy collectively submitted a letter to the central party, suggesting the "urgent need" to promote basic research in high-tech areas, which resulted in the state's decision to carry out a high-tech development plan, later known as the 863 Plan. This was followed by the launching of the Torch Plan in 1988, which is often regarded as the starting point of China's high-tech dream in the Deng era (Feigenbaum 2003; Zhi and Pearson 2017).[3]

The Torch Plan specified key areas of high-tech industries—including electronics and IT, biotechnology, and aerospace—and encouraged the commercialization and marketization of products from basic research through the development of high-tech enterprises. In particular, the plan pushed forward the initiative of establishing high-tech development zones (HTDZs) to realize the goal of "transferring domestic S&T talent into high-tech industries based on China's own technological and economic capabilities." A total of 53 HTDZs were approved as national HTDZs during the 1990s, with the first group of 27 HTDZs approved in 1991, followed by another 25 in 1992 and one in 1997. Like ETDZs, the HTDZs provided beneficial policies in tax rates, tariff rates, bank loans, and land and rental prices, among others. The differences were that (a) HTDZs were mainly targeted at high-tech enterprises instead of all manufacturing industries and that (b) HTDZs emphasized the promotion of high-tech industries among indigenous Chinese enterprises. As will be shown, the creation of HTDZs provided a vital institutional vehicle for the prolocal camp to push forward national policies.

During the first half of the 1990s, the SSTC, together with the State Council, drafted and issued several rounds of five-year and ten-year science and technology plans.[4] Although these plans did not directly criticize the strategy of exchanging market for technology, they aimed to push for the establishment of a vibrant national system that would be conducive to technology innovation and S&T progress. The plans highlighted, in particular, the importance of conducting "independent research" in addition to introducing technology from foreign countries. For China to catch up with advanced technology at the international level, one of the plans argued that China should mainly rely on its own (*yi wo wei zhu*) and should actively promote innovation to achieve major breakthroughs.[5] Several other proposals during this period also emphasized the necessity of going beyond a simple mode of depending on foreign countries, through learning, digestion, and exploring the technological capabilities of the Chinese firms themselves. Furthermore, the decision to develop and provide assistance to nongovernmental (*minyin*) technology enterprises through enterprise incubators was also made during this period (Segal 2003: 34).

In the late 1990s, the goal of "exchanging market for technology" gradually devolved into a justification for FDI-dependent development. Strong criticism started to emerge in policy and academic circles. The term *Latin Americanization of China* was widely used in the 1990s to express worry about China's overdependence on foreign capital, depicting a gloomy future of growth without development. As the development zone fever grew, it sparked heated debate among domestic and foreign observers on whether China had already become another Latin America and whether a growth process based on relentless attraction of FDI would be sustainable. At the same time, various studies and news reports pointed out that the reliance on low wages, low taxes, and low-priced land in competing for FDI had generated ruinous competition that caused severe damage to the environment. Others pointed out the danger of "mindless" economic growth without innovation. Adding to the anxiety was China's entrance into the WTO and the prediction that most of China's firms lacked the capability to compete with MNCs (Nolan and Wang 1999; Nolan and Zhang 2002).

Building on the momentum from the public criticism, the Ministry of Science and Technology (MOST) (since 1998), in collaboration with several academic institutions, carried out a wide range of in-depth studies on key industries such as electronics and IT, automobiles, telecommunications, and aviation in the early to mid-2000s. These reports, which were widely distributed within the government and later partly published through the national media, revealed the fact that two decades after China's reform and opening, domestic enterprises in most of the key sectors still lacked an independent capacity for developing new products and the incentives to conduct R&D. The reports further attributed such problems to the so-called exchanging market for technology strategy, which triggered unprecedented competition for FDIs among government officials at the expense of abandoning indigenous innovation. As a result, most domestic firms of these industries remained at the level of "assembly factories" or peripheral component suppliers, with limited progress in technology and learning capabilities since the 1980s (Lu 2006).

It was also among these reports and various associated publications that the concept of "indigenous innovation" formally emerged in the public sphere in the mid-2000s (Liu et al. 2011).[6] Despite various interpretations, the concept was largely taken to mean that an enterprise or a nation has mainly relied on itself in developing technological capabilities and achieving technological innovations. The word *indigenous* shows a strong reaction against the FDI fever associated with the strategy of "exchanging market for technology." Proponents of the concept argued that there was nothing wrong with introducing and borrowing foreign technology but that this process would not automatically translate into learning and innovation capacities. Furthermore, dependence on foreign firms as a source of technology often reduced or eliminated the desire among domestic firms to innovate. As a result, domestic firms often fell into the vicious circle of "lag–import technology–lag again–import again" (Wen and Hua 2006). Although innovation in the common sense was by definition independent and indigenous, they argued that the term *indigenous innovation* was especially important for the Chinese context, where dependence on foreign technology and later on FDI often *displaced* the independent process of product development and technological innovation.

The criticism in the publications was immediately circulated within the Ministry of Science and Technology and received increasing attention from other central government agencies. Translating the concept of innovation into practical guidance, however, took more efforts over an extended period.[7] When "innovation" started to catch national attention, it was understood in various informal ways, with no single interpretation being able to dominate. The Hu-Wen leadership later produced a standard meaning that decomposed the concept into three categories: original innovation, integrated innovation, and secondary innovation based on adaptation of foreign technology. Although this interpretation became the most frequently cited source in public talks, it did not provide policy guidance by itself. Thus, despite the broad meaning that "promoting indigenous innovation" could take theoretically, in the policy contexts of China it eventually boiled down to further developing high-tech industries and enterprises.

In May 2001, the State Development and Planning Commission (SDPC) and the MOST jointly published the "Tenth Five-Year Plan of Science and Technology Development."[8] The plan adopted the term *indigenous innova-*

tion for the first time and pointed out that one of the major overall goals for the next five years was to "dramatically raise the country's overall level of science and technology and the capacity of indigenous innovation." The central strategy in realizing such major goals was to accelerate the pace of industrial upgrading and continuous technology innovation in several key high-tech industries that were of vital importance to the national economy, including electronics, optoelectronics, IT, biotechnology, aerospace, and new materials industries. The eventual long-term goal was to build a national innovation system in which enterprises were the major agents for innovation, supported by institutions that brought together industry, university, and basic research (*chan xue yan jiehe*). In the same year, several decisions and regulations drafted by the MOST (2001) were also announced in support of the development of high-tech industries, including a detailed regulation on managing the 863 plan.

The theme of developing high-tech enterprises was also reinforced when MOST hosted a national meeting in 2001 with the mayors from all of the cities where national HTDZs were located. The meeting called for a "second undertaking" (*di erci chuangye*) among HTDZs, which was later published as the "Decision on Providing Further Support for the High-Tech Development Zones" by MOST in 2002 (Pi and Wang 2004). Referring to the decades since the late 1980s as the "first undertaking of HTDZs," the decision proposed that all HTDZs enter a new stage of a "second undertaking." The first stage established a favorable environment and laid the primary foundation for developing high-tech industries, and the new stage was aimed at taking several key measures in improving innovation capacity. These included developing and improving enterprise incubators, establishing service platforms for industries, extending supply chains, and increasing the added value of high-tech products.

The momentum provided further justification for the rapid spread of HTDZs across the country, and HTDZs started to play pivotal roles in local industrial growth. In 2006, for example, national HTDZs accounted for more than 11 percent of China's total industrial output, with the within-zone industrial added value increasing to eight times the value of 1998. Meanwhile, among 53 national HTDZs, 33 of them accounted for more than 20 percent of the industrial added value of the city in which they were located, 22 of them accounted for more than 30 percent, and 9 accounted for more than 40 percent (The Statistics Department of the Center for Torch Plan 2007). Between 2006 and 2011, another 30 HTDZs successfully passed their application to become national-level HTDZs, increasing the total number to 83. This was a much faster approval rate than in the period between 1997 and 2006, when the total number remained at 53. These recent figures for the proportion of HTDZs do not include the thousands of local development zones that were applying for but have not yet been approved as national zones. Yet, even examining only state-level development zones, it is evident that HTDZs have become an engine for national and local economic growth.

By 2010, a total of 90 ETDZs and 83 HTDZs established by local governments across the country were successfully approved by the central government as national development zones. Meanwhile, thousands of development zones, established as ETDZs, HTDZs, or other forms (but not necessarily at the national level), emerged rapidly across the country. For example, there were 3,837 development zones in China in 2002, and this number increased to 6,686 by the end of 2003.[9] These development zones were established by city, county, or township governments that were actively seeking the approval of the zones at the state and provincial levels.[10] It was estimated that, in 2005, 68 percent of China's GDP and 87 percent of China's exports came from all types of development zones at the national and the local levels. In fact, the zone fever was so far out of control that the state council decided to crack down in 2004 (Yang 2006; S. Li 2008: 271).

A caveat that has to be added is that not all these zones are targeted at developing manufacturing industries or any type of industries at all. Some have been established for real estate development that contributes to GDP but not to industrial (*shi* ye) development. For any development zones that are mentioned in the rest of the chapter, therefore, I generally refer to the type of ETDZs and HTDZs that, relatively speaking, target industrial development.

Competitions and Compromises

After two decades of development and change, the national economic agenda has become increasingly dominated by two coexisting paradigms. By the first decade of the 2000s, both paradigms showed the ability to be sustained over a considerable amount of time, despite ongoing reinterpretations. Proponents of the first paradigm started with an argument based on "exchanging market for technology" and eventually took a strong pro-FDI stance, as they interpreted FIEs as being the major source of technological

TABLE 3.1.
Two national economic policy initiatives.

Initiatives	FDI attraction	Domestic upgrading
Time period	1990s to early 2000s	Mid-2000s to present
Main argument by the central government	By opening the domestic market to foreign investment, China can benefit from foreign advanced technologies using its low-cost labor	It is essential to build indigenous technology and innovation capabilities; cautions against overreliance on FDI
Major policy goals	Attracting FDI and promoting foreign firms to have spillover effects on the domestic economy	Promoting high-tech enterprises and enhancing indigenous innovation capacity
Major central proponents	Ministry of Commerce (previously the Ministry of Foreign Trade and Economic Cooperation)	Ministry of Science and Technology (previously the State Science and Technology Commission)
Supporting development zones	Economic and Technology Development Zones (ETDZs)[a]	High Technology Development Zones (HTDZs)
Supportive tax policies	15% income tax for foreign firms within ETDZs; those planning to stay for 10 years or longer could be exempted from income taxes for the first two years and submit 7.5% corporate income taxes for the third to fifth years; 24% for foreign firms outside of ETDZs, and among those, 15% for industries encouraged by the state (compared to 30% for all other production enterprises); 40% to 100% return of previous taxes when the firms used profits to reinvest in the zone; all foreign firms in the zone were exempt from investment adjustment taxes. Due to the policy shift, starting in 2008, income tax rates for foreign and domestic enterprises were unified at 25%.	Abolish the income tax exemption for foreign firms; all enterprises should submit 25% income taxes unless they fall into categories encouraged by the state; 15% income taxes for enterprises within the zones, 10% for enterprises that export more than 70% of their gross output; new enterprises are exempted from income taxes for the first two years; income tax exemption for the first 30,000 RMB used for technological transfer and services; exemption of income taxes for high-tech products; domestic enterprises exempted from investment adjustment taxes if building factories for technology development; 15% income tax rates for all state-recognized high-tech enterprises within or outside of HTDZ zones, starting in 2008
Government funding	Decided by local government	The State Innovation Funds, the 863 Plan, and the Torch Plan (implemented through local governments). Various types of local government funds for enterprise startup, enterprise renting, and enterprise R&D. Government rebates for patent applications, enterprise recruitment process, and science and technology activities
Supportive finance policies	Preferred enterprises were matched with banks by governments	Banks are encouraged to provide loans to high-tech enterprises within the zone.
Supportive trade and tariff policies	All export products produced within an ETDZ were exempted from tariffs; all products except oil were exempted from industry and commerce taxes; imports of machinery, office devices, raw materials, parts and components, and so on, were exempted from import tariffs, product taxes, and/or value-added taxes.	High-tech enterprises are exempted from export tariffs. The imports of raw materials and machinery that cannot be purchased domestically are exempted from tariffs.
Other policies	Infrastructure and land policies decided locally	Localized personnel policies for the salary, bonus, and welfare of highly educated personnel

[a] The name "Economic and Technology Development Zone" does not directly indicate its function because it was first created in the 1990s to attract foreign investment and develop export-processing zones. The function, therefore, differs from the High-Technology Development Zone.

spillover for the domestic economy. The paradigm was supported by government agencies associated with foreign investment and trade, such as the OSEZ, MFTEC, State Economic and Trade Commission (SETC), and Ministry of Commerce (MOC) (since 2003). The second paradigm, which emerged as a critique to the first, emphasized the importance of indigenous innovation capacity and translated such spirit into the development of high-tech industries. Supporters of the paradigm mainly consisted of government agencies in charge of science and technology policies, such as the SSTC before 1998 and MOST since 1998. Underlying each paradigm are various preferential policy packages in taxes, credit, land, and funding aimed at promoting FIEs or high-tech enterprises.

A cursory look at the pattern of competition between the two paradigms, as some domestic and foreign observers tend to make, may very well lead one to simply conclude that domestic upgrading is taking the lead. After all, two important facts have clearly signaled this tendency. The first is shown in the increasing contributions of HTDZs to the national industrial and economic growth. The second lies in the revision of the discourse from the pro-FDI program and the increasing national unity around the goal of indigenous innovation. An examination of the articles published in *People's Daily*, the mouthpiece of the Chinese Communist Party, suggests a sharp rise in the number of times that the term *indigenous innovation* appeared in news article titles, in comparison to the term *foreign capital*, as Figure 3.1 illustrates.

ETDZs and HTDZs have been racing each other since the 1990s, in terms of the number of zones approved at the national level and the major economic indicators. Beginning at the turn of the century, national HTDZs started to catch up with and, in some cases, surpass ETDZs in terms of major economic indicators, such as industrial output, total tax revenue, and total exports. For example, in 2003 the average industrial output of national HTDZs reached 32.5 billion yuan compared with 21.7 billion yuan for ETDZs. In 2007, 54 national HTDZs generated a total industrial output of 4.44 trillion yuan, total tax revenue of 261 billion yuan, and exports of 173 billion yuan (Ministry of Science and Technology 2008). These numbers for the 54 national ETDZs were, respectively, 3,842 billion yuan, 203 billion yuan, and 178 billion yuan (S. Li 2008: 273). Except for exports, all other indicators of HTDZs have surpassed those of ETDZs.

The rise of "indigenous innovation" not only produced a significant impact on the national economy but also seemed to succeed in forcing the

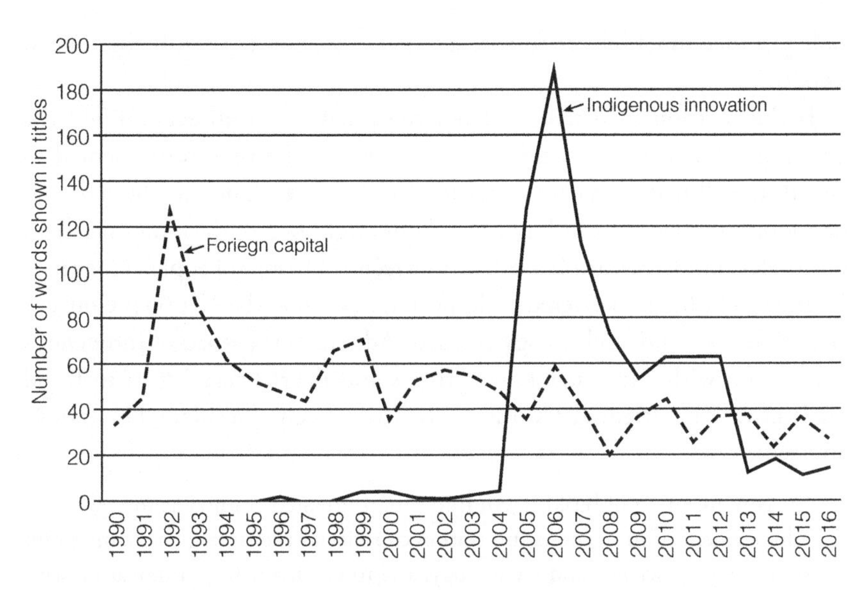

FIGURE 3.1. The number of times that *People's Daily* articles mentioned *indigenous innovation* and *foreign capital* in the title.

SOURCE: *People's Daily* 1990–2016.

pro-FDI camp to make concessions in their discourse. In 2004, the MOC launched the "second undertaking" among national ETDZs, just as MOST did among HTDZs. The core task, as Vice Premier Wu Yi specified in the national convention of ETDZs, was to go beyond the pure focus on the amount and scale of investments in the past two decades and devote attention to the quality of such investments. To replace the previous three "major focuses" of the mid-1980s, the convention established three new "major focuses" and two "commitments" as the goal of ETDZs within the "new context." As such, ETDZs should "focus on improving quality in attracting foreign investment, on developing modern manufacturing industries, and on improving the export structures"; meanwhile, they should commit to developing high-tech and high-value-added industries. The convention pointed out that, to enhance indigenous innovation capacity, development zones should encourage FIEs to outsource production activities with higher added value and to establish R&D centers in China. For the first time in their public discourse, pro-FDI advocates officially endorsed the importance of building "high-tech industries" and "indigenous innovation." By showing that they were not against innovation and in fact could incorporate the element into their own strategy, they seemed to have moved their policy stance much closer to that of their competitors than before (Yuan 2008).

If the revision of discourse from the pro-FDI camp exemplified the growing influence of the indigenous paradigm, the year 2006 seemed to signal its full-fledged victory and its decisive ascendance to the national development strategy. On January 9, 2006, right before the announcement of the eleventh five-year plan by the fourteenth National People's Congress, President Hu Jintao delivered an important speech at the National Convention of Science and Technology entitled "Adhere to the Road of Indigenous Innovation with Chinese Characteristics and Exert Every Effort to Build an Innovation-Oriented Country." In the speech, President Hu (2006) stressed:

> The core meaning of building an innovation-oriented country is to regard the enhancement of indigenous innovation capacity as the strategic starting point for developing science and technology, and to break a path of innovation with Chinese characteristics. It means that enhancing indigenous innovation is the central step in adjusting industrial structure and changing the previous pattern of growth . . . It means that enhancing indigenous innovation is the national strategy which guides the various aspects of modernization and inspires the innovative spirit of the entire nation.

In the same convention, Premier Wen Jiabao (2006) also delivered a speech on indigenous innovation:

> Indigenous innovation is the soul of science and technology development, the source for a nation's development, and the backbone for the rise of the country. Without indigenous innovation, it will be hard for us to gain a fair standing on the international arena, hard to gain a nation's dignity, and even hard to stand up among the world of various nations. In the fierce international competition, the truly core technologies *cannot* be acquired by exchanging them with market, *cannot* be bought by money, and introducing technology and equipment *does not* mean introducing innovation capacity. We should mainly rely on ourselves for our development . . . and let it guide the [development of] all industries, sectors, and regions . . . so as to build our country into an innovation-oriented country. (emphasis added)

For proponents of the second paradigm, the 2006 speeches symbolized the central state's recognition and encouragement of their decades of effort in developing indigenous high technology. On January 9 the front page of the CCP mouthpiece *People's Daily* (2006) endorsed the event as another "spring of science," after the one in 1978. Since then, both speeches have been widely cited in news media, public talks, government-issued documents, and academic publications as support for "indigenous innovation" and building an "innovation-oriented country." The two goals were also naturally incorporated into the Eleventh Five-Year Plan and have spawned a number of related slogans in the party state's key publications, calling for fundamental changes, such as "from a large economy to a strong economy," "from producing for foreign brand to producing for own brand," and "from 'Made in China' to 'Created in China.'"

The "policy blueprint" for the Hu-Wen speech and other slogans was the "The National Medium- and Long-Term Plan for the Development of Science and Technology (2006–2020)" published by the State Council. The ambitious plan, which caught significant attention both home and abroad, specified several key goals to be reached by 2020, including an increase in China's R&D expenses to 2.5 percent of GDP or greater, the contribution rate of science and technology to economic growth reaching 60 percent, the degree of dependence on foreign technology to be lowered to 30 percent or less, and China becoming one of the world's top five countries in terms of number of patents from domestic applicants (State Council 2006).

In fulfilling the plan blueprint, MOST and National Development and Reform Commission (NDRC) have been leading the process in making a whole package of innovation policies, such as the promotion of "indigenous innovation products," a reevaluation of and continued support for "high-tech enterprises," the establishment of "enterprise technology centers" and "engineering research centers," as well as the cultivation of "indigenous innovation demonstrating areas." In all of these policies, the state established a matrix of indicators for evaluating whether the policy targets (products, centers, or areas) were qualified before they could enjoy associated beneficial policies. These targets were accordingly labeled as "nationally recognized" products, enterprises, centers, and areas, just like state development zones. Further exemplifying the effort was the more recent megaplan for the "National Technology Innovation Project," which was proposed by MOST and jointly launched with six state agencies in 2009. The project reemphasized the "central" role of enterprise, the "guiding" role of the state, and the "directing" role of the market in establishing a national innovation system. It also called for building strategic innovation alliances in key industries and asked for the support of all other institutions, ranging from education and research institutions and enterprise service platforms to banking and financial systems. The Ministry of Information Industry (and Ministry of Industry and Information Technology, since 2008), which sought to show its alliance with the new agenda and, perhaps more important, to show its own distinctive function in industrial upgrading, announced its program of evaluating and recognizing the State Industrial Park for the Electronics and IT Industry.

Given all the slogans and policy initiatives, it is not surprising that many domestic and foreign observers tend to argue that "indigenous innovation" has replaced other paradigms in becoming the national priority for twenty-first century China. This argument seems to be further confirmed by the state's implementation of the Law of Income Taxes for Enterprises in 2008, which abolished the differences in tax rates between FIEs and domestic enterprises. As described by the U.S. Chamber of Commerce in a more aggressive way, "Indigenous innovation is a massive and complicated plan to turn the Chinese economy into a technology powerhouse by 2020 and a global leader by 2050" (McGregor 2010). Along with the observation of the rising technonationalism are warnings about the restrengthening of state capitalism and the mercantilist subsidies for domestic producers against foreign firms, which were seen as a serious backlash against China's reform and opening process (Miles 2011; Dean, Browne, and Oster 2010; Bradsher 2010). On top of all of these worries is the growing fear of China as a rising economic superpower, threatening the positions of the United States and other developed countries that were experiencing economic downturns and shrinking manufacturing industries.

Transformation on the Ground: Competing Paradigms at the Local Level

Against the heated discussion over the rise of domestic upgrading in place of the pro-FDI paradigm, the two paradigms coexisted and competed with each other across many of the localities where I conducted research. Unlike the central government, which typically shifts policy paradigms from time to time, typically according to changes in political contexts and the ideas of the major leaders, local governments have to find ways to achieve domestic transformation and maintain policy continuity at the same time. Once foreign-invested firms were established in these localities, these firms became important business allies of local governments, and the different types of global firms that localities attracted during the pro-FDI period laid the basis for the government's adoption of particular upgrading strategies. In other words, local governments created distinctive ways—based on their long-established interests, policy tools, and patterns of state intervention—of linking the two paradigms. They also tried various ways to achieve this transition, from attracting FDI to using global firms to promote industrial upgrading and indigenous innovation. These distinctive local approaches are embedded in the varieties of capitalism in China and have reflected the struggles, competition, and reconciliation among the narrower top-down and broader bottom-up styles of industrial policies, among policy makers both within the local governments and at the level of industrial firms. Only in a selective number of locales, however, did the two paradigms achieve harmonious coexistence with each other. In many other places, the transformation simply became trapped in struggles for resources among bureaucratic coalitions, each with its own business clients.

An economic transformation at the central level has thus become a political issue at the local level. Exploring the politics of such local transitions not only is the key for understanding the variation among Chinese localities but also allows us to tease out political, economic, and institutional factors that contribute to the success and failure of the transitions. As will be shown, the initial alliances that local governments stroked with foreign businesses profoundly affected the ways in which local bureaucrats fought over resource allocation and transited to the stage of domestic upgrading.

CHAPTER 4

Local Policy Making, Globalized Coalitions, and Resource Allocation

> Why are we trying so hard to promote the interests of our own business clients? Forget about those big words such as making our city a better place; we have to get concrete benefits for ourselves. That was the biggest reason and the real reason.
>
> *City government official in Suzhou, 2010*

For many scholars and observers, changes in China's policy paradigms often seem to proceed in a top-down fashion. In fact, as Chapter 3 illustrated vividly, Beijing constantly shifts economic policies or announces new ones, so much so that experts studying the country often view it as a fast-moving target. Yet, contrary to the expectation that autocrats enforce their decisions coercively, the processes of carrying out policies and establishing institutions on the ground are often open to question. Even policies can be shifted relatively quickly from the center (although one should not simply assume that this is so), and local governments must deal with the realities of implementing policies, for such implementation often takes place in a heterogeneous environment with advocates for both old and new policies. Therefore, understanding the politics of local economic decisions in large multilevel countries such as China is key. When do new policies succeed, and when do they fail, at the local level?

This chapter brings to the forefront the local politics of economic policy making in response to national paradigm change from FDI attraction to domestic upgrading.[1] The key insight of this chapter is that local governments' previous attraction of foreign businesses, as discussed in Chapter 2, is important for the success or failure of new policies and institutions at the city level aimed at domestic upgrading. New initiatives are most likely to be impeded by a coalition with a vested interest that comprises city government bureaucrats in charge of international commerce. These bureaucrats are likely to form a cohesive coalition to combat and/or manipulate the new policy when foreign firms overlap with exporters in a city. At the same time, such a coalition is likely to gain political influence over top city leaders when industrial sales of foreign firms are concentrated in large firms. Taken together, these two conditions contribute to cohesive and strong vested interests. Such circumstances exacerbated the difficulty for agencies advocating for domestic upgrading to push for new policies or to provide government support. Two sets of institutions governing local politics, the cadre evaluation system and the informal rule of fragmented bureaucratic competition, have enabled and channeled the influence of foreign firms.

This chapter explores in-depth mechanisms of how the configuration of foreign firms has affected government–business coalitions and bureaucratic competition based on case studies and personal interviews conducted during 18 months of fieldwork. The argument is then tested using a newly constructed dataset that covers most jurisdictions of prefecture-level Chinese cities for which statistical data exist between 2007 and 2010. The analysis highlights the local challenges to implementing central developmental initiatives, especially during the tumultuous times when potential winners and losers tend to fight. In so doing, the chapter sheds light on both path dependence and change in the local implementation of economic policies and developmental strategies.

Central Policy Shifts and Local Responses

Since the Hu-Wen leadership formally launched the agenda of indigenous innovation in 2006, significant changes have taken place across localities. The initiative legitimized and encouraged science and technology expenses among prefecture-level cities, making the end of 2006 and the beginning of 2007 an important departure point for expenses across Chinese cities (Figure 4.1). At the same time, the beneficial policies in government funding, taxation, land, and utilities enjoyed by foreign firms would be gradually abolished. Before 2007, income tax rates for foreign firms were only 15 percent, less than half of the 33 percent charged to domestic firms, and many foreign firms enjoyed five to ten years of tax breaks with zero to 5 percent taxes. After 2007, favorable tax policies for foreign-invested enterprises (FIEs) were phased out, and both domestic and foreign firms are now subject to an income tax of 25 percent.[2]

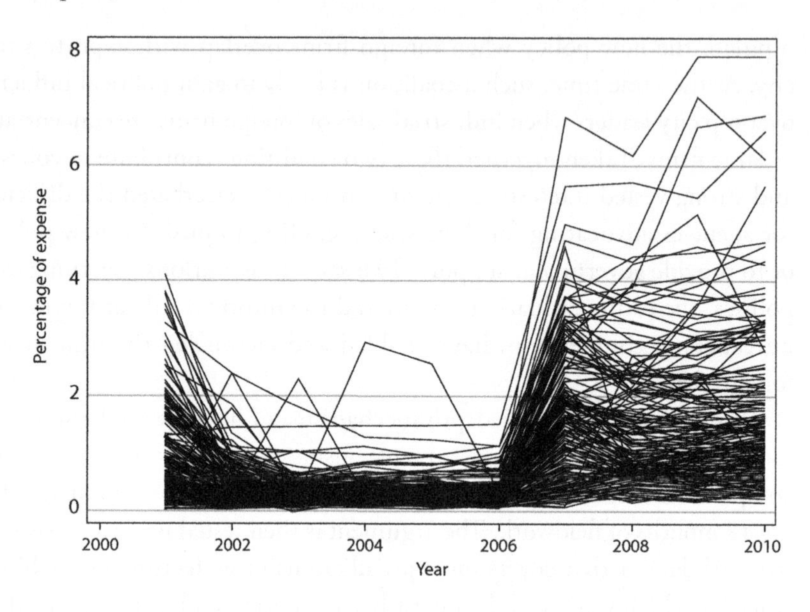

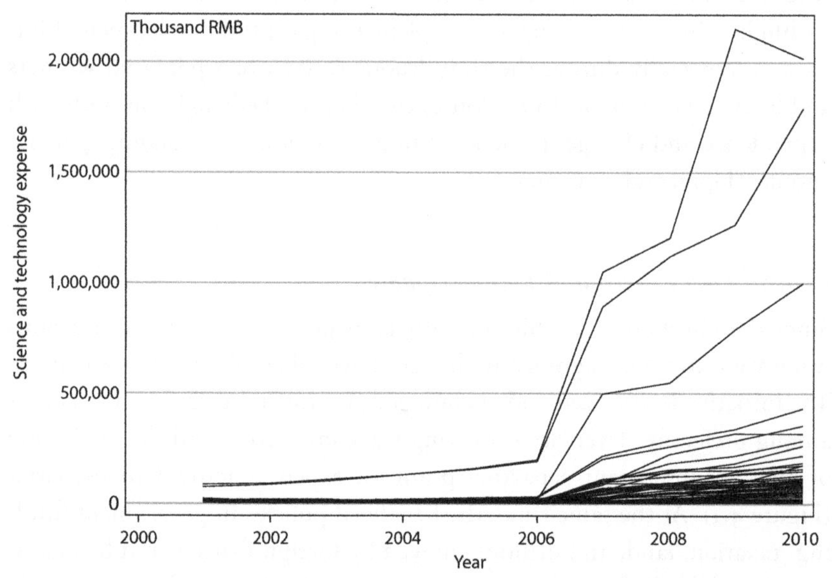

FIGURE 4.1. Government support for domestic technology in prefecture-level cities, 2000–2010.

The central government played a pivotal role in signaling the overall national goal; to put it in colloquial terms, the government indicated "which way the wind was blowing."[3] Local governments, as always, announced corresponding policies that served as supportive gestures. However, within local governments, bureaucrats' attitudes were far from uniform, and struggles were intense. This variation most significantly manifested at the prefecture-city level, which is why I have chosen this level as the unit of analysis here. The province level is simply too broad to capture the vast variation among cities, as will be shown. The county level, in contrast, often does not possess decision-making power over many industrial policies concerning government funding and tax breaks for domestic competitiveness, as has been suggested by field research. The prefecture-city level, in contrast, often controls budgetary resources for science and technology and a certain degree of autonomy independent of the provincial government for allocating budgetary spending.[4]

Figure 4.1 indicates that although many cities experienced a spike in 2007 in terms of science and technology expenditure, others immediately saw this expenditure drop or flatten; that is, some did not have any increase. In 2008, for example, in government funding at the firm level, science and technology activities expressed as a percentage of GDP differed across prefecture-level cities (Figure 4.2). Moreover, this variation does not correspond to provincial borders. Field research suggests that a seemingly well-intentioned policy or reform initiated by the national government—in this case, upgrading domestic technology—often entails unintended outcomes stemming from the complicated process of local coalition politics and tension.

Bureaucratic Coalitions and Globalization

The policy shift in the mid-2000s involved the interests of two groups of agencies within city governments (see Table 4.1). The first group consists of departments of international commerce, such as the Foreign Economic and Trade Bureau, the Bureau of Investment Promotion, and the Economic and Technology Development Zone Committee.[5] These departments were the major beneficiaries of FDI-attraction and export-promotion policies that began in the 1990s; as a result, the resources associated with these departments significantly increased. With the rise of the new paradigm and the loss of some foreign ownership benefits in the mid-2000s, these departments became major (potential) losers. The second group consists of newly emerged policy-implementation agencies intended to promote domestic technology, including the Bureau of Science and Technology, the

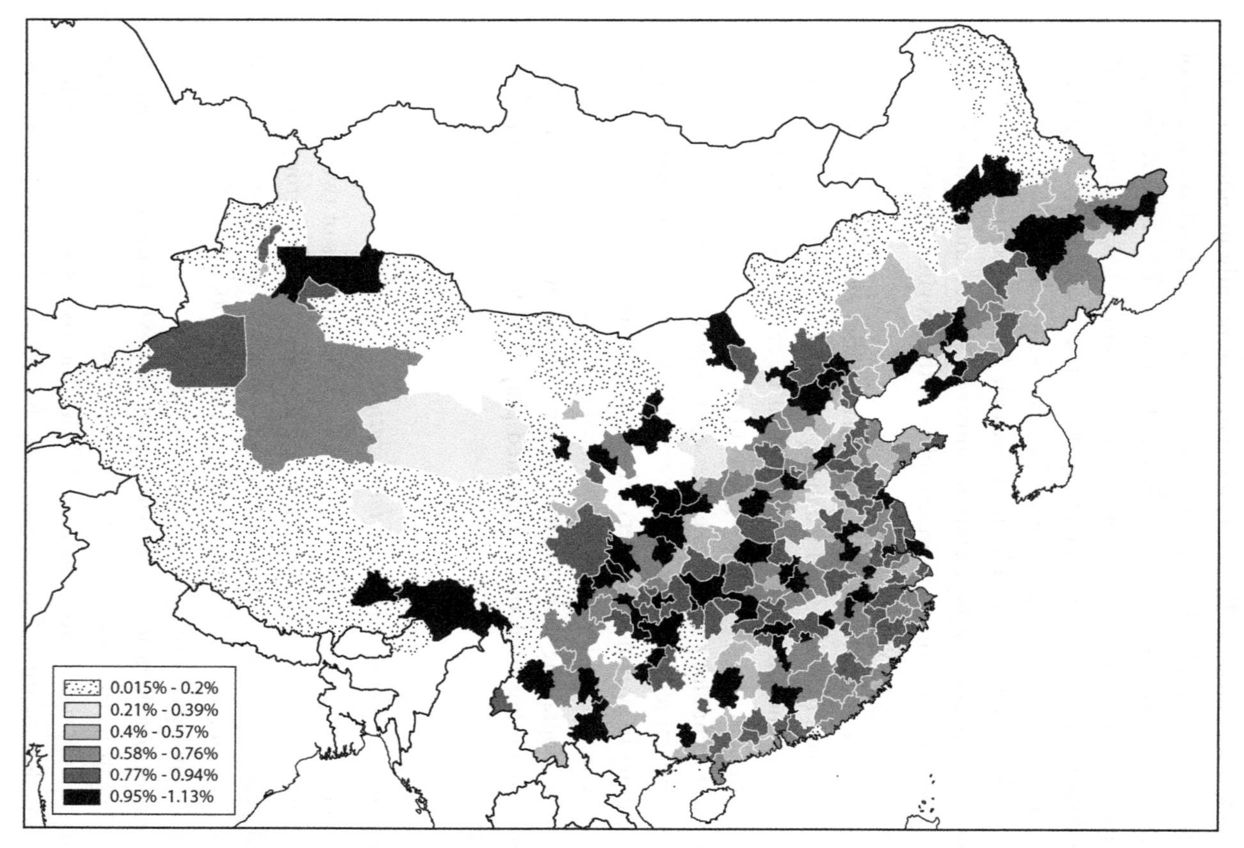

FIGURE 4.2. Prefecture city government funding for firm science and technology activities as a percentage of GDP in 2008.

SOURCES: Based on data from China Economic Census 2008; *China City Statistical Yearbook 2009*.

TABLE 4.1.
Policy paradigms and supporting government agencies in the mid-2000s.

Initiatives	FDI attraction and export promotion (previous)	Domestic technology (new)
Major policy goals	Attracting FDI and promoting exports by using low-cost labor	Promoting the technology competitiveness of domestic enterprises
Central proponents	Ministry of Commerce (previously Ministry of Foreign Trade and Economic Cooperation)	Ministry of Science and Technology (previously the State Science and Technology Commission)
Local implementers	Foreign Economic and Trade Bureau,* the Bureau of Investment Promotion, and the Economic and Technology Development Zone Committee	Bureau of Science and Technology, the Economic and Information Commission, and the High-Technology Development Zone Committee
Supporting development zones	Economic and technology development zones	High-technology development zones

* At the local level, most of the Foreign Economic and Trade Bureaus have changed to the Bureau of Commerce since 2010.

Economic and Information Commission, and the High-Tech Development Zone (HTDZ) Committee. The primary responsibilities of these agencies consist of enhancing and improving the technological competitiveness and innovational capacity of firms to facilitate firm-level learning and to provide high-tech firms with government support and policies. These agencies were (potentially) empowered by the policy shift toward domestic technology upgrading (that is, indigenous innovation).

During the Hu-Wen regime, Chinese localities became arenas in which departmental interests (*bumen li yi*) became the "biggest challenge" for policy implementation, according to China's current premier, Li Keqiang (2015). These departmental interests are embodied in the long-entrenched logic of "where you stand is where you sit" in Chinese politics (Shirk 1993). Bureau heads within departments typically rally division heads (one level below bureau heads) and ignite struggles with other bureaus or commissions to further their own department's interests.[6]

To explore the coalition dynamics behind the policy process, I visited four of China's coastal cities. They share a similar range in terms of population (7 to 10 million), per capita GDP, exports, level of FDI (6 to 8 percent of GDP), and first instance of FDI.[7] These cities differ, however, in terms of the composition of their foreign firms. Suzhou and Wuxi in Jiangsu province, Ningbo in Zhejiang province, and Shenzhen in Guangdong province

TABLE 4.2.
Cases in comparative perspective.

	High concentration of foreign firms	Low concentration of foreign firms
High overlap between foreign firms and exporters	**Suzhou** Cohesive vested interests from international commerce; strong bargaining power	**Wuxi** Cohesive vested interests from international commerce; weak bargaining power
Low overlap between foreign firms and exporters	**Ningbo** Noncohesive vested interests from international commerce; a few individually based proposals, which are dispersed; bureaucratic competition restricted to domestic technology	**Shenzhen** Noncohesive vested interests from international commerce; weak bargaining power; bureaucratic competition restricted to domestic technology

each represent a "type," as shown in the two-by-two matrix, with respect to FIE exporter overlap and degree of FIE concentration (see Table 4.2). These cities were chosen for a comparative case study due to their importance in manufacturing industries and their similarity in basic economic conditions.[8] In each city, I carried out semistructured and in-depth interviews (averaging 1.5 hours) with bureaucratic officials in city government departments; these officials were in charge of international commerce and domestic technology. There were 29 officials in Suzhou, 32 in Wuxi, 36 in Ningbo, and 21 in Shenzhen. Interviews were used both to shed light on the implementation process and to act as semistructured surveys of the four cities.

My discussions and interactions with bureaucrats in these cities showed that, in general terms, the two basic rules of Chinese bureaucracy dominate economic policy processes in local governments. The upward accountability created by the cadre evaluation system that governs millions of bureaucrats in China is still prevalent. Unlike Western democracies, the ruling political elites are motivated by accountability from above rather than from below. The cadre evaluation system has shaped the incentives of top leaders (party secretaries, mayors, and vice mayors of cities), who are evaluated on the basis of policy targets and promoted by provincial-level officials (Manion 1985; O'Brien and Li 1999; Li and Zhou 2005; Liu and Tao 2007; Landry 2008).[9] Thus, city leaders also place downward pressure on rank-and-file bureaucrats within city governments, who then maximize policy targets to obtain political promotion and economic bonuses.

In addition to the urgency of achieving policy targets, Chinese bureaucracy also features fragmentation. Rather than a coherent bureaucracy defining economics policies, as in the East Asian developed states, Chinese bureaucracy exhibits pervasive fragmentation and competition, as captured by the notion of "fragmented authoritarianism" and the "policy enforcement market" noted by other scholars (Lieberthal and Oksenberg 1988; Lampton 2013; Mertha 2006, 2009). Therefore, the pressure of cadre evaluation placed on various departments certainly generates competition to establish political achievements and to supersede policy goals (Jing, Cui, and Li 2015). Furthermore, the redundancy in bureaucratic functions of multiple agencies with overlapping authorities, coupled with the fact that financial resources are almost always insufficient, exacerbates this turf war (Pearson 2005; Lampton 2013: 86). Overall, struggles revolve around three key areas.

First, bureaucratic departments compete for their own political survival. Due to the overlap of government functions, government agencies are frequently reorganized, merged, and even abolished during government restructuring.[10] Within such a context, government agencies compete to survive by showing the "necessity" rather than the "redundancy" of their functions, which is also associated with the bureaucratic ranks officials care so deeply about. When national priority shifted (that is, when FIEs became less important), bureaucrats associated with FIEs worried about the legitimacy of their existence and sought to demonstrate their continued relevance.[11]

Second, authority and control over key policies (*shiquan*) provided government agencies with the opportunity to establish political achievement and to increase their power over other government bodies by setting local rules. The ascendance of the pro-FDI paradigm in the early 1990s significantly strengthened international commerce departments' penchant for establishing local economic rules. The paradigm also created numerous opportunities for political achievement and led to promotion at various levels. In contrast, prior to the 21st century, the role of science and technology departments was mainly restricted to guiding research institutions, with a weak role in economic activities.[12] The rise of the domestic competitiveness paradigm substantially enhanced their role in economic and industrial affairs. Ironically, this explains the rise in bribes of domestic technology officials after the policy shift.[13]

Third, the preferential policies legitimized by policy paradigms provided bureaucrats with the resources to build and consolidate patron–client relationships with businesses.[14] A business is identified as the *client* for a government agency if the agency's function mainly involves regulating the business and the business also relies on that agency for preferential policies.[15] Unlike other policies, such as birth control, tax collection, and pollution reduction, which typically cause implementation headaches, economic and industrial policies are often "resource-bearing" policies that bureaucrats yearn for. Controlling these policies translates into budget increases and new institutions (platforms, zones, and research centers). Moreover, it translates into receiving the authority to approve preferential policies granted to firms, including, but not limited to, tax exemptions, government funding, credit allocation, and land and utility discounts for business clients. For instance, Foreign Economic and Trade Bureau (FETB) and the ETDZ Committee had the authority to decide and negotiate whether a foreign enterprise would fall within the "encouraged" (instead of "restricted") industries, thereby determining, essentially unilaterally, the years of tax exemption the enterprise could enjoy. For their part, the Bureau of Science and Technology and the HTDZ Committee controlled the authority to evaluate and grant an enterprise the title of "high tech," with its concomitant funding benefits. In exchange, the patron–client relationship provided government bureaucrats with economic benefits (such as bribes) as well as records of political achievements that could be drawn on for future political promotion.

Although bureaucrats in all four cities—Suzhou, Wuxi, Ningbo, and Shenzhen—agreed that bureaucratic competition is just a fact of life, it is puzzling why the policy process and outcomes during the policy shift differ so greatly. Previous studies shed little light on this discrepancy, for bureaucratic competition sometimes impedes and other times facilitates policy implementation. To understand this discrepancy, one must consider the role of foreign firms and the way in which they enable and strengthen bureaucratic coalitions.

In the process of coalition formation, bureaucratic competition impedes policy enforcement when a group of bureaucratic competitors outside the functional area of domestic technology (rather than within it) mobilize to challenge implementing agencies. This is far more likely to occur when foreign firms and exporters overlap in a city because it unites bureaucrats in international commerce. The primary responsibilities of these bureaucrats are (a) attracting foreign investment (which, by default, is done by foreign firms) and (b) promoting exports in the city (which can be done by foreign and/or domestic firms). When foreign firms and exporting firms de facto overlap in a city, bureaucrats focused on international commerce become the primary regulators for foreign firms; hence, these bureaucrats see foreign firms as their long-term business clients. The rise of new policies hurts the interests of international commerce bureaucrats and elicits a coherent voice of opposition.[16] In contrast, even when a city has many foreign firms, if it has less overlap between foreign firms and exporters, bureaucrats dealing with international commerce can have clients that are domestic exporters as well as foreign firms. Such a mix of clients mitigates the foreign–domestic struggle. In the latter case, most bureaucratic competition has been kept within departments in charge of domestic technology and the implementing agencies of the new policy, which can facilitate the speed of implementing policies.

In terms of coalition strength, when FIE production in a city is concentrated in a few large global firms, vested-interest groups are found to have more bargaining power—and are, therefore, more likely to be strong—compared to those in which output is shared among small and medium foreign firms. City party secretaries and mayors have tended to favor and develop close relationships with bureaucrats who boost city indicators significantly and rapidly. In economic decisions regarding budget and resource allocation, the vested-interest group can use the existence of large foreign firms and wield power with top city leaders, preventing a domestic technology coalition from increasing its resources.

THE FORMATION OF THE VESTED-INTEREST GROUP

Although the rise of new policy could make international commerce departments potential losers, this does not necessarily mean that vested-interest groups emerge in every city and fight against new policies. Rather, their emergence depends on the existence of a consistent and coherent perception among potential losers. It is precisely here that the existence of foreign firms made a difference. As previously discussed, when foreign firms and exporting firms overlapped in a city, international commerce bureaucrats interacted mostly with foreign firms because any "international" elements in the city (foreign investment *and* export) are conducted by foreign firms. Therefore, foreign firms are viewed as their long-term business clients. Domestic firms, on the other hand, were regarded as irrelevant to the bureaucrats' interests as they were neither foreign investors nor major exporters. These bureaus in international commerce quickly gained traction in city governments during the 1990s and early 2000s because FDI attraction and export promotion occupied China's attention during this period (Zheng 2014; Tao 2006).

Suzhou and Wuxi (which modeled its FDI zone after that of Suzhou) are typical examples of cities in which foreign firms have been the primary exporters. Many of these foreign firms were brand-name multinationals that dominated the major exporting channels, whereas domestic suppliers focused on manufacturing peripheral components instead of final products. Between 2001 and 2005, about 75 percent of exports in Suzhou and 60 percent of exports in Wuxi were done by foreign firms. As such, most business clients of bureaucrats working in international commerce departments in charge of foreign investment and trade were foreign firms. There was a sharp division of labor among bureaucrats along the line of ownership of their business clients.

Figure 4.3 shows the results of the author's semistructured interviews with bureaucrats in the two departments. When asked, "In your daily work, which types of firms do you often interact with and regulate?" most

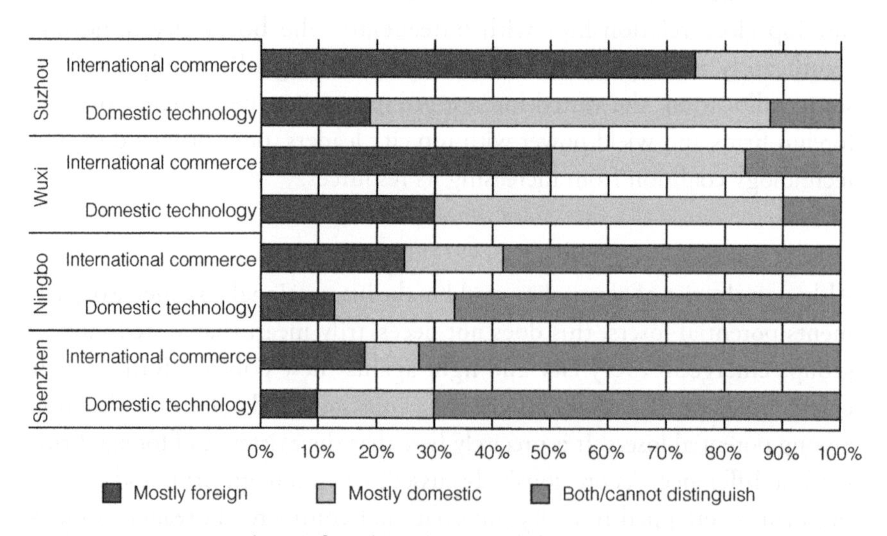

FIGURE 4.3. Business clients of city bureaucrats (scaled to percentage).
These charts depict, in percentages, local officials' answers to the author's question: "In your daily work, which types of firms do you often interact with and regulate?" The total numbers of bureaucrats interviewed were Suzhou (29), Wuxi (32), Ningbo (36), and Shenzhen (21).

bureaucrats in the international commerce departments of Suzhou and Wuxi identified foreign firms as the major business clients with which they interacted. In contrast, officials in domestic technology departments mostly viewed domestic firms as their business clients. Taken together, 93 percent of bureaucrats in Suzhou and 87 percent of bureaucrats in Wuxi (of officials who responded to the semistructured interviews in both departments) chose one type of firm or the other as their regular business clients, leaving only 7 percent and 13 percent in each city who considered themselves to interact with both types of business. In fact, when a Suzhou official in the Economic and Technology Development Zone (the FDI zone) was asked about the development of domestic firms, or when a Wuxi official in the Bureau of Science and Technology was asked about a foreign firm in the city, they both answered that the firm(s) in question "have nothing to do with my job."

Given this division of labor, it is not surprising that the ascendance of the domestic technology paradigm evoked intense reactions in Suzhou and Wuxi. Bureaucrats in the international commerce departments—whose clients were almost solely foreign businesses—saw the change as a severe threat not only to their business clients but also to their own political careers. The adoption of the 2007 tax reform, which phased out the original half-income tax rate and other beneficial policies for income taxes on foreign firms, also caused widespread worry. As a senior official from the Foreign Economic and Trade Bureau commented,

> We summoned an urgent meeting with the Bureau of Investment Promotion and Economic and Technology Development Zone, as all our current institutions were built to support these foreign firms. Why did they suddenly abandon foreign firms and want to emphasize the technology capacity of indigenous firms? The entire plan originated from officials in the science and technology system, who apparently were trying to expand their power. But we have come up with our own ways to deal with it.[17]

This type of panic echoes comments from bureaucrats in the international commerce bureaus in Wuxi, who found the new policy "biased," "threatening," and "annoying."[18] They interpreted the new policy as a threat to their interests and, in reaction, mobilized a coherent group of bureaucrats from various international commerce departments, who blocked policies and competed with domestic technology departments. In both cities, officials disclosed that bureaucratic competitors of the domestic technology group came from the international commerce departments. In Suzhou, for example, one finds a battle between two camps. On one side, there were the domestic technology departments (Bureau of Science and Technology and Economic Information Committee), which applauded the new policy as the coming of a "spring" for science and technology. On the other, there was the Foreign Economic and Trade Bureau, which pushed back against the change.[19] The former reported that they pressed for an increased government budget, tax breaks, and land discount policies for innovative domestic firms in government meetings, though they confessed to little success in reality. The latter, however, actively competed by stressing the importance of foreign firms and the "unfinished" mission of attracting foreign investors in various official meetings and written reports submitted to city leaders. These meetings, per an official working in the city party committee, highlighted the substantial costs and risks to the local economy of losing foreign clients, especially when a city signaled that it would have to allocate too much budget and too many resources to support domestic firm technology.

At the same time, bureaucrats also sought to placate foreign firms by simply blocking the influence of policy changes. A senior official at the ETDZ in Suzhou informed me without hesitation that within the zone and in any media outlet, it was prohibited to mention the concepts of "national brand" or "indigenous technology." He stated:

> We informally barred those words so that at least foreign firms within the zone would be less worried about the possibility of changing our long-term investment attraction policies and would not cease their investment. It is an open secret among bureaucrats.[20]

In this regard, Wuxi faced a similar situation. The city integrated its ETDZ and HTDZ to mitigate coalition-related fights. Because of land limitations, the former department advocated the expansion of export zones for foreign firms far beyond the original boundaries of ETDZ to the extent that this increase would have encroached on the territory/size of the HTDZ.[21] As a result, the domestic technology departments, a coalition that was newly formed and emerged, had to face the mounting challenges to their push for more resources. Wuxi's domestic technology upgrading, according to a Wuxi official, can be characterized as "more talking and less doing." That is, one often saw them in internal government documents, but real changes were slow to manifest. As will be seen in the next section, there were indeed some changes when opportunities opened up, but they were still quite limited.

Ningbo and Shenzhen displayed levels of FDI dependence similar to those of Suzhou and Wuxi, with FDI accounting for about 7 percent of GDP. However, foreign firms and exporters overlapped less. In these two cities, 28 percent and 40 percent of exports, respectively, were from foreign firms by 2005. The perception of international commerce departments regarding policy change was far less threatening because their business clients included a mixture of foreign and domestic businesses. As Figure 4.3 indicates, in Ningbo and Shenzhen, bureaucrats interviewed in the two departments found it hard to determine whether their business clients were foreign or domestic. Including both international commerce and domestic technology departments, 64 percent of officials in Ningbo and 71 percent of officials in Shenzhen answered that they could not distinguish ownership of their business clients. In fact, when asked about whether they primarily regulate foreign or domestic businesses, a bureaucrat from the Shenzhen Bureau of Science and Technology remarked:

> This question is simply laughable. We stopped making a distinction between foreign and domestic businesses ages ago. We now regulate both types as they are connected anyways. Our major function was to encourage them to embark on technology development. Other departments such as the commerce side deal with domestic and international business environments and rules.[22]

Even if a few bureaucrats or their businesses felt threatened by the policies, it was unlikely to lead to the creation of a coherent vested-interest group to systematically combat the reform. Furthermore, many domestic exporters—by being related to international trade and domestic technology upgrading—are business clients for the two coalitions at the same time. There were cases in Shenzhen in which they helped bring together bureaucrats from different camps to sit and talk. The perception that there was a struggle, in the style of "us versus them," was missing. Instead, departments focused on different stages of business development, ranging from help set up businesses to nurturing initial growth and making them stronger.[23]

Note, however, that these cities also experienced bureaucratic competition; nevertheless, the focus of this competition was different in that departments within the issue area of domestic technology competed among themselves, rather than with an external vested-interest group. Figure 4.4 summarizes officials' answers to the question on the major source

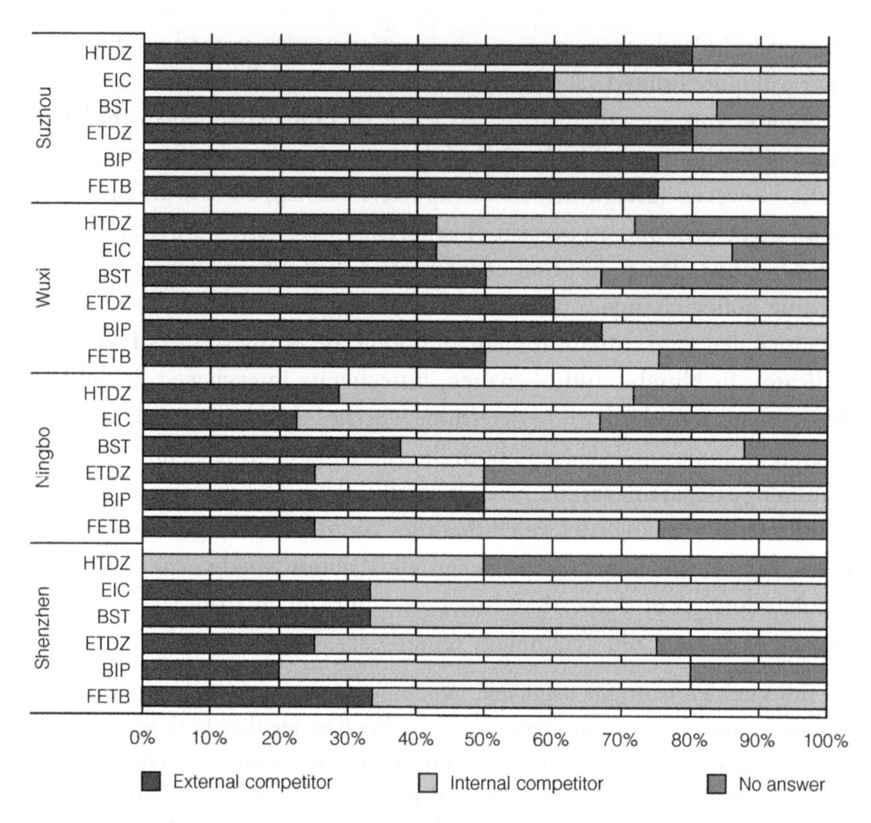

FIGURE 4.4. Internal and external competition among bureaucrats.
The charts illustrate local officials' answers to the question, "Without identifying the specific department, where do you think the major competition for your department comes from? You can choose from two groups of departments or choose not to answer the question." The "international commerce" group includes the Foreign Economic and Trade Bureau (FETB), Bureau of Investment Promotion (BIP), and ETDZ Committee. The "domestic technology" group includes the Bureau of Science and Technology (BST), Economic and Information Commission (EIC), and HTDZ Committee. When a bureaucrat identified competition outside of his or her own group, the answer was coded as external competition; otherwise, it was coded as internal competition. The number of bureaucrats interviewed was Suzhou (29), Wuxi (32), Ningbo (36), and Shenzhen (21).

of competition. It suggests that, in Suzhou and Wuxi, most officials viewed members of international commerce as their competitors, whereas in Ningbo and Shenzhen (more in Shenzhen), most officials viewed members of domestic technology as their competitors.

In Shenzhen, the battle was mostly fought between the Bureau of Science and Technology (BST) and the High-Tech Development Zone Committee, both of which had their functions within the area of domestic technology.

Each established a leadership group under its name to expand its influence by competing to gain support for its own business clients. Although the BST became the promoter and regulator of firms outside of the HTDZ, the HTDZ Committee gained control over resources within the zone.[24] Regardless of the shifting balance of power, however, the competition was kept within the issue area of technology. It led to a race to attract investors, entrepreneurs, and overseas returnees interested in launching research and technology-intensive firms as well as existing businesses that engaged in newer technology. In 2008, the City People's Congress passed the Shenzhen Act to Facilitate Science and Technology Innovation, which became the first innovation act passed by any Chinese city.

Ningbo experienced similar competition between the Bureau of Science and Technology and the Economic and Information Commission, which were both government agencies concerned with domestic technology. These two departments competed to create a number of supportive rules for innovative enterprises, incubators, and enterprise-related R&D centers. This competition was on full display during a government consultation meeting in which the author directly participated as an observer.[25] The meeting aimed to draft the Ningbo Act to Facilitate Science and Technology Innovation. Despite some quarrelling between the two departments, which both wanted to play the leading role, the meeting eventually led to the passage of the Ningbo Act, an act that increased funding as well as fiscal and financial resources for domestic firms and created detailed measures to help start-ups and incubators. Ningbo became the fourth city to pass this type of legislation in China, following Shenzhen, Zhuhai, and Chongqing. In each case, the competition did not come from a vested-interest group outside of the area of domestic technology. Instead, the competition pushed agents within the issue area to gain traction even faster.

LARGE FIES AND THE BARGAINING POWER

The overlap of foreign firms and exporters did indeed lay the foundation for the emergence of a coherent vested-interest group that constantly fought new policies, yet it was the concentration of foreign firms in large global firms that made it even more likely for the vested-interest groups to win. Arguably, the empowering role of large foreign firms can be both direct and indirect. Large foreign firms often have direct access to bureaucrats and city party secretaries or mayors, and they made use of this access when threatened by the new agenda.[26] Granted, it is hard to deny the direct lobbying effects of large foreign firms, but direct influence has its limitations. Field research suggests that large global firms often negotiate with the city government behind closed doors to attain policy deals that favor these firms rather than the entire industry or all foreign firms in the city. This means that, instead of systematically affecting a city's overall pattern of spending resources on domestic technology, the outcomes were highly customized and tailored to specific large foreign firms.[27]

This is why the coalitional effects that these large foreign firms had through city bureaucrats became essential. Large foreign firms often provided the international commerce coalition with more persuasive power toward city leaders. Based on the rule of "delegation by consensus," tensions among bureaucracies are often settled by higher-level officials, who are top city leaders.[28] Top city leaders (*lingdao banzi*)—usually comprising the secretary and vice secretary of the CCP committee, the mayor, and the vice mayors—have the ultimate authority to decide the direction of policy and institutional changes. Therefore, they are the "arbitrators" of bureaucratic conflicts. In the language of Chinese politics, rivalry along vertical lines (*tiao*), which divides bureaucrats according to their professional functions, is balanced by the city government, or the horizontal piece (*kuai*), with each coalition seeking to persuade and exert pressure on the leading group.[29]

Why would party secretaries and mayors not simply impose their decisions on bureaucrats instead of opening up policies for bargaining? Not only are departmental interests and fights hard to overcome, as many studies on bureaucracy have found, but city leaders themselves have also learned that allowing bargaining may increase the odds of implementing a new policy because officials are often more willing to accept the result than a decision imposed unilaterally.[30] That said, top leaders do have preferences.

The motivations of top leaders were predominantly driven by the cadre evaluation system, as mentioned (see Appendix 4.2 for an example). These leaders headed the Target Inspection Committee to stay on top of target accomplishment. Policy targets that carried the heaviest weights in the cadre evaluation system include traditional performance indicators (such as GDP, revenue, and industrial output) and newly added targets in the wake of the paradigm shift (such as the number of high-tech enterprises, the output and exports of high-tech products, and patent applications). Large foreign firms, such as Samsung, LG, Foxconn, and Intel, have been simultaneously influential in all these crucial indicators, and they are far more visible than smaller foreign firms.

These features have allowed international commerce departments to enhance their position through selective interpretation and extrapolation. In Suzhou, the Foreign Economic and Trade Bureau interpreted the new paradigm as a signal of the center's dissatisfaction with the "low technology" of foreign firms. The priority on technology competitiveness was therefore understood as a move from backward, lower-end (*diduan*) technology to higher-end (*gaoduan*) technology (Zhong and Zhang 2009: 55.). Officials from the Foreign Economic and Trade Bureau and the directors of the Economic and Technology Development Zone pointed out that most foreign firms, such as LG, Philips, and Samsung, had mastered advanced technology. In contrast, domestic enterprises were so backward in technology that it would require at least two decades for them to make initial progress or "produce any results."[31] A further examination of these claims, however, shows that a majority of "high-tech" foreign firms were almost always "lower end" in that they located only labor-intensive sections of the production chain in the city, repeating the past pattern of FDI attraction and processing trade.[32]

But such narratives helped vested interests seize the reform initiative from the domestic technology coalition and push the latter into the backseat (Wang 2009). At the end of each lunar calendar year, when cities started to set budgetary expenses, bureaucratic contests in front of top city leaders became extremely intense, especially given that prefecture-level cities' budgets were curbed relative to expenses after the fiscal reform (Liu and Tao 2007). Even though the party secretary and the mayor had the final say on the budget, bureaucrats from each department typically went to vice mayors in charge of their department to request budget increases.[33] Hence, vice mayors often rallied the corresponding departments and lobbied on behalf of, or together with, these bureaucrats in front of top city leaders in budget-setting meetings.[34]

When the Bureau of Science and Technology, the Economic and Information Commission, and the vice mayor in charge of domestic technology in Suzhou pushed for more city-level funding for enterprise innovation at these meetings, they often encountered a louder voice from international commerce (and the corresponding vice mayor), as the international commerce pointed to the vital role of large foreign firms in bringing economic and high-tech benefits. Furthermore, the international commerce departments in Suzhou pushed for grafting part of the institutions and funding from domestic technology into their coalition.

Although the Target Inspection Committee set increased funding for domestic technology in Suzhou, the international commerce departments bypassed the Bureau of Science and Technology, negotiated with the High-Tech Development Zone, and moved newly invested large foreign firms into the zone. They proceeded to co-opt the zone into their coalition and created their own policies of funding and tax exemptions for foreign firms under the rubric of domestic technology.[35] Officials in the zone committee initially resisted but realized that, because they did not have many resources, their career paths would probably be improved if they kept quiet and let the international commerce coalition stay in the driver's seat. Given that the international commerce coalition often backed up its arguments with indicator creation, it tended to have the ear of the mayors and party secretaries.

As a result, the voice of the domestic technology coalition was substantially subdued. In light of budget limitations and an emphasis on revenue creation concerns for revenue, city leaders provided a limited number of firms with funding and tax breaks. A winning vested interest often made it hard for reform advocates to push for the increase of resources for domestic technology, and this was typically ranked as a lower priority than issues such as expanding infrastructure in an Economic and Technology Development Zone. As an official in the Bureau of Science and Technology complained,

> The promotion of domestic technology competitiveness is a crucial function of our bureau, and we saw that as a signal that the central state had begun to take domestic technology seriously. The bureaus in international commerce, to our surprise, were also championing technology and innovation, but in their own ways. They moved ahead of us and seized the initiative from our hands to consolidate their own authority.[36]

Wuxi and Shenzhen provide interesting comparisons with Suzhou and Ningbo. Wuxi has also seen a fairly strong mobilization among its international commerce coalitions. However, foreign firms in Wuxi are more dispersed, that is, there are more small firms, which did not allow vested-interest bureaucrats to wield much power. Thus, despite the rise of a relatively coherent vested interest, the opportunity for this vested interest to successfully make its case in Wuxi was more limited than in Suzhou.[37] This was particularly true when Wuxi saw itself lagging, in terms of economic and technology indicators, behind its peer cities; in response, Wuxi provided limited openings for top city leaders to consider offering opportunities to domestic technology. An internally circulated document by the city government urged,

> In terms of total industrial growth and output in 2008, the gap between Wuxi and Suzhou has widened. Moreover, there is the pressure to prevent being surpassed by Guangzhou and caught up to by Hangzhou in the next round . . . In terms of high-tech industries, Wuxi's high-tech output accounted for 15.2 percent of provincial output in 2006, which still lagged behind Suzhou (36.9 percent) and Nanjing (17.8 percent). (Wuxi Government 2009: 3)

A government decree to "build Wuxi into a leading innovative city" issued by the CCP committee and the municipal government enabled Wuxi to be one of the first cities to attract scientists and engineers to the Wuxi New District, many of whom were educated abroad. At the same time, the district also fomented the development of solar energy, mobile Internet devices, and biomedical products. On one hand, this initiative enabled the city to make some progress in these new industries. On the other, due to the presence of a vested interest in international commerce, the Bureau of Science and Technology always had to be careful to ensure that the industries they were supporting did not directly compete with any foreign firms being brought in or likely to be attracted in the future, many of which were in the areas of IT and electronics.[38]

Ningbo seemed to be the mirror image of Wuxi. It saw less mobilization among the vested-interest coalition due to the city's lower overlap between foreign firms and exporters (see the previous section for more information). Nevertheless, it has several large foreign firms, such as Samsung, ExxonMobil, and Philips. A few bureaucrats (individual) argued that rather than abandoning foreign firms, more joint ventures between these large foreign firms and state-owned enterprises (SOEs) should be set up to allow foreign firms to take advantage of the new paradigm as well.[39] There was an economic basis for such an argument, as a mixture of foreign firms and domestic exporters were clients of international commerce, yet the argument lacked the support of a cohesive group. This weakness was also noticed by an official in the Bureau of Science and Technology's Research Office, as he commented sarcastically:

> A lot of times, those bureaucrats actively seeking to take advantage of foreign capital end up being taken advantage of by foreign capital (*Liyong waizi hui fan bei waizi liyong*). This is a phrase created by us, and they deserve it. They [the

> bureaucrats] probably need to come to realize their relative weakening position and let the indigenous force drive the process.[40]

As a result of the lack of coherence. the discussion of these joint ventures led to tailored policies for individual foreign firms in the Economic and Technology Development Zone (the FDI zone) that did not systematically influence the outcomes of budget allocation and government funding for domestic technology upgrades at the city level.

The Ningbo high-tech zone rose quickly compared to the FDI zone. The former not only contributed 10 to 15 percent of the cost of technology transformation for traditional enterprises, it also used tax and funding tools to increase the amount of new technology in the incubator.[41] In August 2008, the high-tech zone also succeeded in acquiring sufficient budget, and it organized an investigation team of eight local officials in the city government and 180 supporting cadres in the high-tech zone to conduct in-depth interviews of 162 enterprises, gathering information and identifying problems that enterprises may encounter or did encounter (Ningbo Government 2008). In 2010, the number of authorized invention patents in Ningbo surpassed 10,000, and party secretaries and mayors began praising and rewarding the city's Bureau of Science and Technology with an expanded budget allocation.[42] In 2011, the number of authorized patents in Ningbo topped Zhejiang province and the rest of China, which placed Ningbo in the second place (right after Shenzhen) for the number of authorized invention patents (Xia 2012).

In Shenzhen, to begin with, there was no such mobilization of a strong vested-interest group; moreover, the average size of foreign firms was too small to empower individual international commerce bureaucrats. As mentioned in the previous section, the bureaucrats from domestic technology focused their attention on competing internally to build leadership groups and obtain resources. Shenzhen was the first city to pass a city act known as the Supporting Science and Technology Innovation Act, and the city was the best-known coastal city to pioneer a number of policies that served as templates for other cities, including the Adjustment and Revitalization Plan for the Electronics and IT Industry and Guidelines for Using Technology Development Funds for Enterprises. Not surprisingly, Shenzhen has been the home of most competitive private firms, such as Huawei, Tencent, Skyworth, in the electronics and IT sectors for domestic and international markets. In fact, Shenzhen's city government, not enterprises, introduced

TABLE 4.3.
Comparison of city government support for domestic technology.

City	Government S&T expense (percentage of GDP) 2007–2010 average[a]	Increase in government S&T expense (percentage of GDP) 2006–2010	Government funding for firm S&T activities (percentage of city expense) 2008	Tax breaks for S&T firm activities (percentage of city industrial sales) 2008
Suzhou	0.30	0.31	0.41	0.0073
Wuxi	0.33	0.38	0.49	0.0099
Ningbo	0.43	0.40	0.62	0.018
Shenzhen	0.86	1.01	0.83	0.037

SOURCE: Based on data from China City Statistical Yearbook (2008–2011); China Economic Census 2008.

[a]Please note that this indicator is different from R&D expense as a percentage of GDP, which typically includes all R&D expense in the economy. Here "S&T expense" refers only to the amount of budget that a city government spends on science and technology.

and developed the earliest venture capital model in China (Jin 2010: 14, 20). The expansion of the high-tech zone to include various incubators and innovation valleys for hatching smaller start-up technology firms showed the success of the domestic technology coalition in pushing for the establishment of new institutions. The most recent development of the initiative was the 345 million yuan support that the Shenzhen government pledged to 12 R&D teams in microelectronics and biotechnology.

In general, we can view Suzhou and Shenzhen as two extremes of a continuum. Wuxi and Ningbo, which have either a coherent vested-interest coalition or bargaining power, can be seen as mixed or intermediate types. Table 4.3 summarizes the various support measures—budgetary expense, government funding, and tax breaks—that these four cities have provided since the launch of the paradigm. The results support the argument advanced here, with Suzhou and Shenzhen having the overall highest and lowest degrees of support provided, with Wuxi and Ningbo ranked between the two.

Other Possible Explanations?

Before the chapter proceeds further, it is necessary to address other factors that may be at work and may confuse the outcome. The first factor is the possibility of city-level outcomes differing simply because the overall level of dependence on FDI. As the four cases discussed here suggest, and many more cases will soon show, even at a similar level of FDI (between Suzhou and Shenzhen as well as Wuxi and Ningbo), cities still end up with contrasting degrees of support for the new policy. Clearly, more important than the general FDI are bureaucratic channels that enable the influence of foreign firms in a city, which often do not have direct access to top city leaders in a city's decision-making processes. Also, foreign businesses cannot use money to buy votes for their favored politicians.[43]

It is also fair to ask if the backgrounds of bureaucrats and top city leaders affect outcomes. As mentioned, these backgrounds could play a pivotal role, but no systematic evidence has been found to support the notion that the directors of domestic technology departments in Shenzhen and Ningbo or the directors of international commerce departments in Wuxi and Suzhou have a stronger political background. Party secretaries in the four cities also had a variety of previous backgrounds, ranging from agriculture, social science, and natural science to the humanities, and they had been constantly shuffled from one city to the next according to the rule of city leader appointment in China. In fact, Wang Rong, the former party secretary of Shenzhen, served as the party secretary in Wuxi, Suzhou, and Shenzhen during the 2000s, which covered *three* of the four cities studied here.

The final possible explanation is a region's long-term tradition of implementing or resisting central policies. Yet, here, the opposite seems to be the case, suggesting that one needs to examine the policy area with more detail. Ningbo and Shenzhen are located in Zhejiang and Guangdong, two provinces often perceived as more likely to resist central policies, but they ended up with stronger implementation performance. For their part, Suzhou and Wuxi are in Jiangsu Province, which has a reputation for agreeing with and closely following central policies (Landry 2008; Shen and Tsai 2016). Therefore, the crucial aspect is not whether, but how, regions interpret and implement industrial policies, which necessarily entails local structural and institutional constraints.

The Broader Picture across China: Testing the Argument

How would the insights generated from the case studies apply across China? The four cities discussed in this chapter are important cities on China's eastern coast, a region that accounted for 63 percent of China's industrial output in 2010. Yet, even when applying the perspective to China's inland regions in the south and west, where there are different levels of economic

TABLE 4.4.
Globalization and city government science and technology expense 2007–2010 (arranged by the last column).

City name (province)	FDI/GDP (percentage)	Overlap between foreign firms and exporters (percentage)	Concentration of large firms (percentage)	Government science and technology expense as a percentage of total city expense
Ji'an (Jiangxi)	Medium high	High	Medium high	Low
Songyuan (Jilin)	Medium low	High	High	Low
Lhasa (Tibet)	Low	High	High	Low
Shanwei (Guangdong)	High	High	High	Low
Xingtai (Hebei)	Medium low	Medium	High	Medium low
Jixi (Heilongjiang)	Low	Medium	High	Medium low
Maoming (Guangdong)	Low	Medium high	Low	Medium low
Chongqing	High	Medium low	High	Medium low
Deyang (Sichuan)	Medium low	Medium	Medium high	Medium
Guiyang (Guizhou)	Medium low	Low	Medium low	Medium high
Wuhan (Hubei)	Medium high	Medium high	High	Medium high
Changsha (Hunan)	Medium high	Low	Medium high	Medium high
Chengdu (Sichuan)	Medium high	Low	Medium	Medium high
Wenzhou (Zhejiang)	Medium low	Low	Low	Medium high
Tai'an (Shandong)	Low	Low	Medium	Medium high
Huzhou (Zhejiang)	High	Low	Low	High
Taizhou (Zhejiang)	Medium low	Low	Low	High
Wuhu (Anhui)	Medium high	Low	Medium	High

SOURCE: Data from China Economic Census 2008; *China City Statistical Yearbook* (2007–2010).

development, the findings analyzed herein still largely hold. Table 4.4 provides an example of 18 cities located in various provinces across China, arranged by city government expenditure on science and technology as a percentage of total city expenditure between 2007 and 2010 (the last column). In general, the amount of overlap between foreign firms and exporters and the extent to which foreign firms are dominated by large firms are negatively associated with the city's willingness to spend on science and technology. In contrast, a city's overall level of dependence on FDI (shown as a percentage of GDP in Table 4.4) has no strong association with a city's expenditure on science and technology.

To examine whether the observed relationships hold across Chinese cities, this section tests the arguments with quantitative data. The analysis uses data from several sources, including China's National Survey of Industrial Firms, the China National Economic Census in 2008, and *China City Statistical Yearbook*. The survey of industrial firms and the economic census were initiated by the State Economic Census Center of the National Bureau of Statistics (NBS), which implemented the survey through more than 3 million local enumerators from the local survey teams organized by the province-level Bureau of Statistics. With permission from the NBS, I accessed the original database of all above-scale industrial firms (with sales over 5 million RMB) across more than 300 prefecture-level cities in mainland China. It is worth noticing that data gathering within NBS, like the task of implementing economic policies within governments, was divided between the commerce departments and innovation departments. I also cross-checked the two parts of the indicators to ensure consistency of measurement units.[44]

The dependent variable analyzed here is the support that a city government provided for domestic technology upgrades and innovation. Policies and institutions are notoriously hard to operationalize. The major indicator used is science and technology expense as a percentage of the total budgetary expense of the city government. This ratio variable is transformed by the natural log of the odds. It measures the city government's willingness to spend money on domestic technology upgrading and the city government's perception of the importance of such spending. Here, the assumption is that perception of its importance is directly associated with the strength of the domestic upgrade coalition (BST, EIC, and HTDZ), with budgetary expense resulting from bureaucratic competition within the government. I examine the average percentage over the four years from 2007 to 2010 because the national policy shift and concomitant push for introducing institutions started in 2006.[45]

The first explanatory variable is degree of overlap between FIEs and exporters in a city; it is measured by the sale of exports from FIEs divided by the total sale of exports in a city. An alternative way to measure this variable is to look at the percentage of FIEs that exported, but this approach has theoretical and empirical flaws. Theoretically, I want to know whether the business clients of bureaucrats in international commerce were purely FIEs or a mixture of FIEs and domestic firms. The fact that foreign firms engage in export does not tell us if domestic firms export or if they are also business clients of international commerce. Empirically, most FIEs in China export. Therefore, our primary concern is whether foreign firms are the sole exporters. I use registration rather than capital share to identify FIEs because bureaucrats in international commerce departments also regulate and interact with their business clients based on their registered type, which corresponds to the argument made here: higher degrees of overlap mean more cohesive vested-interest groups.

The second explanatory variable, concentration of production by foreign firms, is measured by the proportion of industrial sales from large FIEs among all sales of FIEs. This variable seeks to capture the empowering role of FIEs on the vested-interest group. Lorentzen, Landry, and Yasuda (2014) measured large firm dominance through the relative influence of the biggest firm in a city. But this measure is taken in the absence of a full list of firms in the city and tends to underestimate large firm influence because a city often has more than one large firm. Given that I have data for all above-scale firms in each city, I focus on the relative dominance of all large firms, which are defined as firms with annual industrial sales exceeding 300 million yuan.[46]

Explaining local variation also requires controlling for potential confounders (see Appendix 4.1 for a detailed description of measurement and sources). To address the concern that I may be simply examining the direct influence of FDI, I control for the general structural effect, measured by FDI as a percentage of city GDP. In addition, I control for per capita GDP and a few other economic variables. The influence of SOEs is included in light of the recent state capitalism literature arguing that the government continues to confer favorable benefits to SOEs at the expense of private enterprises (Huang 2008; Naughton and Tsai 2015). For Western observers, indigenous innovation is often seen as a strategy to strengthen the state sector at the market economy's expense (Lardy 2014; McGregor 2010). It is unlikely, however, that this will be the case for this study, given that the new initiative pushed by the domestic innovation coalition (especially when headed locally by BST) was quite different from the traditional approaches that used science and technology funds as excuses for subsidizing SOEs. Instead, the new paradigm and policy implementations emphasized use of the budget to provide support on a competitive basis to private firms and start-ups. Furthermore, SOEs may not need to lobby through bureaucrats to formally increase budgets and/or resources at the city level due to their direct connection with the government either at the local or central level, along with their distinctive channels of financing.

Table 4.5 shows the results of the estimation for government support of domestic technology upgrades. The results consistently support the hypotheses and suggest that, after controlling for other variables, cities where FIEs and exporters overlap and where FIEs are concentrated in large firms are the least likely to provide support for, and dedicated spending to, domestic technology upgrades. The effects of coalitions remain significant after controlling for provincial fixed effects, indicating that provincial variation cannot wholly capture city-level variation. However, we notice that the general structural influence, measured by FDI as a percentage of city GDP, did not have a significant effect in any of the cases examined. This finding suggests a need to break down the composition of FDI to conduct a more nuanced analysis of differences in their influence. Column 6 of Table 4.5 shows that when using predictors that are averaged value between 2001 and 2005 to estimate the 2007 to 2010 results, the effects for the independent variables are still significant. However, when the same model is applied for the years between 2001 and 2005 for both the independent and dependent variables, no significant relations can be found (column 7). This nonsignificant finding shows that only the launch of new policies after 2006 stimulated varied responses among different coalitions within city governments (and therefore one is able to observe variation of the dependent variable).

Conclusion

As China's turn to FDI on the eve of its reform toward a policy of "open doors" required deliberate action to build support (Shirk 1993), a transition from FDI to domestic upgrades has also required state officials to handle struggles and contention. The policy processes have gone beyond central-level debates laid out in Chapter 3, manifesting in local coalitions, especially among bureaucrats who regulate businesses and rely on such businesses to advance their political careers. Although this study uses the feature of FIEs as an important indicator, it is worth reemphasizing that progress or stagnation in policy changes cannot be explained without paying attention to the articulation and manipulation of local bureaucrats, who have varied perceptions of the paradigm shift and uneven levels of political influence. At the same time, foreign capital interacts and conditions local governments' policy choices and development trajectories.

Estimation of prefecture-level city government support.

DV = S&T expense/total expense (log the odds)	(1)	(2)	(3)	(4)	(5)	(6)	(7)
FIE exporter overlap	−0.414***			−0.277**	−0.276**	−0.541***	−0.360
	0.136)			(0.119)	(0.117)	(0.152)	(0.224)
Large FIE concentration	−0.293**	−0.367**		−0.273**	−0.274**	−0.233*	−0.223
	(0.142)	(0.144)		(0.112)	(0.113)	(0.129)	(0.195)
FDI/GDP (%, ln)	0.0188	−0.00558	0.000853	0.0244	0.0238	0.0752**	0.00256
	(0.0313)	(0.0312)	(0.0323)	(0.0415)	(0.0426)	(0.0370)	(0.0519)
GDP per capita (ln)	0.400***	0.409***	0.355***	0.399***	0.398***	0.338***	0.246**
	(0.0756)	(0.0758)	(0.0741)	(0.0825)	(0.0821)	(0.0734)	(0.114)
Budgetary revenue (ln)	0.277***	0.274***	0.230***	0.257***	0.256***	0.232***	0.139**
	(0.0448)	(0.0447)	(0.0403)	(0.0494)	(0.0473)	(0.0423)	(0.0687)
Fiscal capacity (%)	0.0162	0.0122	0.0195	0.0281*	0.0283*	0.0237	−0.0551*
	(0.0131)	(0.0131)	(0.0133)	(0.0161)	(0.0154)	(0.0165)	(0.0284)
State owned enterprises	−0.263	−0.156	−0.168	−0.299	−0.301	−0.247	0.0386
	(0.210)	(0.209)	(0.181)	(0.218)	(0.224)	(0.181)	(0.279)
Joint ventures	−0.0953	−0.00753	0.0435	−0.00714	−0.00702	−0.0194	0.138
	(0.130)	(0.136)	(0.135)	(0.133)	(0.133)	(0.138)	(0.250)
Ethnic Chinese firms	0.137	0.0668	−0.0271	0.133	0.133	0.0373	−0.115
	(0.149)	(0.147)	(0.136)	(0.160)	(0.159)	(0.109)	(0.177)
Export/GDP (ln)	0.0662**	0.0641**	0.0757***	0.0628*	0.0624*	0.0659*	0.00320
	(0.0266)	(0.0260)	(0.0244)	(0.0350)	(0.0360)	(0.0384)	(0.0436)
East	0.161**	0.110	0.172**			0.131	0.371***
	(0.0753)	(0.0745)	(0.0754)			(0.0899)	(0.106)
Length of FDI					0.000565		
					(0.00354)		
Constant	−11.72***	−11.88***	−11.04***	−11.57***	−11.56***	−9.878***	−9.260***
	(0.612)	(0.606)	(0.584)	(0.765)	(0.750)	(0.617)	(0.875)
Observations	244	244	275	244	244	243	214
R-squared	0.689	0.674	0.675	0.603	0.603	0.684	0.280

NOTE: The dependent variable, city government expense on science and technology as a percentage of total city budgetary expense, uses the average value over the years 2007 to 2010 in columns 1 through 6. Columns 1, 2, 3, 4, and 5 use predictors for this same period. Column 6 uses predictors for 2001 to 2005. Column 7 uses predictors and dependent variables for 2001 to 2005. All variables are average values across the years. Robust standard errors are in parentheses in models 1, 2, 3, 6, and 7. To control for provincial-level effects, provincial fixed effects are used in models 4 and 5, with clustered standard errors in parentheses.

* $p < 0.1$ ** $p < 0.05$ *** $p < 0.01$

In many cases, local institutions and policies did not automatically emerge and had to be carefully crafted and forged. The most formidable challenges often lay in the decision-making and policy-manipulation processes, especially when bureaucrats, acting as patrons for their business clients, put up resistance before any development policies reached the firm level. Under such circumstances, an analytical angle is needed to focus on new policies announced at the state level and to account for the previous context and potential groups that may feel threatened by, or compete with, agencies advocating the implementation of new policies. This is, however, not the full story until we examine the story of policy implementation at the firm level, which, in the end, will be shown to reinforce the policy making at the city level.

APPENDIX 4.1.
Measurement and sources of variables.

Variables	Measurement	Sources
City S&T expense/total expense (%, log the odds)	City government expense in science and technology as a percentage of total budgetary expense	*China City Statistical Yearbook* (various years)
FIE exporter overlap	Ratio between the sale of exports from foreign-invested firms and the total value of exports	*China City Statistical Yearbook* (various years); China National Survey of Industrial Firms
Large FIE concentration	The proportion of industrial sales from large foreign firms to all sales of foreign firms	China National Survey of Industrial Firms
FDI /GDP (%, log)	Foreign direct investment as a percentage of GDP	*China City Statistical Yearbook* (various years)
GDP per capita (log)	GDP per capita in a city	*China City Statistical Yearbook* (various years)
Budgetary revenue (log)	The budgetary revenue of the city government	*China City Statistical Yearbook* (various years)
State-owned enterprises	The ratio between the amount of assets of state-owned enterprises and the amount of total firm assets in a city	China National Survey of Industrial Firms
Joint ventures	The proportion of joint venture sales to total foreign firm sales	China National Survey of Industrial Firms
Ethnic Chinese firms	The proportion of output from foreign firms invested by ethnic Chinese investors (Hong Kong, Taiwan, Macao) to output by all foreign firms	China Economic Census; *China Industrial Economy Statistical Yearbook* (various years)
East coast	92 cities located in Beijing, Tianjin, Liaoning, Shanghai, Jiangsu, Zhejiang, Fujian, Shandong, Guangdong, and Hainan (1 = yes, 0 = no)	*China City Statistical Yearbook* (various years)
Fiscal capacity (%, log)	Budgetary revenue as a percentage of GDP	*China City Statistical Yearbook* (various years)
Export/GDP	Exports as a percentage of GDP	China Economic Census
FDI length	The number of years between the first arrival of FDI in a city and 2007 (note the latest arrival is one city in 2007)	*China City Statistical Yearbook* (various years); provincial statistical yearbooks; news reports

APPENDIX 4.2.
Jiangsu province cadre evaluation system (for evaluating prefecture level cities).

Categories	Number	Targets	Units
Economic development X1	X1—1	Per capita GDP	—
	X1—2	Budget revenue as percentage of GDP	%
	X1—3	Growth in agriculture	—
	X1—4	Added value of service industry as percentage of GDP	%
	X1—5	High tech industrial output as percentage of GDP	%
	X1—6	Contribution of consumption to GPD growth	%
Science and technology innovation X2	X2—1	R&D expense as percentage of sales income	%
	X2—2	Science and technology progress	%
	X2—3	Patent authorizations and invention patent applications per million yuan GDP	Number
Social progress X3	X3—1	Public service expense as percentage of total government expense	%
	X3—2	Coverage of social progress	%
	X3—3	Higher education	%
	X3—4	Public facilities area per ten thousand people in the population	Square meters
	X3—5	Number of work-related deaths per 100 million yuan GDP	Number
	X3—6	Social security index	–
Ecology X4	X4—1	Percentage of reduction in energy consumption per unit of GDP	%
	X4—2	Occupation of land under construction per unit of GDP and percentage of reduction of such land	–
	X4—3	Percentage of reduction in chemical oxygen demand (COD) and SO_2 emissions	%
	X4—4	Percentage of water that reaches quality standards	%
	X4—5	Percentage of days with air quality that is good or above	%
	X4—6	Percentage of green area in urban and rural areas	%
Improvement of life X5	X5—1	The increase in per capita income of urban residents	–
	X5—2	Urban unemployment rate	%
	X5—3	Percentage of population with less than 2,500 yuan annual income	%
	X5—4	Health indicators of urban-rural residents	–
	X5—5	Percentage of households with housing difficulty as proportion of low-income urban households	%
	X5—6	Degree of access to information technology	–
	X5—7	Level of public transportation available for urban and rural residents	–
Public participation		Degree of satisfaction for the progress in scientific development among the population	
Cadre score = $40 \times (X_i - \min(X)) / (\max(X_i) - \min(X)) + 60$			

SOURCE: Jiangsu Government 2008 (acquired through author's field research).

CHAPTER 5

The Microfoundation of State Intervention and Policy Effectiveness

City-level bureaucrats' contention and interpretation of government policies shaped the government's willingness to provide support for domestic technology competitiveness, but the ultimate success of the initiative lies in creating the right incentives for firms. In other words, the program of supporting domestic technological upgrading does not stop at the stage of budget and resource allocation; rather, it also involves coordinating firm relations—foreign and domestic—in local production so as to make such support effective. Policy effectiveness is defined here as the ability to translate state policies into firm behavior. The key question one invariably wants to pursue is: When does government support work? When would firms respond to the "push" from local officials and invest in technological learning and upgrading?

This chapter delves into the microfoundation of state intervention and examines the effectiveness of state development policies.[1] Once again, we have seen a very wide variation among localities, even when we control for the industrial type. The chapter illustrates the sources of such local variation, drawing on China's largest manufacturing and exporting industries, electronics and the information technology (IT) industry.[2]

The chapter then uses economic census data and a unique measurement of policy effectiveness to gauge the level of success across localities. Once again, we need to place development policies into the preexisting context of investment attraction as well as the subsequent relations between foreign and domestic firms. As this chapter shows, the type of foreign firms that local governments attracted influenced the configuration of local production and the sequence of industrial development. Together, they created a context that defines the space and incentives for learning and technological upgrading for domestic firms. In localities where cities attracted large lead firms in a top-down approach, firms also show weaker incentives to respond to policy inducement and to invest in technological competitiveness. Ironically, cities that started with smaller foreign-invested enterprises (FIEs) and those less dominating in export channels saw a more inclusive development trajectory that ultimately has motivated domestic firms to invest in technology learning and innovation. Ultimately, contention over the allocation of resources at the city level, which we examined in Chapter 4, and the effectiveness of policy at the firm level, which we will explore in this chapter, mutually reinforce each other.

Electronics Industry and Waves of Policy Initiatives

The electronics industry is the largest manufacturing industry and the largest export industry in China in terms of the annual value of industrial sales. The rise of the electronics industry, together with the offshoring activities of FIEs, has made China the top exporter of high-tech goods, exceeding the United States (U.S.), Japan, and the European Union (EU) since 2006. The electronics industry gained the central attention in the paradigm shifting process, as it was a major industry in which the Chinese government tried every industrial development strategy. In the joint-venture period in the 1980s, electronics and IT were the focus of the State Council leadership group. In the local FDI-attraction period starting in the 1990s, the electronics industry was the one experiencing the largest wave of global outsourcing and was a major industry for FIEs. In the era of promoting domestic technological upgrading and competitiveness, the electronics industry had become a new target for state support. Furthermore, unlike more centralized industries, such as aviation and energy, most cities in China have manufacturing firms in the electronics industry, making a comparison across localities feasible while also allowing me to control for the industrial type. Typical examples of the electronics industry include the making of computers, mobile phones, electronics, and telecommunication devices. Since the late 1990s, the east coast region of China has become the largest manufacturing base for electronics products. Shenzhen and Suzhou, for example, together manufactured 70 million of the 140 million notebook computers and 360 million of the 1.4 billion mobile telecommunication devices produced globally in 2010 (Mei 2010; Ministry of Commerce 2011).

In the years following the rise of the FDI-attraction and domestic-competitiveness paradigm, the electronics industry became the pillar industry of most development zones—whether Economic and Technology Development Zone (ETDZ) or the High-Tech Development Zone (HTDZ)—across China. In fact, local city officials recognized it as the most "advanced" and important industry after the promotion of the automobile industry back in the 1980s and the 1990s. The industry was important enough to capture the attention of top city leaders, but it was not so sensitive or strategic as to be monopolized and controlled by the central state, such as air and space or nuclear power. Therefore, it testified to the effectiveness of city-level industrial policies. Although the east coast in general has been the engine of production for electronics and IT products, the competitiveness of domestic firms and their willingness to invest in technological learning and upgrading differ tremendously. If we agree with the business school literature on the importance of business motivation, incentives, and ambitions for achieving competitiveness, the success of using policies to arouse these incentives can be observed only in some cities instead of others. For that matter, we have to go back to the varied strategies and patterns of attracting FIEs. The following section illustrates such dynamics, drawing on the comparative case studies of two important electronics manufacturing cities.

Suzhou and Shenzhen were chosen for this chapter due to their importance and their similarities, which provided for ideal control in basic economic conditions. Jiangsu and Guangdong accounted for 60 percent of the total electronics output and exports among all 31 mainland provinces in 2009. The cities of Suzhou and Shenzhen were, respectively, the manufacturing center of each province, producing 35 percent of electronics products and 40 percent of electronics exports in China among the 341 prefectural-level administrative units. Furthermore, the local governments of Suzhou and Shenzhen pioneered the two typical upgrading strategies that localities emulated widely within and outside their provinces. Finally, the two cities share similar national ranks in terms of gross domestic product (GDP), gross industrial output, and population, and they are at similar stages of development in the electronics industry (Table 5.1).

Despite these similarities, domestic firms in Shenzhen and Suzhou showed very different motivations for upgrading. The contrast is clear when

TABLE 5.1.
Basic economic and industrial conditions in Suzhou and Shenzhen (2008).

City	GDP (billion yuan)	Gross industrial output (billion yuan)	Population (thousand)	Electronics output (billion yuan)	Electronics output by FIEs (billion yuan)	Employment in the electronics industry (thousand)
Suzhou	670	1,863	9,217	645	628	1,132
Shenzhen	781	1,585	8,768	911	633	902

SOURCE: Based on data from *Jiangsu Statistical Yearbook 2010*; *Guangdong Statistical Yearbook 2010*.

TABLE 5.2.
Suzhou and Shenzhen domestic electronics firms compared (2008).

Upgrading indicators	R&D expense (thousand yuan)	R&D expense/ industrial output (%)	New products output (thousand yuan)	New products output/ industrial output (%)	Number of new product projects	Number of new product projects per person	Number of patents applications	Number of patents per person
Suzhou per domestic firm	1,320	1.065	12,560	3.906	0.63	0.004	0.60	0.003
Shenzhen per domestic firm	13,356	2.035	125,412	10.160	3.53	0.010	14.17	0.006

SOURCE: Economic Census Center, National Bureau of Statistics in China.

one compares the firm-level data of Suzhou with that of Shenzhen (Table 5.2). Compared to Suzhou, Shenzhen domestic firms on average had 10 times the research and development (R&D) expense, 10 times the new product output, 6 times the number of projects in new product development, and 24 times the number of patent applications. This difference is striking even when one takes into consideration the difference in the scale per firm and compares the indicators by each firm in proportion to the industrial output and total employment.

Several potential causes exist for the divergent outcomes, none of which can provide a fully satisfactory explanation. The first is that Suzhou may have had a lower starting point and a weaker industrial base than Shenzhen did. However, the reverse seems to be true. Suzhou started developing its electronics industry in the 1950s, three decades earlier than Shenzhen did;

so, by 1979 (the beginning of the post-Mao era), Suzhou had at least 25 domestic electronics enterprises, and Shenzhen had only one. By 1991, a decade into the reform era, Suzhou achieved a total industrial output of 58.4 billion yuan, almost three times Shenzhen's 19.7 billion yuan (Suzhou Statistics Bureau 1993; Shenzhen Statistics Bureau 1993). Jiangsu not only had a much stronger electronics industrial basis during the prereform period but also was among the strategic localities that the central state selected for developing electronics industries in the postreform era. Recall that (in Chapter 3) the major billion-yuan investment projects in microelectronics in the early 1990s, such as Huajing in Wuxi and Huahong NEC in Shanghai, were all located within or right next to Jiangsu Province. Although Shenzhen did open up for foreign investment in 1979 as opposed to 1985 in Suzhou, Figure 2.1 in Chapter 2 suggests that it was not until after 1992 (Deng Xiaoping's southern tour) that real waves of FDI started in all regions of China. Before 1992, the amount of FDI shown in the figure is too sparse and miniscule to observe. Furthermore, the widening gap between the two developmental approaches in Figure 2.2 shows that Suzhou is not simply replicating an earlier stage of Shenzhen.

Second, the fact that Shenzhen is geographically close to Hong Kong and that Suzhou is adjacent to Shanghai may explain their diverse paths. Ethnic Chinese firms have, however, invested in both regions. The real difference is that only large ethnic Chinese firms, such as Taiwan's Compal, can qualify for the Suzhou government's attention. Similarly located on the Pearl River Delta near Taiwan and Hong Kong, Xiamen City of Fujian Province has only 13 percent of its electronics produced by ethnic Chinese, whereas foreign firms from other regions (especially OECD countries) produced 81 percent of the electronics (China Economic Census 2008).[3] In both Xiamen and Suzhou, it is the government's selectivity regarding firm size rather than geographic distance that keeps smaller FIEs from investing. Third, one may suspect that the Shenzhen government has more experience in promoting industrial upgrading than does that of the Suzhou region. Quite the contrary; Suzhou was *the* epitome of a local developmental state in the 1980s, and the entire Southern Jiangsu (*sunan*) region is associated with a strong historical record of coherent planning and the implementing of industrial policies.[4] Finally, human resources may contribute to the difference between these two localities. Both the Yangtze and Pearl River Deltas have abundant labor, each employing about 30 percent of the 200 million migrant workers in China. In terms of the number of science and technology personnel in the electronics industry, Guangdong (where Shenzhen is located) did exceed Jiangsu (where Suzhou is located) in the 2000s. However, Jiangsu had three times the personnel of Guangdong in the early to mid-1990s and has been overtaken by Guangdong only since 1998 (National Bureau of Statistics 2002). This fact suggests that Jiangsu did not lack human resources from the beginning of the upgrading period. The differences may result from its upgrading policies and hence each region's attractiveness to entrepreneurs and scientists. The rest of the chapter examines and compares the two cases.

Suzhou: Developing the Electronics Industry under the Sunan Model

Suzhou, along with Wuxi and Changzhou, constituted the Sunan (Southern Jiangsu) area, which was the wealthiest region and the earliest place for rural industrial development during the post-Mao era. Geographically, Suzhou includes seven city districts and seven county-level cities (Changshu, Zhangjiagang, Kunshan, Wujiang, and Taicang).[5] In Suzhou's electronics industry, collective enterprises in both rural areas and urban districts have provided initial capital accumulation, employment, and equipment for the industry and accounted for 76 percent of the total number and 70 percent of the total electronics output in Suzhou. The four "little giants" (the most successful brands in consumer electronics and appliances in the 1970s and 1980s), Xiang Xuehai, Great Wall, Peacock, and Chunhua, all started as collective enterprises in Suzhou (Suzhou Gazetteer Committee 1995c).[6] Electronics firms acquired technological support through various channels. Large-scale collectively owned enterprises (COEs) and state-owned enterprises (SOEs), most of which were set up under the City Bureau of Electronics Industry, tended to rely on importing machinery from Japan and Germany with state subsidies (Suzhou Foreign Trade and Economic Relations Commission 1991).[7] Small and medium-sized enterprises often built market linkages with large firms and sought to "steal" technology from SOEs through "weekend engineers," technicians and engineers who were formally employed within the SOEs and worked for nonstate enterprises during weekends (Pan 2003: 107; Shen 2009).

During this period, Suzhou's electronics industry benefited from Shanghai both in direct and indirect ways. Directly, Suzhou officials sought to gain technology for local enterprises either through the purchase of machinery and technology licenses or through the formation of joint-venture enterprises (*lianying qiye*) with, or by subcontracting production from, Shanghai SOEs. Indirectly, Suzhou was able to attract military electronics firms and their technicians through a Shanghai–Inland–Suzhou pattern. In the 1970s, following the "Third Front" strategy that Mao Zedong developed; many Shanghai technicians and engineers were sent to develop military industries during the Cultural Revolution in the hinterland, such as Sichuan, Guizhou, Jiangsi, and Shaanxi. These local talents were looking forward to returning to Shanghai in the 1980s, but their requests were often rejected due to the limits of the Hukou system. Local officials in Suzhou, and especially those in Kunshan, made many trips to the hinterland and played a crucial role in attracting these "Third Front" enterprises to relocate to Suzhou (Zhong and Zhang 2009: 9, 47–48; Xia and Xuan 2000: 25, 281). The flow of thousands of talented people to Suzhou not only contributed to local human resources but also brought along electronics industries and technologies as firms transformed from military to civilian electronics enterprises. These enterprises initiated the development of products such as televisions, wireless cables, capacitors, and telecommunication switches. Although most of the electronics still relied on imports from Japan for crucial components, a number of the large public firms started to have product development platforms and were able to produce end products with their own brands. A number of brands, such as the four little giants, also started to enter international markets during this period (Suzhou Foreign Trade and Economic Relations Commission 1991). Medium to small firms focused mostly on producing electronic components. Thus, the decade of the 1980s saw the steady development of the electronics industry in Suzhou and in the Sunan area in general.

From Promoting Collective Enterprises to Attracting FDI

Although the role of COEs and local developmental states in the 1980s captured most of the attention from scholars studying this period, the unfolding of another process at the same time often went unnoticed. This process started with an initial FDI wave in Kunshan, spread across numerous other localities, and eventually washed away the township and village enterprise (TVE) period by launching a new era in the 1990s when FIEs became the major development allies with local governments. Many important events took place in the critical juncture of the late 1980s and early 1990s, such as the Tiananmen crackdown in 1989, the beginning of the privatization of TVEs in the 1990s as they ran into fiscal difficulties, the State Council's decision to open up the Pudong District in 1990, and the southern tour of Deng Xiaoping in 1992. In retrospect, these events unleashed critical transformations that led to the downfall of COEs and the rise of FDI-centered development. This transformation produced a long-lasting impact on the indigenous upgrading capacity in China.

The role of COEs faltered, however, and the golden years for COEs came to an end. After performing well for a decade, the electronics firms ran into trouble. All four giants in consumer electronics started to encounter loss in 1990. The cause of the decline is still up for debate, and studies have proposed various explanations for the phenomenon, largely revolving around the mismanagement of COEs themselves and the inability of collective firms to compete with growing local private business.[8] Each explanation is partial in the case of electronics firms in Suzhou. The mismanagement explanation fails to account for the sudden occurrence of the problem in 1990 rather than earlier. The loss was indeed caused by intense competition, but competition itself would not necessarily cause the downfall of Jiangsu's COEs, as we will later see how electronics firms in Guangdong grew stronger from the competitive pressure.

The problem instead lies with the fact that, in the face of decreasing sales from local enterprises, neither the Jiangsu government nor the Suzhou government viewed the further improvement of technology capacity as the way to meet the challenge. Instead, as the "exchanging market for technology" paradigm was spreading across the country, forming joint ventures (JVs) was seen as the treatment for the backward Chinese firms. The state's need to reform these enterprises converged with the interests of the FIEs, which were anxious to enter China's domestic markets in the 1990s and which were most capable of buying off the assets from loss-making enterprises.[9] For example, Peacock formed a JV with Philips in 1992, Kunshan IRICO Electronics formed a JV with Sakurai Densi Kogyo and Kobun Kogyo from Japan in 1994, and Xiang Xuehai formed a JV with Samsung in 1996. A precondition for forming these JVs, however, was to abandon the product platform of their original brands and to produce under foreign brands so as to create market shares for foreign products. As such, these domestic firms stopped their original production lines completely and became assemblers for foreign firms.[10] Thus, rather than forming strategic JVs to *reform* these larger enterprises, FIEs *replaced* these domestic enterprises, which led to the de facto disappearance of the domestic brand-name companies.

Most of the small and medium-sized enterprises that were associated with the SOEs and large-scale COEs were at the same time privatized in a top-down manner in the 1990s. The 1989 Tiananmen crackdown led to the reform and regulation of TVEs by conservative leaders (such as Li Peng and Yao Yilin), preventing them from either further establishing linkages or competing with SOEs (Zweig 2002: 120; Huang 2008: 128–129). Ironically, this conservative backlash pushed local governments toward the same direction as the decision to open Pudong District and Deng's southern tour in 1992. Whereas the former weakened the basis and constrained the development of local enterprises, the latter encouraged China's opening up to coastal cities. It was during these political and economic changes that local governments in Sunan started to shift their development partners from COEs to FIEs.

Thus, as COEs were declining, FDI-centered development was quietly and rapidly rising. Kunshan, a county-level city in Suzhou, had the earliest start on attracting FIEs in Jiangsu. Like other localities, Kunshan used to build electronics industries with the help of Shanghai SOEs and the inner-land "third front" firms in the early to mid-1980s. Examples include Kunshan Golden Star Television, which was a branch of Shanghai Golden Star Television, and Kunshan Wanping Electronics Company, which was set up jointly with the "Third Front" 897 Firm (Xia and Xuan 2000: 26). Among all 43 Kunshan electronics firms in 1985, six of them were large to mid-sized county level firms, and 37 of them were TVEs. If one measures the degree of openness by the amount of exports, Kunshan's export performance actually lagged far behind any other regions in 1985. Unlike Wujiang, Changshu, and Zhangjiagang, where TVEs had fairly good export performance, Kunshan's export had remained at a very low level up until the mid-1980s (Suzhou Foreign Trade and Economic Relations Commission 1991; Zweig 2002: chapter 3). Kunshan, however, soon stepped on another road that enabled its rapid integration into the world production system, not through exports from domestic firms but by attracting the inward FDI exported to the world markets.

In 1984, Kunshan established an "industrial district" based on self-raised funds, which was later approved as the state-level ETDZ. In contrast to the first group of national ETDZs that were established in state-designated localities, Kunshan's ETDZ was the first self-funded development zone established through the initiative of local governments. In 1985, Kunshan succeeded in attracting the first FIE and in the early 1990s the first electronics FIE. In a decade, the total amount of FDI in Kunshan's ETDZ rose from $1.5 million in 1984 to $612 million in 1995. The change of industrial structure was even more impressive. Starting with a Japanese glove-making firm in 1985, the city, only about a half-decade later, had already marched into the top electronics industries in the 1990s, such as notebook computers and LCD screens.

To a large extent, local governments in Jiangsu quickly rechanneled their developmental energy from promoting collective enterprises in the 1980s to FIEs, beginning in the 1990s (Zweig 2002: 109). Building on the legacy of a strong state in the past, government officials rather than local business became the major factor determining the type of investment made in the localities. This trend was clearly observed when a new FIE came to invest in the region, where networks with local officials rather than with local firms mattered most for the eventual investment decision. It is true that most businesses in China are likely to perceive friendly relations with local governments to be important, but the fact that such networks dominated new investments made Suzhou distinctive. For example, the presidents of the WUS circuit and Sanmina-SCI were attracted to invest in Suzhou due to the newly established personal networks with Suzhou FETB officials (Xia and Xuan 2000: 28; Zhong and Zhang 2009: 49). Another example was the Taiwan Shunchang Group, which made their initial investment in Kunshan largely because the personal driver for the ETDZ director (later the vice mayor) happened to be a relative of the company's president (Zhong and Zhang 2009: 50). In fact, it became almost common knowledge among foreign businesses that, in the Sunan area, a business must first approach the officials through various channels rather than local business in the investment-to-be location, whether in a city, county or township (Xin 2005: 53).[11]

Top-Ranked MNCs, Group Offshoring, and Incentive Deprivation

As many of the Jiangsu cities settled on the strategy of using large MNCs as the "dragon's head" to drive local industrial output, they seemed to be able to leapfrog into the global technological frontier by directly attracting the world's most successful MNCs. With both a high volume of foreign investment and a large number of high-tech enterprises, Jiangsu certainly invites many envious eyes. The Achilles' heel for this model, however, lies in creating local indigenous capacities. As the process of outsourcing unfolded, and as China started to promote domestic upgrading in the 2000s, the model's drawback became clear.

The logic behind the upgrading strategy that Suzhou uses was that large electronics MNCs would play the role of the "dragon's head enterprises" that were expected to drive (*daidong*) the development of local firms midstream and downstream on the entire production chain. "Once these dragon's head enterprises were set up and linked to the local industry," reasoned local officials, "smaller enterprises on the dragon's tail would automatically follow up. And therefore we should do well in upgrading."[12] The main measures were encouraging FIEs to localize a larger segment of production to domestic producers through local purchase requirements so that MNCs would adopt more electronics components that local electronics suppliers manufactured. Local firms were supposed to benefit from the driving force of the MNCs and to gain learning experiences by producing for the technologically advanced MNCs. Thus, MNCs as dragon's head enterprises also provide the impetus for dragging local producers up the value chain.

In reality, however, the model does not work. Chapter 4 identified the reason why not enough government resources were allocated. However, when the limited resources were eventually granted through the domestic technological officials to firms, implementation problems surfaced at the firm level. Because most of the FIEs in electronics that first came to Jiangsu were large-scale, wholly foreign-owned MNCs that adopted the advanced design and frontier technology of the industry, it was hard for these firms to find key component suppliers and the appropriate producers of original equipment manufacturing (OEM) or original design manufacturing (ODM) locally at the time in which they came. These firms initially made their investment decisions largely based on the attractiveness of government policies rather than on local industrial fit. A few FIEs were willing to try using local suppliers initially but often stopped the contract after the first batch of orders arrived. For example, Kunshan IRICO, which was reformed in 1994 to manufacture cathode sleeves for VCRs, was based on entirely different technology from the LCD that computer manufacturing was seeking. When they finally started to manufacture an LCD substrate, OEM firms, such as Compal, found their quality to be extremely wanting and not suitable for the level that their clients (LG, Samsung, and the like) demanded, and therefore they switched back to Japanese suppliers. As such, there was often a considerable "gap" between the type of products that MNCs demanded and those that local firms were able to supply.[13] To use a metaphor from an MNC manager, the problem was essentially that those electronics MNCs playing the role of "dragon's head" often had a hard time directly finding a "dragon's body and tail" among domestic firms.[14] Nurturing local suppliers would take a significant amount of time, not only for producing key components—microprocessors and motherboards for computers from Intel, glass substrates for thin-film transistor (TFT)-LCD and chips of mobile telecommunication equipment—but even for slightly advanced components, such as backplanes, resistors, and batteries.

Neither local bureaucrats of international commerce, who are driven by short-term economic indicators and achievements, nor FIEs, which seek immediate business returns, wanted to wait. In the end, the dominant strategy that emerged was "group offshoring." Instead of relocating single firms to China, the entire production chains were brought to the same locality, often with brand-name firms leading a group of suppliers that had already established long-term preexisting production networks. The lead firms had the organization resources and willingness to do so, and officials in international commerce also embraced such strategies, as it caused FIEs to invest more and to stay longer. As such, a distinct configuration of local electronics production was established with the top, middle, and downstream areas of the production chains populated by WFOEs, from product design and development (United States, Japan, Europe, South Korea) and key component production (United States, Japan), to OEM and ODM production and midtech components (Taiwan and Singapore), and even peripheral components and subcomponents. Local producers that entered the electronics industry often could find space only at the bottom of the value chain for the production of peripheral components or the peripheral phases of the assembly.

As local officials realized the advantages of group offshoring, they spearheaded, coordinated, and fully embraced the strategy as an industrial policy. Instead of bringing in a single foreign-invested firm, officials preferred to bring in an entire value chain and proudly termed this pattern as "when one flies in, the entire flock flies in" (Zhang 1997). As an official of BST retold the locally popular story in the 2000s:

> There is a well-known story that our vice mayor joined officials from the investment promotion bureau in disaggregating a notebook computer into 1,000 components. Did we do that for reverse engineering? Not really. We did so to identify the composition of the production chain as a basis to attract the best foreign investment.[15]

The strategy was highly appealing to the interests of local bureaucrats who were seeking to build their political achievements within the cadre appointment system. First, it raised the efficiency of attracting high-tech FDI, allowing Suzhou ETDZ to attract an average of $6 million of FDI *each single day*, more than the amount that Cambodia attracted in the entire year of 2011 (Suzhou Industrial Park 2011). Second, it fulfilled the local purchasing requirement and provided bureaucrats in international commerce with the hard indicators and statistical evidence to win support from top city leaders. The "dragon's head" enterprises, FETB argued, were driving the industrial capacity of the entire electronics industry as well as local GDP (Suzhou Bureau of Science and Technology 2010; Suzhou HTDZ Management Committee 2011; Zong 2008). Furthermore, the ETDZ contended, firms in the industry were increasingly "localized." A report that ETDZ conducted suggested that while a leading computer FIE purchased only up to 5 percent from Chinese electronics suppliers during the 1990s, the domestic procurement ratio increased to 85 percent in 2006, providing a "door to door" direct purchasing system. In reality, my interviews suggest that these "local" suppliers were WFOEs, which were as foreign to the local context as to the lead firms (Zhang and Zhang 2007: 153; Kunshan ETDZ 2009).

The model also traveled beyond the Yangtze River Delta. Huchet (1997: 262) finds that Japanese electronics FDI in Dalian city of Liaoning Province followed a pattern where both big Japanese corporations and Japanese SMEs invested in a common industrial district. Huchet sees this strategy as a recreation of the Japanese *kereitsu* system in the Chinese context, which was in line with the chain-outsourcing model in Suzhou. Yeung, Liu, and Dicken's (2006) study of Nokia's investment strategy in Beijing's ETDZ reflected a similar pattern. Building on previous lead firm–supplier networks, Nokia colocated the flagship firm and its major international suppliers to the same industrial park in the ETDZ. Both Huchet and Yeung attribute this strategy to MNCs—the dense networks within the Kereitsu system and Nokia's capacity to nurture external linkages with suppliers. Although major MNCs were essential in inventing the strategies, the case of Suzhou suggests that governments had played a crucial role by encouraging, actively creating, and coordinating the chain-outsourcing model.

How about "real" local firms that were domestically owned? As bureaucrats of international commerce attracted large, top-level MNCs and embraced the chain-offshoring model, it created a harsh environment for bureaucrats of domestic technology to push for its upgrading. As detailed in the last chapter, obtaining budgetary support at the city level was difficult for these cities. Arguably, though, even with a limited resource, one could put such a resource to good use. However, effective government support means cultivating firm incentives to invest in technology learning, and chain-offshoring was inimical to such incentives. The upgrading space was substantially limited, and, as of 2010, it was getting worse for domestic manufacturers.

Shrinking Developmental Space and Incentive Quashing

Due to the standardized production process in the peripheral components on which the majority of domestic firms focused, including resistors, diodes, light-emitting diodes, and capacitors, firms needed only to come up with standard products while keeping their costs as low as possible. According to a firm-level survey that I conducted in 2011, 77 percent of the surveyed domestic electronics firms in Jiangsu did not receive technological guidance from FIEs, and 75 percent of them based their production on the already existing blueprints or imported machinery. Due to the similarity in the nature and quality of products, price rather than quality became a crucial determinant for getting orders. Interviews suggest that even when there was a rare case of learning by doing, the type of knowledge accumulated at the peripheral component level seemed to have little use in developing knowledge about the product at the higher level of the value chain.[16] Due to the similarity in the nature and quality of these products, price became a crucial determinant for customers to place their orders. As managers of the private enterprises commented, firms that were able to come up with standard-quality products at low costs would be most likely to receive orders.[17] Furthermore, sometimes FIEs, even offshore, outsource low-value-added components or low-cost-category products directly to the same locality, further squeezing the developmental space.

Moreover, and at a fundamental level, the hierarchical production order with each node that FIEs populated imposed high barriers of competition and quashed the aspiration of local entrepreneurs, leading them to hold a pessimistic view of the possibilities of innovation and upgrading. The geographical closeness of the lead firms and their suppliers produced by chain outsourcing not only further consolidated the top positions of lead MNCs but also benefited midstream and downstream MNCs, both in terms of their networks with upper-stream customers and in terms of their patron–client relations with bureaucrats of international commerce. This was in stark contrast with domestic entrepreneurs, who had to engage in cutthroat competition for survival and who viewed themselves as not in the "same club" as the foreign firms. Although most domestic electronics producers complained about the bitter experience of competing with cheap labor and razor-thin profit margins, they viewed upgrading to the higher segment of the production chain as impractical and unfeasible.[18] Investing in upgrading meant directly competing with FIEs at the higher level of the chain, which may very well be their own customers to whom they had sold products. Even if the FIE was not their own customer, they offered advantages in terms of capital and technology, sales channels (including export channels) with upper-stream customers, and, above all, established networks of local officials. In evaluating the high risks involved in upgrading, firm owners and shareholders were far more likely to expand existing production lines rather than investing in new product development, design, and technology.[19]

Ineffective Government Support

In such circumstances, making government support effective is challenging. Resources were granted to firms to introduce incentives for technology upgrading—typical of many industrial policies implemented elsewhere. The quandary, however, was that the large MNCs blocked the direction toward which the policy was pushing the firms. To be sure, even in cities that obtained a moderate resource of support, such as Wuxi, one can still identify a number of firms receiving startup funds, innovation funds, subsidies, and tax exemptions for encouraging enterprises to engage in R&D and patent applications. Yet firms that received these funds did not engage in any of these activities due to the lack of incentives. Contrary to the widespread belief that many Chinese firms would innovate if the patent application system were better, a Bureau of Science and Technology (BST) official complained to me:

> I constantly urge domestic firms to apply for patents and fight with the other officials to get approval for certain rewards or certain tax exemptions. I even asked the consulting companies that linked with us to write up application for them. All they need to do is to submit the application. However, after these firms took the money they wanted, many of them simply do not have the need and the incentive to do so. I felt that I am like a policeman, trying as hard as I can to catch these managers in order to force them to apply for patents—it is really for their own good!

Many officials at the Economic Information Committee echoed similar views, suggesting that there seemed to be a chicken-and-egg problem, where the more trapped that these interviewers were at the bottom of the value chain, the more likely they would lack incentives to upgrade, thus becoming more trapped. Government support was supposed to help them to get out of the trap but only when the composition of local production did not block the upgrading space. "Most local government officials and firms here understand and talk about the importance of upgrading, but it was simply hard for firms to do so for the given environment," an official remarked.

Domestic electronics producers, on the other hand, ironically believed that governments rather than firms benefited more from patent applications and new projects in high-tech products, as patents and projects mainly contributed to government statistics. One popular saying among local businesses is that "in China, if a firm does not innovate, it is waiting to perish; but if it does innovate, it is seeking to perish."[20] Despite the sarcastic tone, this observation was not uncommon among electronics entrepreneurs in the Yangtze River Delta.

Figure 5.1 shows the recent much-boasted effort of Kunshan to build the world's first-class "Optoelectronics Valley" in Kunshan ETDZ. Drawing on the impact of Compal, the valley was able to attract lead firms, such as LG and Samsung, and core component producers, such as AGC, to outsource from various segments of the value chain between 1992 and 2010 so that it had one of the most complete global production networks in TFT-LCD in China. The network included brand-name lead firms, core component suppliers, core component makers, OEM/ODM producers, midtech component producers, peripheral component producers, and assemblers. FIEs that were at the higher and middle levels of the value chain were business clients for bureaucrats of international commerce. Domestic Chi-

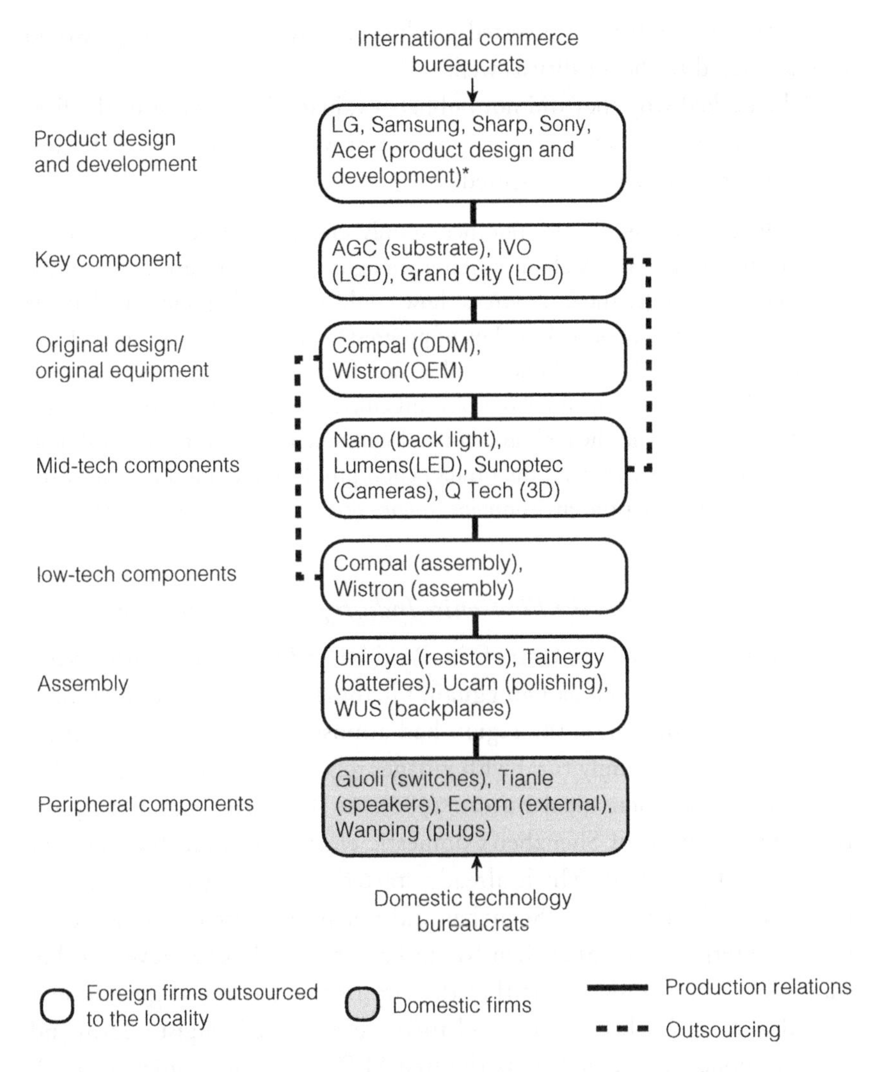

FIGURE 5.1. The government's upgrading initiative in Kunshan's Optoelectronics Valley.

nese firms, which focus on peripheral components, were business clients for domestic technology bureaucrats.[21] Guoli and Wanping, for example, have both received government funding and tax cuts for investing in more sophisticated technologies, but both they and BST bureaucrats complained that they had a hard time moving up the value chain; on top of that, they feared that newly foreign-invested producers of switches and plugs would be outsourced to the locality as well.

When asked why they did not publicly evaluate the progress of the firm after granting the fund or tax cuts so as to provide extra incentives for upgrading, a BST official commented:

> We did evaluate the process, but there is only so much that we can do and will be willing to do. Think about it. After we fight with other bureaucrats in the government to get these resources, how could we simply point out that the funded firms were not making lots of progress? Saying that would mean hurting ourselves, as the government will refrain from giving us more money next time. We cannot complain about our difficulties in this way—top city leaders will not understand the real problem and will take it to be a sign of weakness. Yet, to be honest with you, the fundamental problem does not lie in us or the domestic firms, but the environment (*huanjing*) and the institution (*tizhi*).

Shenzhen: Developing the Electronics Industry in the Early Years

Shenzhen constituted the core of the Pearl River Delta along with several other major cities, such as Dongguan, Guangzhou, Foshan, and Zhuhai. Between 1956 and 1978, the region had almost no independent business and was overwhelmingly rural with villages relying on fishing (Vogel 1989: 327; Guangdong Statistical Bureau 1986). At the beginning of the post-Mao era, the basis of Shenzhen's domestic electronics industry was very weak. Unlike Suzhou, which already started developing the electronics industry in the late 1950s, Shenzhen did not have its first domestic electronics enterprise, the Shenzhen Radio Factory, until 1972. Several other state-owned electronics firms that the city or the provincial government owned were established in 1979 and 1980. Because the Dengist reform and opening policy set Shenzhen as the first SEZ, these electronics firms all started businesses by processing and assembling products for foreign firms. Government officials facilitated the linkages between domestic and foreign firms by acting as active brokers between the two. The Shenzhen Radio Factory and the Xinhua Electronics Factory began to process radio main boards for their Hong Kong partners in 1978 and 1980, respectively. Shenzhen Huaqiang Electronics Corporation also started to assemble Sanyo radios and tape recorders from Japan in 1980. A number of other firms also started processing or manufacturing adaptors, radio and recorder components, and electronic watches (Wei, Zhang, and Guo 2010: 2–3; Zeng 2004:

15–22). Given the weak industrial basis of Shenzhen's electronics industry then, however, only a few firms were actually able to process and assemble products as independent enterprises in the startup period. In most areas of Shenzhen, the electronics industry before the mid-1980s was dominated by informally contracted firms between local governments and guerilla foreign investors, the majority of which came from Hong Kong.

The period between 1979 and 1985 was crucial for achieving the first stage of transition. On the one hand, with practice in processing and assembling based on materials and blueprints that foreign firms provided, domestic electronic firms began to engage in the exports of complete knockdown (CKD) or semiknockdown (SKD) components (Wei, Zhang, and Guo 2010: 5). Although these components were not the highest-value-added parts, production based on knockdown kits involved coordinating groups of components, thus providing richer expertise and knowledge about the manufacturing process of the final products rather than a single peripheral step or component. The knockdown kits also allowed producers to go beyond a sole customer and adapted production for multiple sources of orders. The momentum of progressing into more complete component production emerged between foreign customers and local business, but the pace was especially quickened after the establishment of the Shenzhen Electronics Industry Development and Coordination Committee in 1983, which represented a joint effort among the Ministry of Electronics Industry, the Guangdong Bureau of Electronics Industry, and the Shenzhen government (Wei, Zhang, and Guo 2010: 8). Since then, facilitating the localization of technology-sophisticated components became the major focus of the committee. This included encouraging investors both to outsource more complete package orders to local suppliers and to subsidize local firms to engage in the manufacturing of packages of circuits, transistors, and transformers.

On the other hand, the Shenzhen government also encouraged electronics firms to experiment in developing their own product platforms at the same time as they promoted processing trade. Unlike factories that foreign investors invested in and controlled, most of which later turned into FIEs, the domestic processing firms could make independent decisions regarding whether and how to develop their own products. It was a tough process for local firms to both conduct processing and to develop an independent product platform when their own technological bases were still weak. As employees of Huaqiang Electronics recalled, when they went beyond processing radios and attempted to produce their own brand-name single-cassette and quad-band tape recorders, they had to combat both the poor working conditions and the backward technology. With limited initial capital, they "worked in shabby factory buildings and lived in thatch huts that were vulnerable to wind and rain" (Zeng 2004: 17). Despite the rough start, the decision to move up the value chain led them down the road to become a leading electronics producer.

The prevailing mode of technological learning that Huaqiang and other enterprises adopted during this period was "combining technology acquisition with trade" (*ji mao jie he*), which means that firms earned foreign reserves through processing trade and then used them to import equipment, technology, and key components, which served as the basis of manufacturing their own products.[22] Domestic electronics firms could simply use imported technology, but more ambitious firms began adapting technology to local markets. Aiwa was an example that relied mainly on imported technology. The company nonetheless achieved production of scale in a few years and progressed relatively quickly in substituting imported materials and product diversification, laying its foundation for becoming an OEM producer in the 1990s. Kangle Electronics, in contrast, was an example that directly adapted its own technology. After importing sample cassette players from Hong Kong in 1982, the company modified the player by using its own adapters, speakers, capacitors, and antennae, and it adapted the cassette doors and external shells for domestic markets. These improved players substantially increased the company's market share and reversed the firm's profit-losing situation from before the adaptation. Enterprises took the lead in such processes of learning and adaptation, but Shenzhen Development and Coordination Committee helped to introduce the *ji mao jie he* method to other companies and encouraged the experimentation of producing a wide range of products, such as cassette players, cassette recorders, radios, telephones, televisions, and calculators. A number of those companies started to develop their own brands, including tape recorders from Huaqiang, Jinghua, Kangle, Baohua, Lanhai, and the Shenzhen Radio as well as calculators from Nanhe and Aiwa (Wei, Zhang, and Guo 2010: 5–6; Zeng 2004: 17–18).

By the end of 1985, the total number of electronics enterprises in Shenzhen increased to 170 compared to only a couple in 1980. The total industrial output increased 113-fold from one million yuan to 1.375 billion yuan. The number of product types also expanded from 10 to 400. Shenzhen certainly shared similarities with Suzhou in the starting period of the electronics industry, as publicly owned enterprises initially took the leading role among domestic enterprises, with steady progress in making more complicated and self-branded products. Nevertheless, the major differences of the two trajectories already began to emerge.

Subcontracting, Local Linkages, and the Broadening of Production Networks

The electronics industry in Shenzhen and in the broader Pearl River Delta therefore took off with *san lai yi bu* firms set up by guerilla investors, and the number of firms at the bottom of the value chain began to expand. Throughout the 1990s, Shenzhen and Guangdong were often denounced as sweatshops for lower-end (*di duan*) production, especially compared with Jiangsu localities, which had a much higher starting point by attracting only higher-end (*gao duan*) MNCs. It is thus ironic that Shenzhen domestic firms were eventually able to gradually climb up to the higher segments of the production chain. How did this process take place?

Because most FIEs initially invested in Shenzhen were located at the bottom of the value chain, the technology gap between foreign and domestic firms was manageable, unlike the huge technology gap between MNCs and domestic firms in Suzhou. After Chinese entrepreneurs and managers gained initial hands-on manufacturing experience and knowledge and learned to meet production standards, an increasing number of overseas investors began to feel confident in subcontracting complete orders to domestic producers without intervening in the daily management of production. This change provided Chinese entrepreneurs—coming from both within and outside of the region—the opportunities to develop the capabilities of managing orders independently and adapting to multiple customers. They became the first group of entrepreneurs to establish indigenous electronics firms (Zeng 2004: 17). Over time, an increasing proportion of FIEs in Shenzhen and the Pearl River Delta also began to purchase electronics components locally. The small sizes and limited organization resources of these FIEs prevented them from group outsourcing. Local domestic electronics firms that produce for these FIEs, as they started to manufacture independently, also began to establish their own sales channels domestically and export channels overseas *in addition to* supplying components to FIEs.

The emergence of these domestic firms that subcontracted production from FIEs was a crucial step in the upgrading process.[23] Although some of these domestic enterprises initially registered as fake FIEs so as to take advantage of lower tax rates implemented by the central government, these firms were de facto Chinese producers. They acquired orders from FIEs and engaged in *san lai yi bu* production, but the relationships between the two parties were often compensation trade or processing trade instead of joint ventures or mainland branches of FIEs. Thus, rather than disrupting the development process of domestic firms as MNCs did when they offshored to Jiangsu, the guerrilla investors contributed to the expansion of the number of domestic producers in Shenzhen at the end of the value chain through the subcontracting system.

In addition to *ji mao jie he*, the government also tacitly allowed the licensed leasing among enterprises. The Chinese central state imposed regulations on the entrance to electronics products, such as televisions and mobile phones, through production licenses and granted them to only a handful of SOEs and MNCs. Chinese firms in the Pearl River Delta invented the informal arrangement of license leasing between holders of licenses and nonholders.[24] Over time, the lessee became the OEM producer for the lessor, although the two might or might not share the same distribution channel and after-sell service. Products sold under such relationships had the logo of the licensed firms or logos of both firms on them. TCL was an example that initially entered the production of colored televisions by renting a license from Shaanxi Rainbow and later became a leader in domestic consumer electronics (Xu 2009). In the mobile phone industry, license leasing persisted until the mid-2000s, with the lessee paying the lessor 80 to 100 yuan per mobile phone produced. Many SOEs started simply earning profits through license leasing with little real engagement in production.[25] Again, the local bureaucrats who were in charge of regulating the "illegal" phenomenon often preferred to "open one eye with the other closed," sometimes even actively collaborating with enterprise in the practice.[26] The license leasing strategy helped overcome the barriers of entrance in the electronics industry and broadened the developmental foundation of electronics among domestic enterprises.

In response to the rise of this new policy paradigm, officials in the Shenzhen Science and Technology Innovation Committee took measures to continue to facilitate global–local linkages at the bottom of the global value chain, encouraged self-experiment with domestic products, and promoted indigenous high-tech firms, which all contributed to a distinctive path for the city's electronics industrial competitiveness. After the domestic business

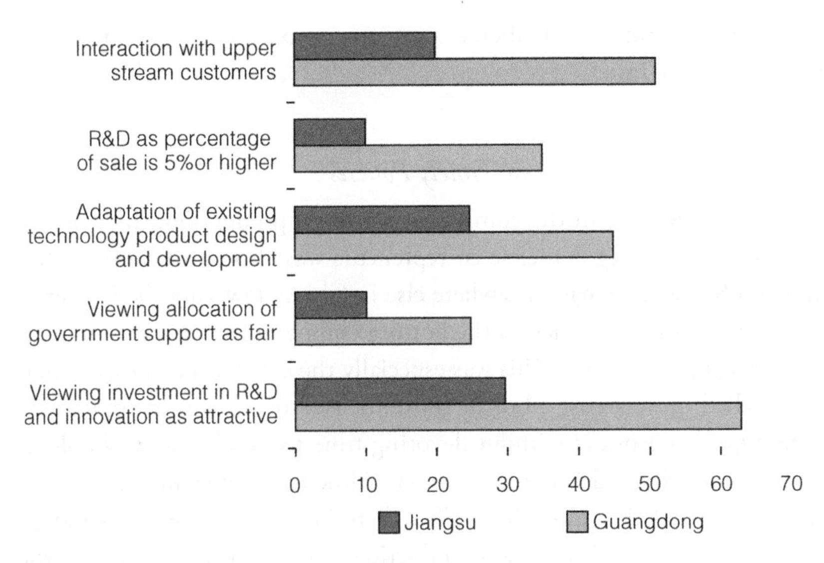

FIGURE 5.2. The upgrading incentives and behavior of domestic firms.

SOURCE: Based on data from 2011 firm survey conducted by the author.

basis of the government industrial policies was broadened, the promotion of indigenous high-tech firms further pushed domestic entrepreneurs to invest in higher value-added activities. Although both the Suzhou and Shenzhen government established HTDZ to support high-tech domestic firms, the Shenzhen government did not predesignate the winners or "dragon's head" MNCs at the beginning but instead encouraged and mobilized investment in the electronics and information industry from various types of enterprises, especially private enterprises. The initiative incubated a number of electronics enterprises, such as Huawei, ZTE, Legend (Lenovo), Great Wall, Shenghai, Shida, and Huihuang, which were then hardly known start-up firms and later became the leaders in the electronics industry (Xu 2008; Jin 2010: 9–10). In addition, a torrent of less technology-intensive private electronics SMEs focusing on various stages of electronics components also started to flourish in the Huaqiangbei area of the Futian district.

As Figure 5.2 indicates, 51 percent of enterprises in Guangdong (as opposed to 20 percent in Jiangsu) had interactions with upper-stream customers, among which 70 percent had constant interaction. In other words, local governments' earlier alliances with small FIEs enabled FIEs and local producers to be linked through a set of production networks that were far more dynamic than those in Suzhou, in addition to the

Shenzhen government's deliberate measures to push domestic producers up the value chain.

Incentives Enhancement and Timely Policies

Given the difference in the composition of local production, the demand for upgrading among domestic entrepreneurs was also significantly different from Suzhou. As with anywhere else in China, lowering the barrier of entrance often led to a race to the bottom competition that drove numerous firms out of business. This was especially the case with enterprises that solely relied on low-cost labor or those focused on getting market share by manipulating prices without devoting time to developing technological capability (Lu and Mu 2003: 68–69). Although some still competed at the lower end of the value chain, Shenzhen domestic managers saw long-term commitment to innovation production processes as the key to exit the cutthroat competition and expressed much stronger motivation in climbing up the value chain.[27] This finding corresponds with the survey finding that 63 percent of Guangdong firms (more than twice the percentage of Jiangsu's 30 percent) viewed investment in upgrading as an attractive option. Furthermore, there were also larger proportions of firms that invested 5 or more percent of sales in R&D and engaged in adapting and improving existing products.

A key reason that competition at the bottom provided incentives for firms in Shenzhen rather than in Suzhou to upgrade was that, in the Suzhou case, the hierarchical barrier between foreign and domestic firms was so strong that it trumped the recognition of the possibility for upgrading in the firm managers' belief systems. In assessing the overall situation, a firm's management level would vote against the idea of taking a big risk on a product and the process upgrading. What made Shenzhen different, in contrast, was that on the one hand the intense competition among a large number of foreign-invested and domestic firms forced a number of firms to recognize the unsustainability of the race to the bottom approach in the long run and the urgency of developing proprietary knowledge. On the other hand, the configuration of production in Shenzhen provided the "ladders" to technology progress. Upgrading was viewed as inviting, despite the challenge, in Shenzhen.

Local entrepreneurs were typically noticed for their "boldness" and their aspirations to challenge upper-stream firms and even global lead firms.

Competition was inevitably intense, yet the availability of higher-value-added opportunities facilitated the aspiration for upgrading. Huawei and TCL, for instance, both made initial profits by importing HAX telecommunication switches from Hong Kong and selling them in the domestic market. As numerous firms entered, profits plummeted within half a year, causing 95 percent of firms to go out of business. This propelled Huawei to use 60 percent of its initial annual sales to conduct R&D (later kept at a 10 percent level) in its own switches and TCL to develop its own platforms for telephones and televisions. Skyworth started its business in 1990 by making remote controls for televisions, and its profits shrank from 50 percent to 10 percent within a year. It was then that Huang Hongsheng, the founder of the Skyworth, made the determination to invite a group of scientists and technicians from Hong Kong and produced their first large-scale IC television (Jin 2010: 17).

Under such circumstances, the Shenzhen government's supportive policies in domestic upgrading came in time and further provided impetus for a wider range of firms to take the high road of learning and innovation. There was no doubt that bureaucrats of domestic technology, like those in Suzhou, often lowered the standard of R&D set by the central government in evaluating enterprise performance.[28] The important point, though, was that government support was more likely to produce results as domestic producers had both the urgent need *and* the possible space for upgrading and investing in learning and innovation. Mr. Zhuo, a manager from the P Group, shared a story from his own company:

> We used to be an assembler of mobile phones for a leading multinational corporation, L, during the late 1990s and early 2000s, which brought us huge annual sales, the highest reaching 3.78 billion yuan. But our highest profits were only 30 million. This low profit margin pattern showed signs of running out of steam. The city government encouraged us to conduct research on our own products and introduced to the president of our group the opportunities of various innovation funds and tax policies. The company decided to give it a try, and we began to produce brand products in LCD screens and mobile phones. Despite that, our current annual profit is still around 30 million yuan, not huge; it is made out of an annual sale of 600 million yuan, in which case the profit rate is raised more than sixfold compared to before.[29]

Within such a structure of production, domestic firms usually enter the industry from the bottom of the global production chain through

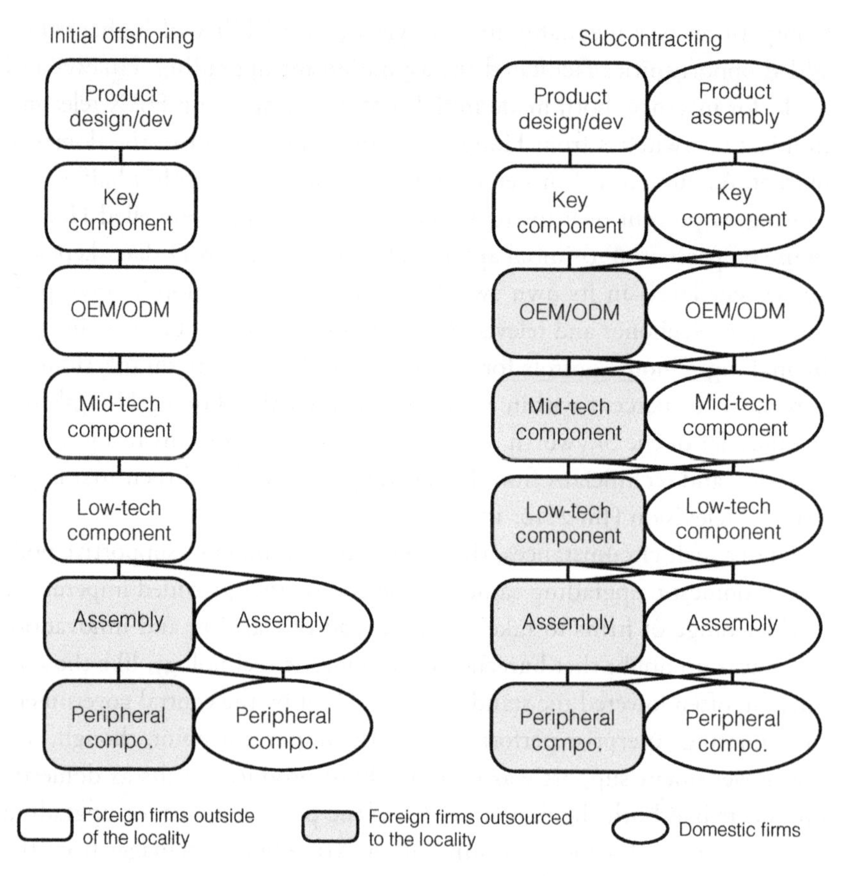

FIGURE 5.3. The path of industrial upgrading for Shenzhen's domestic electronics producers.

processing trade for FIEs, learning to upgrade their own products by selling them in China's huge domestic markets and eventually competing on the international market (Figure 5.3).[30] The specific upgrading approaches were dependent on firm situations. Some met the challenge head on by conducting R&D in core technology. Examples include the ZX500 and ZXJ2000 switches from ZTE and the first 10,000-line switch, the C&C08 2000 switch from Huawei in the early 1990s (Harwit 2007; Xu 2008: 23–26; Wu and Ji 2006). Other enterprises, such as Xianke, engaged in flexible learning by importing the core technology and adapting it to the domestic market. Finally, an increasing number of small-scale component producers began to cluster in Huaqiangbei and produce telecommunication computer components through imitation and adaption of existing technology and designs. Not surprisingly, FIEs in Shenzhen also constantly felt competitive pressure from local enterprises, instead of resting very comfortably at the top of the hierarchy as MNCs did in Suzhou. To use the words from Mr. Chan, the founder of a Taiwan electronics FIE:

> The growing of numerous electronics enterprises indicated the coming of a new age for us. In the "old days," when overseas investment was the major source of capital for the electronics industry, we often felt that we were children being spoiled by the local government. Now came the time that we were not the only child and the government had to spread its love for everyone. These domestic competitors started by getting orders from us and were now competing with us.[31]

The competition that Mr. Chan mentioned came from Chinese entrepreneurs who showed much more ambition in achieving competitiveness compared with their Suzhou counterparts. Unlike in Suzhou, where entrepreneurial initiatives were often suffocated by pro-MNC institutions before generating any fruits, Shenzhen entrepreneurs were embedded in norms that often encouraged them to challenge existing successors.

As firms grew competitive in domestic and international markets, collaboration among domestic enterprises and between domestic and foreign enterprises also started to emerge. MTK, a Taiwanese chip producer of mobile phones, established close cooperative relationships with many newly emerging domestic design houses, top among which were Ginwave and Topwise, CK Telecom, and Longyu. These design houses increased rapidly in the mid-2000s as technicians who specialized in design works and entrepreneurs who had enough capital came together to set up design businesses that served both domestic and foreign mobile phone producers. Similarly, VIA, a rising Taiwan netbook chipmaker, established an "open industrial strategic alliance" with 20 domestic personal computer makers and more than a hundred smaller suppliers (B. Li 2008). Both MTK and VIA were strongly supported by the Shenzhen government due to their broad connections with domestic private enterprises, and both had entered Shenzhen HTDZ in the early 2000s. These collaborations posed significant challenges to leading chip makers in OECD countries such as Qualcomm and Broadcom in mobile phone chips and Intel in computer chips. In response, they were also pressured to adjust their strategies by establishing production relationships with domestic producers.

The subcontracting institutions and the ways in which government coordinated relations between foreign and domestic businesses thus effectively countered the reinforcement of hierarchical segregation between foreign and domestic businesses. Furthermore, it facilitated the effectiveness of government policies in promoting upgrading and technology learning by providing spaces and opportunities for these activities. It should be emphasized that although the configuration of local production provided the initial condition of upgrading, it did not *determine* the outcome of upgrading success. Rather, the argument is that, by starting with smaller FIEs at the lower section of the value chain, domestic firms had a greater incentive to engage in upgrading and that the "push" from domestic technology officials through offering funding and tax breaks were more likely to produce results.

Applicability across the Country: Disaggregating the Monolithic Picture

The case studies in the previous section suggested that, in the electronics industry, when cities attracted predominately large-scale, top-ranked FIEs, domestic firms were less likely to engage in upgrading and less likely to respond to the industrial policy tools that government used to induce firm behavior in technology development. In contrast, cities that attracted smaller, less-well-known FIEs were more likely to have firms engaging in technology innovation and upgrading, and the industrial policies were more effective in producing results at the firm level. In other words, the "global allies" that local government chose influenced the effectiveness of domestic development policies. How does this observation hold across other cities in China? This section uses national economic census data to test the generalizability of the argument developed from the two cases.

The major challenge in identifying the causes for varied policy outcomes lies in the fact that both the characteristics of individual firms and local contexts affect firms' decisions on whether to invest in upgrading. At the firm level, factors such as capital, employment, sales, and state support received are always important determinants of how many resources firm management is willing to invest in the upgrading activities of R&D, new product development, and patent applications. At the local level, economic, political, geographical, and cultural conditions can also potentially affect the upgrading behavior of firms that are located within their jurisdiction. Moreover, given the uneven nature of economic development in China, different cities have different numbers of firms and thus have very unbalanced sample sizes and variance.

Hierarchical linear modeling (HLM) provides an ideal analytical tool for teasing out factors at both levels. HLM specifically deals with data having a hierarchical structure, such as individuals or firms nested within social groups, neighborhood districts, and regions. This allows for the completion of the essential tasks of (a) estimating the effects of government support across individual firms while controlling for other firm level variables and (b) estimating the different magnitudes of such effects associated with government policies across different localities. The first provides the microfoundation for our model by taking into consideration individual firm characteristics and, in particular, by gaining a sound measurement of government policy effectiveness at the firm level within each city. The second dimension allows us to explore the heterogeneity of estimation across cities and to examine the city-level determinants for the variation in firm behavior and their response to state policies. This study thus uses HLM for two levels of analysis, the firm level and the city level.

Data used in this section were gathered during China's 2008 National Economic Census. With permission from the NBS, I was able to gain access to the original database that consists of the entire population of the 421,833 above-scale firms in 41 industries located across 300 prefecture-level cities (2,000 counties) in mainland China as of the end of 2008. What is unique about the dataset is that it not only contains economic information as industrial surveys do but also contains science and technology information such as government support for science and technology activities and firm-level R&D spending and patents applications.

Based on the original dataset, two sets of hierarchical data were constructed for both the electronics industry and all manufacturing industries. For the electronics industry, the hierarchical dataset includes data on 6,740 domestic private electronics firms at the first level and data on 159 cities that these firms are located in at the second level. These cities are localities that actually have domestic private firms in the electronics industry and have at least one FIE in their jurisdiction.[32] For all the manufacturing industries, the dataset includes data on 322,138 domestic private firms across 321 cities (out of the total 341 prefecture-level units in China as of 2008), again including cities that have domestic- and foreign-invested firms. Three key variables are worth detailed discussion.

FIRMS' TECHNOLOGY UPGRADING BEHAVIOR: THE FIRM-LEVEL DEPENDENT VARIABLE

Mobilizing firms to upgrade was the key goal of China's upgrading and indigenous innovation policies over the past two decades. Evaluating and explaining the success or failure of such policies requires, in the first place, understanding and measuring firm innovation behavior in a reliable way. Because upgrading is a notoriously difficult concept to operationalize, this study focuses on whether a firm devotes any effort to upgrading activities rather than on the general economic performance of the firms. I measure upgrading behavior by examining whether a firm has invested resources in R&D and whether it has patent applications.[33] I chose these measures for two reasons. First, these measures are the most relevant to the goals of state upgrading policies. By offering various beneficial policies in land, tax, government funding, finance, tariff, and intellectual property protection, the Chinese government has aimed to encourage domestic firms to change their habits in low-value-added manufacturing and learn to conduct R&D and new product development and to apply for patents. In fact, these are the benchmarks that the government uses to evaluate whether firms are eligible for state support policies. Second, these measures are also most relevant to the theoretical framework advanced in this study. My field research between 2008 and 2011 suggests that the crucial condition for Chinese firms to exit competition at the bottom of the value chain lies in whether the firm executives have the *motivation* to invest resources in learning and innovation. These decisions are based on management's perceptions of the risks, benefits, and urgency of engaging in upgrading, which are deeply shaped by the local political and economic contexts in which firms are embedded.[34] Thus, to the extent that state policies have influences on firm upgrading behavior, after other economic variables are controlled, they are expected to have the most significant effect on the observed efforts that firms put into technology development.

THE UPGRADING AND TECHNOLOGY POLICIES OF THE STATE

The two key measures for state upgrading policies used in this study are whether a firm receives government funding for R&D activities and government tax exemptions for the purpose of engaging in technology development in 2008. As previously mentioned, China's domestic technology policies cover a broad range of areas, yet my research suggest that the core policy areas affecting a firm's innovation decisions are government funding and tax cuts. The finance policy certainly matters tremendously for firms, but a preliminary examination of the data suggests that state policies do not vary significantly across firms and/or across localities. This is because the majority of domestic electronics firms are private firms, and banks across China are almost unanimously biased against providing loans for private firms, despite supportive measures specified in the state upgrading policies.[35] Land policy is another important area, but, given the sensitivity of the issue, the economic census database (and most existing statistical datasets in China) does not provide indicators at the city level, not to mention at the firm level. Therefore, this study will use the amount of government funding and the amount of government tax exemption as proxies for the amount of government support that a firm receives. These two variables were also clearly specified in the questionnaire of the national census as "government funding for R&D" and "tax reduction or exemptions for technology development" so that firms would not be confused and provide information on government support for other purposes.

THE EFFECTIVENESS OF STATE POLICIES ACROSS LOCALITIES

The effectiveness of state policies is measured by *the relationship between the probability that a firm receives state support and the probability a firm devotes any effort to upgrading, when other firm-level variables are controlled.* When policy effectiveness is high, having state funding or tax breaks is associated with a relatively high probability of a firm's investment in upgrading and innovation. In contrast, when policy effectiveness is low, having state support is associated with relatively little change in firm behavior or may even reduce the amount of effort for innovation at the firm level.

The control variables are factors in addition to state policy support that are likely to affect a firm's decision to invest in innovation. These firm-level control variables include: (a) the total assets of the firm (with log transformation); (b) the profit rate of the firm; and (c) the capital labor ratio measured as fixed capital divided by total employment (with log transformation). These variables were selected to control for the general size and economic conditions of a firm as well as for the influence of world markets

TABLE 5.3.
Government support and firm upgrading behavior in China (the unconditional model).

Fixed effect	R&D expense	Patent applications
Independent variables		
Government funding	2.638*** (0.171)	2.058*** (0.113)
Tax break	1.833*** (0.314)	1.305*** (0.248)
Control variables		
Assets (log)	0.550*** (0.034)	0.625*** (0.042)
Profit rate	0.432 (0.286)	1.305*** (0.314)
Capital–labor ratio (log)	0.024 (0.035)	−0.037 (0.041)
Intercept	−2.165*** (0.093)	−2.774*** (0.077)
Random effect (variance component)	R&D expense	Patent applications
Intercept	0.510***	0.121***
Government funding	0.817***	0.058**
Tax policy	1.451***	0.790***

Firm level N = 6,740; city level N = 159
*$p < 0.10$ **$p < 0.05$ ***$p < 0.01$ Robust standard errors are used

but without creating strong correlations among them. The statist literature leads one to hypothesize that when other factors are controlled, the amount of state support received should in general produce positive effects on firm upgrading behavior. The findings based on case studies also suggest that, when implemented in different local settings, the same state policy would create different outcomes.

Therefore, the two hypotheses for a basic two-level hierarchical model at the firm level and at an unconditional city level are:

1. Overall, firms that receive more government support for technology activities are more likely to engage in technology activities, all other things being equal.
2. Firms located in different cities vary significantly in terms of their average level of upgrading and in terms of the effectiveness of government policies.

Table 5.3 presents the unconditional two-level model using full maximizing likelihood to estimate the effects of government funding and tax policies on domestic electronics firms across 159 cities, controlling for assets, profit rate, and capital–labor ratio at the firm level. The coefficients represent the mean coefficients across the 159 cities when firm-level estimation was performed within each city. The results support both hypotheses. On average, across the 159 cities in which the 6,740 firms were located, government policies of funding and tax reduction have generated significantly positive effects on firm upgrading behavior. In the table, fixed effects of government funding and tax breaks represent the average slopes for two government-support variables across these cities. For example, having government funding is on average associated with 2.638 units of increase in log the odds ratio for a firm's probability to engage in upgrading activity. Returning the value to the odds, this means that having government funding increases the odds 13.98 times. Similarly, having tax breaks is associated with an approximate 1.305 units of increase in a firm's log likelihood to have patent applications, which means that the odds ratio increase is 3.686. As clearly indicated in the table, the percentages of changes that government support policies have brought are in most cases greater than other firm-level variables, implying that government funding has greater elasticity.

An equally important finding is that when firm-level upgrading behavior is estimated within each city by the two independent variables of government support and the three control variables, the results vary substantially among cities. This is indicated in the model by the random effects for the intercept, the effect of government funding and the effect for tax policy, which are all significantly different from zero. We can thus confirm the second hypothesis that cities vary significantly in the average upgrading behavior of domestic firms (measured by the intercepts) as well as the effectiveness of government policies (measured by the value of coefficients for government policies). Figure 5.4 shows a random sample of 50 cities when running a hypothetical regression in each city. The sharper the slopes, the more effective government funding policies are. This result suggests that a single regression among all the 6,740 domestic private firms would not capture or account for the variation among cities, and we should further examine explanatory factors at city level, accounting for between-city differences.

Before proceeding to predictors at the city level, however, we can take advantage of the unconditional model and get a substantive idea of how cities vary from each other. Due to space constraints, I focus on showing the variation in policy effectiveness. The empirical Bayes coefficients generated for each city through the sum of fitted value and residuals allow us to

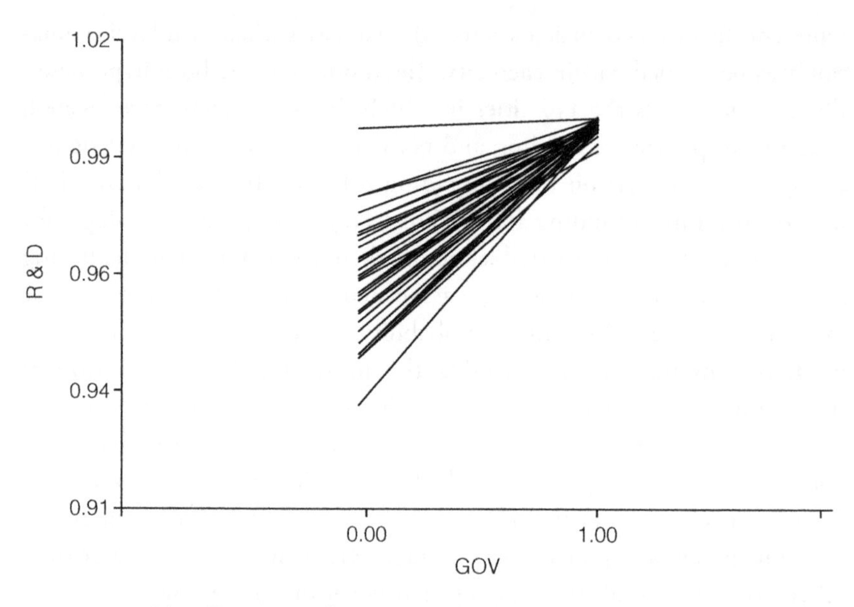

FIGURE 5.4. The effectiveness of government funding in encouraging firm-level R&D.

compare the slopes of government funding and tax breaks—indicators for policy effectiveness—across the 159 prefecture-level cities. Figure 5.5 maps out the national picture using the mean value of coefficients measured in four indicators across the two models. It distinguishes the levels of policy effectiveness according to quartiles of low, medium low, medium high, and high. The variation among cities is striking. Although neighboring cities sometimes display similarities, provincial borders are too broad to capture the diverse outcomes. Note, however, that cities with high levels of policy effectiveness do not necessarily have strong degrees of government intervention. Rather, having a higher level of policy effectiveness means that when regression analysis of firm-level variables is conducted for the city, one unit of government support is associated with larger changes in firm upgrading behavior.

To explain variations of effectiveness among these cities, the next step is to introduce city-level predictors. Based on previous case studies, we have a third hypothesis: The larger the median size of the foreign invested firms in a city's electronics industry, the lower the degree of effectiveness that government policies produce among domestic firms, all other things being equal. The measures for the effectiveness of government policies are the

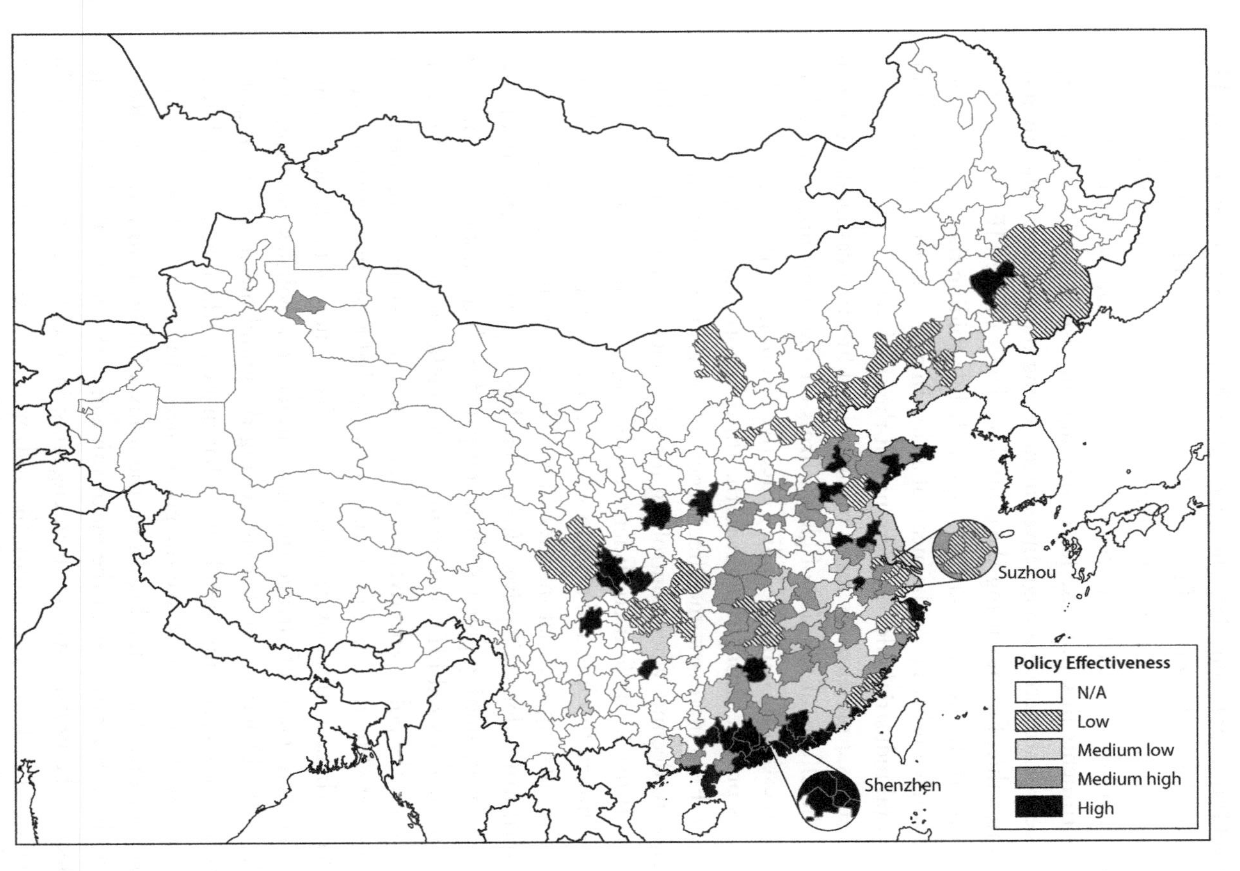

FIGURE 5.5. The effectiveness of state upgrading policies in China's electronics industry across 159 cities.

same as the ones used in the previous model—the coefficients representing the slopes between government support (funding and tax breaks) and firm-level innovation behavior. The *firm size of the FIEs* in a city is measured by the median value of the firm's total assets among all FIEs of a given city. Using assets, rather than employment, as the measure for the firm size is based on the fact that the size of the assets is the major criterion that local governments in China use for evaluating the size of the FIEs during the process of attracting foreign investment. Using the median, rather than the mean value, for measuring the central tendency of the FIE sizes can help reduce the influence of outliers, especially by avoiding the situation where one single outlier raises the mean of a city. In addition, the model controls for total industrial sales of electronics at the city level.

Table 5.4 presents the result of a two-level hierarchical model, estimating the effects of the size of global firms on the mean upgrading efforts of domestic firms and the policy effectiveness of government policies. The results provide strong support to the third hypothesis. As the general size of the FIEs increases, the effectiveness of government upgrading policies tends to decline, when controlling for other city-level and firm-level factors. Three of the four coefficients predicting government effectiveness in government funding and tax cuts were negative and statistically significant. The results suggest that in cities where FIEs are dominated by large-scale global firms, domestic private firms were less responsive to the call of government upgrading policies when compared with domestic firms in cities with smaller-sized FIEs. For example, the coefficient for the size of foreign firms on the policy effectiveness of tax policy was –1.005. This means that one unit of increase in the median size of global firms in a city was associated with 1.005 units of decrease in the effectiveness of tax policies, which is the percentage of change that government tax policies can bring on a firm's R&D activity in that city. Using the grand mean size of all global firms as the base, this would mean that in a city where its median foreign firm size is one unit above the grand mean, the predicted odds of a one percent increase in tax breaks on the firms' likelihood to invest in R&D will be 1.202 rather than the mean value of 3.284 across all the cities, reducing the probability of a firm engaging in R&D from 0.76 to 0.54. In the case of patent applications, the odds were reduced from 1.077 to 0.328 (after deducting 1.188 from the log of odds of 0.074), reducing the probability of firm applications for patents from 0.52 to 0.25. In this case, a firm that received tax breaks that was originally more likely than not to apply

TABLE 5.4.
Effectiveness of government support in local China.

Variables (independent variables in bold)	R&D expense	Patent applications
City-level variables		
Predictors for mean upgrading efforts (intercept β_0)		
Base	−1.934*** (0.096)	−2.87*** (0.091)
Size of foreign firms (log)	−0.185* (0.051)	−0.054 (0.092)
Electronics sales (log)	−0.027 (0.096)	0.057* (0.027)
Predictors for policy effectiveness (slopes)		
Size of foreign firms (log) (for the effects of government funding)	−0.437** (0.172)	−0.045 (0.154)
Size of foreign firms (log) (for the effects of tax policy)	−1.005* (0.541)	−1.188** (0.474)
Firm-level variables		
Government funding	2.304*** (0.158)	2.039*** (0.115)
Tax policy	1.189*** (0.22)	0.074*** (0.246)
Assets (log)	0.495*** (0.051)	0.61*** (0.038)
Profit rate	0.409* (0.233)	1.314*** (0.295)
Capital–labor ratio (log)	0.039 (0.032)	0.028 (0.377)

Firm level $N = 6{,}740$; City level $N = 159$
$^{*}p < 0.10$ $^{**}p < 0.05$ $^{***}p < 0.01$; robust standard errors

for patents is now apparently less likely to do so than otherwise. In other words, although government support has on average contributed to firm upgrading behavior among the domestic private electronics firms in China, the size of foreign firms in a city *interacted* with government intervention in a negative way by reducing such effects on these firms.

Conclusion

This chapter raises a fundamental concern about how globalization has complicated the consequences of state-led development in developing countries. For a long time, the emphasis has been on the conditions that contribute to the rise of a developmental state that shows the willingness and capacity to promote development. Under this view, China was able to get the institutions right, as its decentralized fiscal arrangement provided developmental incentives for local bureaucrats. The argument holds quite well, as long as the developmental allies of the government are largely domestic businesses, as is the case of China in the 1980s and the case of the East Asian developmental states in their catch-up period of the 1960s and 1970s. When global capital penetrated into local settings and became an important ally in local development plans, such as in China or in Southeast Asian countries, the picture became far more complicated.[36] Not only may the "willingness" to promote development and upgrading be dampened by the vested interests within the state, but the effectiveness of such policies was put to question as well. As governmental supportive policies interacted with the influence of global firms, the original goal of promoting domestic industrial upgrading may have been undermined or enhanced by the presence of global capital, as we have seen in the comparison of Suzhou and Shenzhen and in the two-level hierarchical models.

The consequences of such interaction, however, are often not anticipated in the original development plans, and thus the promotion of upgrading in the current era requires a learning process for the state as well. The theoretical and practical lessons learned from this chapter—that global firms of large scale reduce the effectiveness of upgrading policies on domestic firms—are critical for other developing countries similarly located at the lower end of the value chain. This finding highlights the importance for the state to choose global allies that are closer to the developmental stages of domestic producers so as to facilitate a more equal structure of local production and a fairer basis for policy implementation, both of which are crucial for mobilizing the upgrading incentives of domestic firms. The policies of picking winners may not necessarily work when the winners are global firms that tend to draw on group outsourcing strategies, do not leave space for local upgrading, and substantially tilt the playing field into an uneven one.

CHAPTER 6

Varieties of Local Capitalism in Historical Perspective

As we have seen in previous chapters, some cities focused on attracting FIEs at the top of the value chain, which aroused a strong vested interest that curtailed city governments' support for domestic technology. In other cities, where openness to foreign capital started with FIEs at the lower end of the value chain, governments were able to offer a larger proportion of city expenses as support due to the different coalitional alignments. At the same time, some cities ended up with a production structure that reduced the effectiveness of the support on the firm level, whereas others were able to generate stronger incentives at the firm level for engaging in technology upgrading. These two observations, furthermore, are not separate phenomena. The allocation of support for technology upgrading and the effectiveness of such support at the firm level mutually reinforced each other. As Figure 6.1 indicates, cities with lower degrees of support also tended to be the ones that were less effective in motivating firms to upgrade (using the indicator developed for government funding effectiveness in Chapter 5), as these two aspects both resulted from a city's strategy in earlier periods to attract FDI and promote exports.

As more or less successful upgrading results were produced, giving rise to more or less competitive domestic firms, they also generated feedback loops to policy makers, making it more or less likely for domestic technology bureaucrats to acquire funding and other resources from the city government. In other words, major types of FIEs that the government attracted during the 1990s and the early to mid-2000s sowed the seeds for a

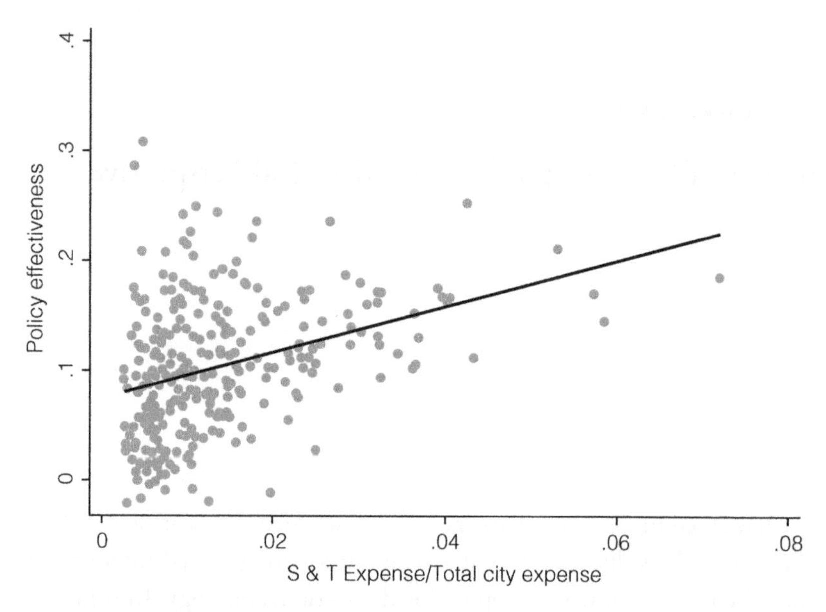

FIGURE 6.1. City government science and technology expense and the effectiveness of government funding across Chinese cities.

region's bureaucratic coalitions, its strategies of technology upgrading, and its likelihood for success.

Why, then, within the same political regime and national economic context, did bureaucrats seek alliances with different types of foreign firms in the first place? Furthermore, why did choices made earlier tend to reinforce options later down the road so that cities ended up with distinct trajectories of development rather than converging with each other? This chapter places China's regional economy into a longer comparative historical perspective. To understand the type of path dependency driving the entire development process, and why it was not easy for a city to switch the course in the past two and a half decades, one needs to explore patterns embedded in varieties of local capitalism over the long term.

Existing works provide interesting insight into the path-dependent nature of regional economies. The first insight emphasizes the previous economic legacies from the Maoist era, which provided the Jiangsu area with stronger collective resources compared to other regions such as Zhejiang and Guangdong (Oi 1999; Whiting 2001; Tsai 2007). Although previous economic conditions are helpful for understanding the public or private ownership type among domestic enterprises in the initial reform period of the 1980s, this explanation still left one wondering about the government's focus on large top-ranked MNCs versus less well-known FIEs when China was increasingly globalized in the 1990s. The second potential cause is that, over the course of several decades, cultural and ethnic Chinese networks have a potential influence on favoring the development of small FIEs in Guangdong rather than Jiangsu (Naughton 1997; Hamilton 2006; Tong and Zheng 2008; Yeung 2009; Kohli 2009; Ye 2014; Hsing 1998). As it has been shown, however, both regions have attracted a large number of ethnic Chinese firms from Hong Kong and Taiwan. Suzhou (and especially Kunshan area), for instance, was the well-known home for Taiwanese firms throughout the 1990s and 2000s, even though it is not geographically adjacent to either Hong Kong or Taiwan. What distinguishes these "China-circle" firms in the two regions is actually the relatively top rank, large size, and dominance of exports in the Yangtze River Delta compared to FIEs in the Pearl River Delta.

This chapter argues that the historical process of state-preference formation is fundamental to the emergence of regional development patterns. It traces the divergent paths in industrial development through a century-long formation and consolidation of the local bureaucrats' preferences in choosing their business constituents for the advancement of their own political and economic interests. The post-Mao political and economic institutions instilled strong incentives for bureaucrats to promote local economic development by seeking an alliance with the business group. They, however, tended to see the building of such coalitions as fulfilling different ends. When bureaucrats have been driven mainly by political purposes, the development process becomes highly politicized. Bureaucrats tended to ally with large businesses situated at the top of the production hierarchy and adopt a top-down mode of development. When bureaucrats were habitually motivated by practical economic gains, they often preferred to network with small businesses in a dispersed manner, resulting in a bottom-up path in the trajectory of development. The reinforcement of different types of capitalism and regional development patterns thus can be attributed to the state's preferences over different types of developmental allies, which were further rooted in the bureaucrats' entrenched perception of their own interests and their ways of carrying out developmental tasks. The development outcomes generated from each period thus show historically persistent variation across the two regions. Although the second mode of capitalism tends to involve small measures of local insubordination or petty corruption, it turns out to have more advantages in the globalized era.

It is particularly worth emphasizing in the beginning that the top-down and bottom-up modes of capitalism are *not* simply a state versus market divide, as is often assumed in previous works (McNally 2012; Nee and Opper 2012). Rather, as will be detailed, both types of capitalism involve active roles of government officials. The difference instead lies in the development strategies these officials adopt driven by distinct interests. Such a difference can also be perceived when regions enter a globalized era. In the former situation, bureaucrats competed to attract investments from large top-ranked enterprises, often undergoing months of negotiation. In the latter situation, bureaucrats tended to develop practical and flexible approaches for seeking small firms that could bring in immediate economic benefits to the locality.

Such divergent perceptions of interests did not emerge overnight. Nor were they entirely determined by the post-Mao regional institutions. Rather, they were formed and developed over a long stretch of time that dates back to the late 19th century. The development of preferences and institutions followed an iterative process in which preferences developed in the previous period were transmitted into the next period through institution building and policy implementations, the result of which further reinforced such preferences. As the pursuit of interests became gradually entrenched in local bureaucratic norms, they defined the basic means for the state to achieve developmental goals and the breadth of state–business coalitions, as well as the particular type of capitalism that emerged in the region. A comparative historical analysis is thus essential in understanding the century-long development of state preferences and local capitalism. The next section begins this effort by tracing the political and economic interests of local states and their preferences for choosing business allies through the historical rise of distinct types of regional capitalism.

Bureaucrats, Businesses, and Dual Patterns of Regional Capitalism from the Historical Perspective

Scholars in the Chinese political economy have been increasingly intrigued by the dualist nature of capitalism in China (McNally 2012). On the one hand, they emphasize a top-down mode of capitalism, coordinated by a strong Leninist developmental state that penetrates into various facets of an economy through strategic planning and intervening tools (White

1988; Yang 2004; Pearson 2005). This mode of capitalism found its extreme version in "state capitalism" or "developmental autocracy," in which the state tilted resources into state-monopolized sectors at the expense of local private enterprises (Huang 2008; Pei 2006; Naughton and Tsai 2015). On the other hand, there is a fundamentally different pattern of accumulation and development that relies on mechanisms from the bottom up, which consists of numerous flexible practices, incremental experiments, and adaptive strategies. Typically representing small-scale dispersed petty capitalism, these bottom-level initiatives are often the engine for institutional adaptation and policy change (Tsai 2007; Arrighi 2007; Heilmann 2011; Nee and Opper 2012).

How can one reconcile the seemingly conflicting nature of the two patterns? Some scholars take a temporal view by arguing that one mode of capitalism tends to dominate in a particular historical period (Huang 2008; Hung 2015). Yasheng Huang (2008), for example, argues that an entrepreneurial decade in the 1980s was replaced by state-sponsored capitalism with a strong urban bias. Others find that, in effect, the two patterns have often coexisted in a dialectic relationship in contemporary China's economic policy making and implementation (Heilmann 2011; McNally 2012). However, what was often missed is a regional perspective of capitalism that has persisted for decades. When going beyond an aggregate national view of China and delving into the country's local economies, one can often discover historically persistent regional pathways based on varied modes of capitalism, with the Yangtze River Delta and the Pearl River Delta each representing a prototype.

The regional capitalism examined in this chapter builds on the previous understanding of the dual patterns of Chinese capitalism to challenge existing perspectives in several important aspects. First, while the top-down mode of capitalism is traditionally associated with state dominance and the bottom-up mode with a free-market economy, in this chapter, the local state bureaucrats are found to be critical players in forging both types of regional capitalism. The distinction is not whether the state is active or dormant but rather that the state is active in different ways. Second, whereas most studies view top-down planning as initiatives taken by the central state and bottom-up adaptations coming from local-level innovations, this chapter finds that local initiatives can be implemented as much in a top-down manner as in the bottom up. Bureaucrats may contribute to the formation of a top-down or a bottom-up bottom trajectory depending

TABLE 6.1.
Varieties of capitalism in Jiangsu and Guangdong.

Regions	Jiangsu	Guangdong
Patterns of development policies	Highly politicized	Focusing on practical economic benefits
Policy tools to achieve the goals	Campaign style; mobilization from above	Guerilla style; builds diverse ties from below
Political and economic rewards	Political rewards; successful in getting promoted	Increased local economic income; petty corruption
Response to central policies	Highly responsive to signals from above; competes to accomplish policy goals in a way that displays achievement but may not benefit local businesses	More identification with local interests; flexible in policy implementation; strong localism
Government–business coalition	Ranks business in a hierarchy; allies with the influential businesses at the very top; discriminates against small businesses; narrow coalition	Nurtures ties with numerous small business at the bottom; attentive to the interests of small businesses; broad coalition
Local capitalism	Top-down capitalism	Bottom-up capitalism

on their perception of interests, their response to central-level signals, and their choices of business allies. Compared with the central-local divide, this finding is more consistent with previous scholarly observations that local officials are sometimes highly protective of local small-scale private enterprises, whereas at other times they discriminate severely against private businesses (Tsai 2006; Huang 2008).

In a path-dependent manner, the degree of political mobilization that developed during the state-building period of the 20th century (1895–1990) drove the state's choice of global allies and further shaped the subsequent trajectories of industrial transformation in the contemporary period starting in the 1990s. The logic of capitalism demonstrated a significant degree of institutional persistence even under globalization. Starting in the late 19th century throughout the 20th century, a top-down mode of capitalism increasingly dominated the Yangtze River Delta, whereas the Pearl River Delta became the quintessential example of a bottom-up pattern of development. During each of the historical periods—the late Qing and early republican period (1895–1920), the Mao era (1949–1978), the post-Mao period (1978–1990), and the globalized era (1990–present)—bureaucrats in the two deltas have prioritized political or economic goals and interests. As a result, they also responded differently to central policy initiatives and em-

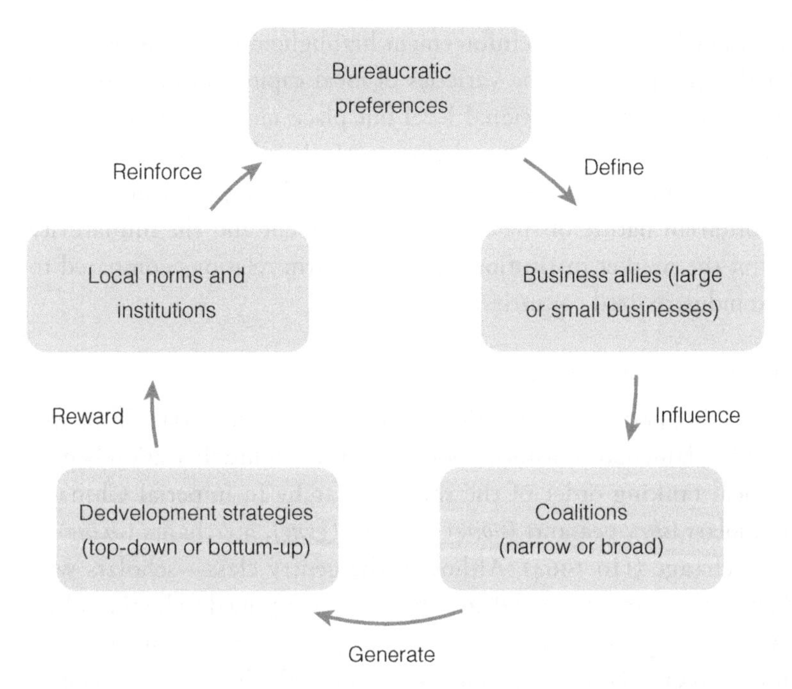

FIGURE 6.2. The reinforcement of bureaucratic preferences and the policy cycle.

ployed distinctive policy tools to achieve these goals. These diverse interests and policy tools helped the state to build narrow or broad developmental coalitions that encompassed different types of businesses (Table 6.1). With repetition and diffusion, the practices gave rise to distinctive types of capitalism in each region. As the developmental outcomes rewarded bureaucrats' behaviors with political or economic benefits and further strengthened local norms and institutions, the bureaucrats' perceptions of their own interests were further reinforced. This enabled the preferences to be carried into the next historical period as legacies of bureaucratic traditions, despite the complete changes of institutional landscapes (Figure 6.2).

The interests of the bureaucrats hence were embedded in and profoundly shaped by local habits, norms, and institutions, rather than being based on functionalist utility maximization. This understanding does not preclude bureaucrats from being calculating (and often more calculating in some areas than others), but it is the local variety of capitalism that shaped their interests in the long term.[1] As Table 6.1 shows, the mutual reinforcement and complementarity of different elements in China's regional capitalism have displayed similarities with the varieties of capitalism frameworks and the institutional inertia and reinforcement highlighted in the historical institutionalist perspective.[2] The varieties of local capitalism not only take the perspective to the subnational level but place more emphasis on the preferences of bureaucrats, their relations with their business clients, and their response to central development policies. This emphasis stems from the authoritarian nature of the Chinese government and the immaturity of many of the market institutions governing firm relations compared to advanced industrialized countries.

THE LATE QING AND EARLY REPUBLICAN PERIOD (1895–1920)

In the late Qing period, the traditional social order of imperial China underwent a fundamental transformation, and initial industrialization began. The classical ranking order of the social hierarchy in imperial China—literati/scholars (*shi*), peasants (*nong*), artisans (*gong*), merchants (*shang*)—started to change (Ho 1964). Although the gentry class—scholars who passed civil exams and became degree holders—continued to be the ruling force in the state apparatus, businesses also began to exercise growing influence in local industrial development.[3] Late imperial China thus developed an economy increasingly dominated by two modes of production, with the tributary mode of production existing alongside the petty-capitalist mode of production (Gates 1996). In the face of expanded foreign intervention since the mid- to late 1800s, local officials came to embrace different approaches for governing local development and industrialization. Over time, they cultivated relations with large businesses. The Yangtze River Delta became dominated by a collusion of bureaucrats and large businesses, whereas the Pearl River Delta preserved the development of small businesses that were relatively independent from the local gentry.

By the late 1800s, the Yangtze River Delta, especially the southern Jiangsu region, had become a major industrial base and China's most urbanized region. The city of Suzhou—the capital of the *liang-jiang* governor-generalship—was viewed as the central metropolis and the most advanced commercial and manufacturing center (Skinner 197:, 3–32; Liu 1984). This successful economic development was forged through a tight coalition between local officials and a selective group of powerful business elites "of great wealth" that excluded small businesses. The experience of the Suzhou's rapid modernization initiative under the leadership of Jiangsu-Zhejiang Governor-General Zhang Zhidong was an especially good example of this.

According to the study of Suzhou by Peter Carroll, the modernization project that began in 1985 was an initiative that grew out of "bureaucratic capitalism" and involved social mobilization and top-down dislocation. With the belief that a "modern, technologically advanced industry was the seminal source of national plenty," Zhang facilitated the establishment of *guandu shangban* (officially supervised and merchant-managed) enterprises with the Commercial Bureau (which also takes the function of an industrial bureau) playing a central role in coordinating business activities (Carroll 2006: 30–31; Feuerwerker 1958: 1–30). The local gentry and bureaucrats were able to rally large businesses around the modernization agenda of the Commercial Bureau by appointing well-connected local elites (such as Lu Runxiang from the Hanlin Academy) to lobby for financial support from other businesses. The idea of promoting modernity and growth through aggressive state intervention grew in influence and helped tighten the coalition between prominent state and business elites. This quest drove the state to build a domestic industrial zone near Suzhou's foreign industrial zone, so as to spur growth and catch up with cities such as Shanghai or Hankou. Ignoring the suggestion that officials and provincial government should reduce their role in the economic planning of the bureau, Zhang went ahead with his original vision by directly supervising the industrial development through the bureau and verifying the alignment of local businesses with the governor-general's agenda (Carroll 2006: 32, 37–38, 50, 85).

An "overt hierarchy" of businesses emerged in local policy, ranking the local state enterprises and classes of businesses according to the perceived benefits that they would bring to the state (Carroll 2006: 85–86). At the top of the hierarchy were large, capital-intensive enterprises and prominent businesses whose roles sometimes intermingled with the role of local officials (examples of which include scholar-industrialist Sheng Hsuan-huai) (Feuerwerker 1958). By contrast, small-scale businesses were situated at the bottom of the government-ranked hierarchy. It was *not* the case that the region lacked small businesses; there were small businesses developing in both of the delta regions (Gates 1996). However, in contrast to the few "honorable" business elites, the small-scale businesses were regarded as "ignorant" and "obstinate" (Carroll 2006, citing Suzhou shanghui: 695–696). These small businesses were frequently removed, repressed, and regulated by urban campaigns and the use of police force so as to forge social cohesion in the achievement of development. The idea of constraining and disciplining the "wicked" small businesses who were undermining the progress of modernization was espoused throughout the republican era (Carroll 2006: 79, 84, 90–95). It is thus not surprising that Suzhou Gazetteer recorded that, although Suzhou was regarded as the "heaven" on Earth for its prosperity, it was only a "heaven" for the gentry bureaucrats and large businesses (Suzhou Gazetteer Committee 1995a: 4). As Carroll commented:

> Indeed, it can be argued that by reining in the activities of small-scale merchants and street vendors, the "motor" of petty capitalism, city authorities actually diminished the volume of contemporary commerce and stunted the urban economy's capacity for future development. (Carroll 2006: 89)

The state's alliance with the big businesses and its discrimination against small businesses were reflected in studies of other cities in the late Qing and republican Jiangsu. Zhang Zhidong's personal secretary, Zhang Jian, became the leading figure in the undertaking of industrializing Nantong through his connections with large bankers, investors, and industrialists. Lipkin's (2006) study of the republican period in Nanjing echoed Carroll's observation of the top-down mobilization of the state and the discrimination against marginal groups. Lynda Bell (1999) highlighted in her study of Wuxi that the local government and prominent economic elites, both in the late Qing and republican eras, collaborated or intermingled to achieve social dominance. They did so by seeking vertical integration and expansion of enterprises and by monopolizing industrial development, which drove out small competitors and strengthened the big businesses (Shao 2004).

In contrast to the Yangtze River Delta, the Pearl River Delta (where Guangdong province is located) grew into a regional economy that preserved the development of small merchants and traders. It also had a lower degree of industrialization and commercialization. Although historical studies of Guangdong's political economy have remained scarce for this period, the existing literature suggests a lack of top-down mobilization based on a coalition of the local bureaucrats and large businesses such as one sees in Jiangsu. Quite to the contrary, Edward Rhoads finds that the same modernization reform launched by the late Qing government was short lived in Guangdong. Despite the establishment of the Commercial Bureau in Canton following the proposition of Zhang Zhidong to the central government, the bureau was not able to gain popularity, nor did it exercise effective coordinating authority among local businesses. Viewing the bureau as representing the government's interest, businesses instead preferred associations that represented their own interests such as guilds and *hui-kuan* (Rhoads 1974: 105).

The gentry group was less mobilized to align with the higher-level state agenda or direct development projects through formal state appointments. Instead, officials entrenched themselves in local settings and lived in their home villages, using connections and informal leadership to exercise "extra-bureaucratic" management in infrastructure and public management of temples, granaries, and schools (Rankin 1994: 5, 33; Faure 2007: 154–155). Merchants and businesses remained relatively separate from each other rather than colluding directly. In Canton, this separation was realized geographically by the domination of gentry in the eastern half of the city and the concentration of businesses on the western half. The suspicions of gentry toward businesses' fear of them added to the separation in self-consciousness (Rankin 1994: 101–102). In places outside Canton and closer to Hong Kong, such as Xin'an County, the predecessor of Bao'an County and later the city of Shenzhen, the economy remained predominantly rural with a focus on the fishing and salt industries. Both the gentry and businesses were widely dispersed, with the latter often having emigrated overseas. The presence of the state was limited to defense purposes due to China's foreign conflicts in the late Qing period and warfare in the early republican period (Shenzhen Gazetteer Committee 2011: 3; Southern Metropolis Daily 2007).

Existing historical studies provide few direct insights into the collusion of local bureaucrats with large businesses in the Yangtze River Delta and the relative separation of businesses and local governments in the Pearl River Delta. Yet what can be inferred from the available information is that the strength of the social norms and institutions that encouraged individuals to seek advancement in the bureaucratic hierarchy varied between the two regions. In Imperial China, bureaucrats were appointed based on the passing of different levels of the Imperial Civil Service Exam, which required sustained preparation in time and economic resources. Historically, Jiangsu had a strong culture and effective academic institutions for encouraging ambitious individuals and families to seek upward mobility by preparing and taking exams at various administrative levels, including *tongshi*, *xiangshi*, *huishi*, and *dianshi*. Embedded in such norms and institutions, Suzhou people were also far more successful than those in Guangdong or any other province in the nation in generating degree holders and high-level bureaucrats.

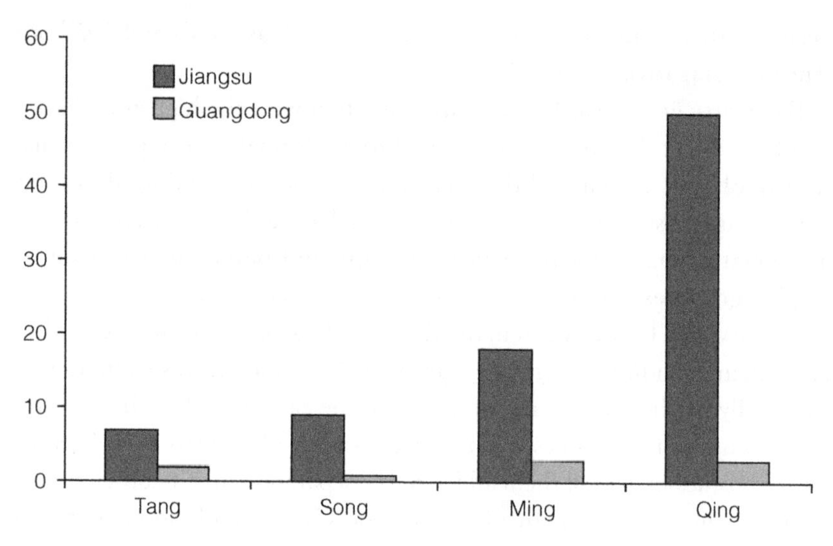

FIGURE 6.3. The number of *zhuangyuan* from Jiangsu and Guangdong in Imperial China.

SOURCE: Data from Hu et al. (2006).

Figure 6.3 compares the number of *zhuangyuan* (the highest ranks) in Jiangsu and Guangdong since the establishment of the civil exam system in the imperial China. Table 6.2 shows the number and the ranking of *jinshi* (degree holders who were eligible for state appointment) and *zhuangyuan* (the one who ranked first in the Palace Exam and gained a prestigious appointment by the emperor) in each of the major provinces. Compared across provinces, Jiangsu had the highest national ranking in the number of both *jinshi* and *zhuangyuan*, whereas Guangdong fell far behind. Viewed in a temporal perspective, the number of *zhuangyuan* in Jiangsu also increased chronologically, reaching an unprecedented height during the Qing Dynasty. The number of *zhuangyuan* from Suzhou during the Qing Dynasty accounted for 22.8 percent of China and 40.8 percent of Jiangsu, which was an achievement unmatched by any other locality (Li 1993: 2; Suzhou Gazetteer Committee 1995a: 4).

Wealthy business families in Jiangsu—especially in Suzhou—tended to invest economic resources in preparing for exams, gaining degrees, and seeking appointment within the state. This process often involved extensive tutoring and bribing of the gentry scholars (Blecher 2010: 3; Finnane 2004). On the other hand, after scholars climbed to a high position in the bureaucratic hierarchy by struggling through various levels of exams, the Confu-

TABLE 6.2.
Jinshi and *zhuangyuan* from major provinces in the Qing Dynasty.

	jinshi		*zhuangyuan*	
Provinces	Number	Rank	Number	Rank
Jiangsu	2,949	1	50	1
Zhejiang	2,808	2	20	2
Hebei	2,674	3	4	5
Shandong	2,270	4	6	4
Jiangxi	1,919	5	3	6
Henan	1,721	6	1	12
Shanxi	1,420	7	0	15
Fujian	1,371	8	3	6
Hubei	1,247	9	3	6
Anhui	1,119	10	12	3
Shaanxi	1,043	11	1	12
Guangdong	1,011	12	3	6
Sichuan	753	13	1	12
Hunan	714	14	2	10
Yunan	694	15	0	15
Guizhou	607	16	2	10

SOURCE: Based on data from Shen (1999) and Hu et al. (2006).

cian ideology of elitism and the maintenance of both an orderly hierarchy and their very own positions drove them to interact with the most well-educated, prominent business people. The ambition of achieving or helping with the large development project at the city or provincial level also rendered it necessary for the gentry to seek support from businesses both financially and through direct appointment (as in the case of the Bureau of Commerce). The gentry also sometimes invested in industries or established large businesses themselves. Over time, the connections between high-level bureaucrats and large businesses were cultivated and strengthened. The coalition was established to consolidate state governance and gain legitimacy from the state rather than to create independent local power (Bell 1999: 6).

Guangdong had weaker institutions and culture for preparing individuals to seek political positions and achieve upward mobility than in Jiangsu. Despite the relative development of Guangdong's academies and degree holders in Qing China when compared to other dynasties, such development was almost exclusively limited to the city of Guangzhou; even there, the gentry tradition remained relatively thin (Grimm 1977; Faure 2007: 32,

244). The story from Miles (2006: 1–2) in which the Guangdong literati were often mocked as lacking education and Guangdong being seen as a "peripheral outpost" in the 19th century suggested the region's status compared with Jiangsu. Even after Ruan Yuan, a native of the city of Yangzhou in Jiangsu, established the well-known Xuehaitang Academy in Guangzhou, the influence of the academy was restricted to urban Guangzhou and was ignored by elite lineages outside of Guangzhou. Therefore, the Pearl River Delta had remained divided between urban Guangzhou and the rest of the hinterland, with the literati having access to different cultural resources and thus developing distinct versions of their Cantonese elite identity (Miles 2006: 13, 202). For this reason, as shown in the national map in Chapter 5, Guangzhou falls into the intermediate category between Suzhou at one end and Foshan and Shenzhen at the other end.

The dispersed businesses showed no interest in politics and had "practically no access to the officials," preventing their interaction with the bureaucrats (Rhoads 1974: 102). The gentry scholars, on the other hand, lacked success in ascending to high-level positions, so they remained at the grassroots level, whereas the formal state officials at the higher level were often appointed from outside of the province; most of these were not popular among locals. Over time, the gentry developed strong interests to identify with the local benefits by directly engaging in small-scale local improvement initiatives—without the need to ally with large business groups or overtly purge the small businesses as Suzhou did. Rather than aligning with the upper-level administration in ambitious projects, the gentry actually sought to expand their local role at the expense of central government officials (Rhoads 1974: 113, 115). The preservation of small businesses and the development of localism among the gentry thus became important legacies in Guangdong during this period.

THE MAO ERA (1949–1978)

China under Mao established a Communist regime that was highly centralized both politically and economically. Politically, the Leninist party established the *nomenklatura* system (or the *bianzhi* system) for controlling the appointment and promotion of cadres at the provincial, prefectural, county, and city levels. Economically, the state nationalized almost all enterprises and relied on vertical central planning for the assignment of production targets and the allocation of resources. The center also periodically launched various ambitious campaigns based on mass mobilization for the achievement of rapid developmental goals. Although centralized as a whole, the Maoist system decentralized more political and economic power to localities compared with the Soviet Union. Rather than bypassing local governments and transmit plans directly to business units, the center left an amount of room for policy implementation by the localities (Oi 1999: 96).

After years of anti-Japanese war and the civil war in the 1920s and 1930s, Jiangsu—especially in Suzhou—grew to become the stellar example of a local communist state that relies on zealous mobilization from above. Bureaucrats ardently embraced Mao's signal at the center and even pushed beyond the planned targets in achieving developmental goals. Shortly after the economic recovery period, Suzhou started a thorough land reform in 1951 that confiscated 31 thousand *mu* (667 square meters) of land from landlords and rich peasants and distributed them to poor peasants. Suzhou also actively implemented the national Five-Year Plan (1953–1957) that prioritized the development of industries, and especially heavy industries, the proportion of which increased steadily. During this period, Suzhou cadres answered to the call of the center by launching a wave of socialist transformation of private enterprises under the "Leadership Team for Transforming Private Enterprises" established by the Suzhou Chinese Communist Party (CCP) committee. By the end of 1957, all but two private enterprises were transformed into public ownership, reducing their proportion of the city's industrial output from 80 percent to 0.02 percent (Suzhou Gazetteer Committee 1995b: 6-9). Although the textile industry remained the city's major industry, Suzhou started to have its own electronics industry by integrating 25 transformed enterprises into the first radio assembly firm.

The zenith of state-led rapid development came during the "Great Leap Forward" between 1958 and 1960. Although development targets set during this period were notoriously unrealistic, Jiangsu cadres stood at the forefront in demonstrating to the center their "political zeal" in exceeding the targets in the competition of overreporting production figures by local cadres. In agriculture, where producer cooperatives were integrated into large communes, a Jiangsu cadre reported to Vice Chairman Liu Shaoqi in September 1958 that one mu of land could produce 5,000 kilograms of rice. This led to Liu's suggestion to set an even higher target by plowing the soil deeper (Gao 2008: 85). In terms of industry, according to the memoir of Jiang Weiqing (2009), then the CCP secretary of Jiangsu, Jiangsu aimed to supersede the central government quota of producing 150,000 tons of steel by generating 180,000 to 200,000 tons. The Jiangsu government thus mobilized state bureaucrats in various agencies and administrative levels—a total of 7 million residents—for steelmaking. Eventually, Jiangsu was able to leap forward from a daily production of 900 tons of steel in early September 1958 to a daily production of 10,073 tons of steel by the end of that month. Jiangsu was celebrated by the *People's Daily* (1958) on National Day as one of the nine "ten-thousand-ton" provinces.

In the electronics industry, for example, Suzhou initiated a new wave of expanding production in electronic components. The city centralized the ownership of enterprises from the district level to the city level and combined and integrated existing collective enterprises into larger-scale state-owned enterprises that represented the "higher stage" of industrial development. More strikingly, after the disastrous Cultural Revolution ended in 1976, Suzhou officials launched a "New Leap Forward" in 1977 to make up the loss during the revolution.[4] The plan for the leap forward was that by 1980 Suzhou would be able to have an annual output of 1,000 integrated circuits, 150 computers, 200 microwave relay switches, 140,000 televisions, 100,000 telecommunication switches, and a total annual industrial output of 1 billion yuan. These goals proved to be highly unrealistic and were not accomplished. However, the way in which Suzhou officials pursued highly ambitious goals out of political zeal and strived to achieve them through rapid industrialization bears considerable similarity to Suzhou's contemporary upgrading initiatives (Suzhou Gazetteer Committee 1995c: 339–340).

Guangdong under Mao was again very different from its Yangtze River counterpart. Although bureaucrats and businesses were relatively independent from each other during the late Qing and early republican period, local cadres became increasingly embedded in society under the Guomingdang regime between 1927 and 1949. Due to Guomingdang's purge of the Communist Party, Communist cadres and guerrilla activities were operated behind enemy lines in a manner similar to secret societies. Over time, the guerrilla cadres were out of contact with northern Communists, and they nurtured dense ties between the cadres and residents through local concerns and local language. These ties gave rise to strong localism and practicalism (Chan 2003; Vogel 1969: 92). Even during the rule of the Nationalist government, Guangdong was seen as having semiautonomy and posed challenges to the central state over economic and tariff issues (Hill 2010). As such, the attempt of the CCP regime to realign the interests of the local Guangdong officials to the central state invariably encountered difficulties.

In response to the various movements and campaigns launched by the center, local bureaucrats in Guangdong displayed much less enthusiasm and much more practical adaptation of, and even resistance to, central policies compared with Jiangsu bureaucrats. For them, the priority was to protect local businesses and producers rather than showing their political "redness" through rapid development. As Vogel (1969) found in Guangzhou during the land reform, the cadres who had established previous ties with landlords found it "profoundly disturbing" to turn against landlords, who not only owned land but were simultaneously the bourgeoisie who contributed to commerce and industry in the cities. To prevent the interruption of economic activities, city cadres played a crucial role in protecting these bourgeois landlords from the purge of land reform by sheltering them as business people in the cities. During the socialist transformation of private enterprises, the government tried its best to protect small private businesses by providing them various loans and assistance, returning their state-controlled properties, and assuring them of gradual transitions without interruptions in production. The government also recruited a considerable number of merchants and industrialists as cadres to involve them in the planning and management of development (Vogel 1969: 102–103, 159–163).

Bureaucrats were thus clearly ignoring the directives from the central-south authorities in Wuhan, and the cadres who were sent down from the center to supervise work in the south (*nan xia gan bu*) were referred to by local cadres as "northerners" and "outsiders." In choosing between being criticized by the center for slow progress or protecting local businesses, most local cadres clearly prioritized the latter and were willing to adapt and water down central policies for local economic benefits and production. This tendency of reluctance and resistance to implement production-disturbing campaigns could be seen in cadres' response to almost every campaign that the center launched, including the campaign to wipe out hidden counterrevolutionaries in 1955, the campaign of socialist education in 1962, the four clean-ups in 1963, and the regulation of the private market in the 1960s. As Vogel observed, the cadres were affected by the increasing "privatism" and turned their energies to private lives; they were not enthused by the Communist utopian ideals. Most of these party and government cadres were Guangdong natives who did not have either the zeal or the access to high official positions (Vogel 1969: 297, 345 375).

Even when the radical Communist transformation culminated on the eve of the Great Leap Forward, power, funds, and personnel were decentralized in Guangdong, providing flexibility for the city government to create a local economic plan. In 1958, at the risk of being branded as rightists, the cadres expressed their caution through the *Southern Daily*, saying, "We must overcome the ill wind of empty talk and false reports" (Vogel 1969: 241). They were later criticized for dragging their feet and resisting orders from Beijing during the Great Leap Forward.

In the Cultural Revolution period, campaigns and class struggles in Guangzhou were extremely mild and the "small freedoms" (private plots, sideline production, and rural markets) were preserved and even encouraged through peasant remuneration (Vogel 1969: 302). In the 1970s, according to Chan, Madsen, and Unger's (2009: 248) study of the Chen Village, when peasants were disappointed with the performance of the collective sector, they channeled their energy into the private economy by growing vegetables in their private plots to mitigate the financial influence of the collective sector. This was long before the decollectivization movement took place in rural China.

The central government thus made repeated (albeit futile) attempts to stir up campaigns and contain growing tendencies of "bourgeois" selfishness and "conservative rightist" tendencies. The local cadres continued to make capitalist concessions by prioritizing economic production. In places less developed than Guangzhou, especially the Shenzhen/Bao'an area, cadres tended to join peasants to escape to Hong Kong for a better livelihood, despite the central government's severe punishment. The waves of escapees started in the 1950s and were heightened in 1957, 1962, 1972, and 1979, as campaigns to tightening control over small plots and markets intensified. Even in Xikeng Village, which was erected as the "flagship village" for anti-escape campaigns and socialist education, most of the population had fled by the early 1970s, including the local cadres (Chen 2010).

The Maoist era thus reinforced the regional tendencies of top-down and bottom-up capitalism that germinated during the late Qing and republican era. Jiangsu bureaucrats maintained their tradition of political zeal by promoting rapid, and often unrealistic, industrial transformation, and they encouraged the expansion of enterprise sizes. They also accumulated abundant experience with state-led industrialization during this period and established an initial industrial base for the post-Mao era. By 1978, Jiangsu had a gross industrial output of 33.77 billion yuan compared with

19.97 billion yuan in Guangdong. By contrast, Guangdong bureaucrats had built on their local practical concerns and were further embedded into the local economy by prioritizing the continuity of economic development. They sought to protect small producers and petty capitalists while showing little enthusiasm for the theme of "politics in command," even during the most politically zealous period in China. These historically developed state interests and policy preferences had profound influences on the post-Mao era.

THE POLITICAL AND ECONOMIC LOGIC OF PRODEVELOPMENT STATES IN POST-MAO CHINA (1979–1990)

Unlike the Maoist period, when state legitimacy was largely based on the Communist ideology that appealed to the interests of peasants and workers, the post-Mao Chinese regime explicitly centered its legitimacy on economic performance (Lee 1990: 412; Lieberthal 2004: 246; Zhao 2009). The Dengist reforms in 1979 placed the task of development as the central priority, replacing the Maoist emphasis on politics in command. Two sets of institutions introduced in the reform period—the cadre evaluation system and the fiscal contract system—have provided political and economic rationales for local bureaucrats to pursue rapid economic growth and industrialization.

First, the hierarchical cadre evaluation system—based on the *nomenklatura* system established during the Mao era—instilled strong political incentives for local bureaucrats to accomplish policy mandates and build political achievements through economic and industrial performances. Initiated in the mid-1980s by the Central Organizational Department, the system is a complex institution that uses a range of policy targets (typically 20 to 30) in various domains of economic and social development to evaluate the performance of the local cadres.[5] Each target has a numerical value and is assigned with different weight, so that cadres receive a score based on the accomplishment of these targets. The major evaluation processes consists of (a) the evaluation of the leading group cadres of a given administrative level by the upper administrative level government and (b) the evaluation of other cadres in various government agencies by the corresponding agencies in the upper-level government or by the leading group cadres of the same level, depending on whether the vertical or the horizontal authority is dominant (Huang 1996: 29-31; Lieberthal and Oksenberg 1988). This means, for example, that the party secretary and other leading officials in Suzhou City are evaluated by a group of leaders from the Jiangsu province, while a cadre in the Suzhou Bureau of Science and Technology is evaluated at different times by the Suzhou Provincial Department of Science and Technology or the leading cadres in Suzhou City. The results of the cadre evaluation are closely associated with each cadre's office tenure, remuneration, and prospects for promotion (Huang 1996; O'Brien and Li 1999; Li and Zhou 2005; Whiting 2001: 268; 2004). Even in provinces and prefecture cities where the formal procedure of evaluation has not been introduced, local officials perceive that political and administrative achievement constitutes the necessary condition for political promotion.[6]

Although the detailed policy targets used in the leading group evaluation vary across localities and over time, they all reflect the dominant policy concerns in that domain, whether the target is the index of public security in the domain of social progress or per capita area of green space in the domain of environmental protection (see Chapter 4). Among all the domains, however, targets in the domain of economic development—particularly GDP, gross industrial output, and fiscal revenue—are almost always ranked at the very top and are attached with the heaviest weight, especially for the evaluation of leading cadres below the provincial level (city, county, and township levels) (Liu and Tao 2007; Mei 2009; Whiting 2004; Jiangsu Government 2008.).[7] This is not to mention the evaluation criteria for government agencies that are directly associated with economic and industrial development. The institutional design generates competitive pressure among cadres who seek to advance their career by building up their political achievements, which propels them to promote the growth and development of local industrial enterprises.

Second, in addition to motivations to enhance political careers, the central–local fiscal arrangement has also provided strong economic incentives for local bureaucrats to support economic development. In the 1980s, the state changed the centralized fiscal system of the Mao era, known as "eating from one big pot," to a decentralized fiscal contracting system, known as "eating in separate kitchens." On the one hand, the decentralization of fiscal institutions granted localities the rights to economic surplus and residuals, allowing them to keep a negotiated amount of income to local coffers generated from the efforts of growth promotion. On the other hand, the arrangement also posed hard budget constraints on localities so that they had to rely on their own instead of on the central government bailouts for local expenses. Both aspects provided local governments with motivation to promote industrialization and economic growth so as to cultivate each locality's own sources of revenue.[8]

It is within such political and economic institutional contexts that local bureaucrats actively promoted growth and industrialization in post-Mao China and achieved a spectacular economic growth. In fact, a spate of literature has labeled the emergence of prodevelopment states in local China during the post-Mao era as forms of "developmental states," "local state corporatism," "entrepreneurial states," and "market preserving federalism" (Oi 1999; Blecher 1991; Blecher and Shue 1996; Duckett 1998; Montinola, Qian, and Weingast 1995). These studies argue that local governments have actively orchestrated local production, supervised and facilitated industrial performances, and lobbied resources for local enterprises from the upper levels of the government.

Most of the studies during this period, however, tended to have a narrow regional focus and neglected the heterogeneity of local development. In particular, southern Jiangsu (composed of Suzhou, Wuxi, and Changzhou) was the best example of successful state-led industrialization through the promotion of collectively owned township and village enterprises (TVEs). In a short amount of time, collective TVEs gained distinctive attention throughout the academic and policy areas and were viewed as the path of China's economic success (Oi 1999; Naughton 2007: 271; Qian and Stiglitz 1996; Rodrik 2007: 87). However, when more data became available, a growing number of studies started to question such findings, pointing out that in other regions of China, especially the Pearl River Delta and Southern Zhejiang, private enterprises started to take off at the same time, albeit often wearing a "collective hat" and registered under a township and village government (Unger and Chan 1999; Huang 2008; Tsai 2006.).[9]

These diverse findings are consistent with this chapter's argument. In the decade after the Dengist reform, places represented by southern Jiangsu achieved miraculous growth in their industrial development by building on the Maoist legacy. The legacy was not only economic, in the sense that the Mao-era bureaucrats passed on many collectively owned resources due to their zealous support of rural collectivization; the legacy was also political and bureaucratic, because the state continued to pursue a top-down planning pattern by changing the political or ideological target from the Mao era into the new goal of economic growth. The state acted as a large, multilayered, and vertically organized corporation in which each level of government was responsible for reaching targets assigned from the upper levels while allocating resources for production to the lower level. Publicly owned firms were ranked and provided credit and subsidies according to their adherence to the state plan (Oi 1999; Walder 1995). The establishment of private businesses and the competition with collective enterprises, however, were constrained and punished by the local cadres (Nie 2003; Sargeson and Zhang 1999). In contrast, in Guangdong and the Pearl River Delta, local bureaucrats continued to collude with and protect local businesses, which were often de facto small privately owned businesses but were registered under the collective umbrella due to the constraint on private ownership during the initial reform period.

In hindsight, it was understandable that the top-down mode of capitalism represented by Jiangsu received far more attention during this period because the region had been dramatically successful in its industrial growth. By 1988, a decade into the post-Mao era, Jiangsu overtook Shanghai and became the province with the largest industrial output in China, reaching 215.3 billion yuan, far ahead of the 131.9 billion yuan of Guangdong in the same year. By 1991, Suzhou achieved a total industrial output of 58.4 billion yuan, almost three times that of Shenzhen's 19.7 billion yuan (Suzhou Statistics Bureau 2012; Shenzhen Statistics Bureau 2012; Jiangsu Statistics Bureau 2011; Guangdong Statistics Bureau 2011).

The success of the local state-led development in China in the 1980s was similar to the experience in other East Asian developmental states (especially 1960s Taiwan). The state mobilized resources, orchestrated production, and strategically focused its limited resources on large enterprises at the upper stream of the production chain. These large enterprises drove the development of the local economy through their connections with midstream and downstream enterprises. For instance, in the initial stage of accumulating capital and technology for the electronics industry in the 1970s and 1980s, the state focused mostly on electronic enterprises that were SOEs owned by the Bureau of Electronics Industry or set up during the Mao-era "third front" initiative. The large collective firms and the smaller firms then became the manufacturers and subcontractors for these SOEs, which were situated in the mid- or lower stream.[10] Note, however, that the local government in China acquired loans, made market decisions, and guided the production mainly as the owner of the enterprises rather than as an investment seeker during the 1980s.[11]

If the emergence of a prodevelopment state based on the institutions of cadre evaluation and fiscal decentralization constitute the precondition for the rise of a state–business alliance, the ultimate formation and consolidation of the alliance rests on the emergence of an investment-seeking state in the 1990s. The success of most public enterprises (both state-owned and collectively owned) in the 1980s was dependent on the soft credit that the state provided. In the 1990s, however, the implementation of a tax sharing system squeezed the local share of budgetary revenue, and the reform of the banking system posed hard budget constraints on these publicly owned enterprises by reducing their access to soft credit. Many of these enterprises experienced losses and substantial debts and became economic burdens for local governments (Whiting 2001: 265–290). As these enterprises were reformed, privatized, or sold, local governments started to search for new ways to build political achievements and increase economic revenue (Tao and Yang 2008; Zhao 2009).

As domestic institutions evolved and as China integrated into the global production system in the 1990s, the local states actively sought external investments, especially foreign direct investment (FDI). The distinctive preferences of local bureaucrats that had been developing and formulating over the 20th century were thus projected onto their choice of global allies, further locking in the modes of regional capitalism in which localities were embedded. As has been elaborated in the previous chapters, although the top-down mode of development was much more successful in the period before China's opening to FDI, one saw a "reversal of fortune" in the globalized era (Acemoglu, Johnson, and Robinson 2001), when the bottom-up approach started to show much more potential for sustained development, innovation, and upgrading, especially since the 2000s.

CHAPTER 7

Making Economic Policies Work

In 1955, when "made in Japan" was still associated with cheap, low-quality products, a small Japanese company was struggling to develop an export market in the United States for its new transistor radios. A well-established U.S. company, the Bulova Corporation, placed a large order of 10,000 radios under the condition that the radios would be produced under the Bulova name. Although the order was worth ten times more than the total assets of the Japanese company, Akio Morita, the founder, decided to decline the lucrative offer and to focus on developing the competitiveness of their own brand's product on the international market, with support from Ministry of International Trade and Industry (MITI). The company later earned a worldwide reputation under the name of Sony.

The story would be very different within the current Chinese context. The Chinese bureaucrats might have stampeded to attract Bulova in the 1990s. Then, with the rising concern for local competitiveness and rapid changing of technology, officials would have responded by fighting to demonstrate that Bulova was still important and relevant and would have encouraged outsourcing production to local producers. Only few of those producers could have made the entire radio and perhaps had their own brand; instead, a majority of the domestic manufacturers would have produced doors, plugs, and shells for the radio. With this in mind, the path of Japan's industrial success may not be viable or even desirable for China.

The Chinese economy, in other words, has been integrated into the world economy substantially differently from the way Japan's had been in the 1950s and 1960s, despite the fact that both countries have been large exporters. In the 1980s, when Chinese local governments and firms were searching for their own ways of developing and building industries, the wave of FDI unleashed a new set of processes and dynamics. The direct involvement of foreign capital in the local economy called for new ways for the government to coordinate relations among businesses, and it has brought substantial changes to the Chinese local economy. At the same time, however, these changes reflected the deeply rooted patterns of local Chinese capitalism that were familiar to local bureaucrats and businesses.

This study precisely explores the way in which local Chinese bureaucrats, under the rules of fragmented competition and cadre evaluation and in pursuit of their political and economic interests, participated in the campaigns of FDI seeking and domestic upgrading in a globalized era. Bureaucrats who lived in a highly mobilized political environment often sought to strike alliances with large global firms that would benefit their political careers. This gave rise to a narrow developmental coalition that exacerbated inequality in local production and dampened the upgrading incentives of local producers. Bureaucrats who lived in a less vertically mobilized environment often individually brokered contracts with small foreign firms, which turned out to broaden the development coalition within the government while providing a more equal developmental space for local producers in the long run. Although these consequences were not necessarily intended by the initial state policies, they were shaped by the institutional context that local bureaucrats established during the process of realizing their own political and economic interests.

Although this book largely focuses on the era of the Hu Jintao and the Wen Jiabao regime, it has important implications for the current era under President Xi Jinping and Premier Li Keqiang. The project contributes to the understanding of the nature of capitalism in an authoritarian China, examining the prevalent role of the state in shaping local institutions and trajectories of development, even in sectors that are increasingly liberalized. Rather than assuming a benevolent or predatory role for the state, the study draws attention to the actual incentives of the bureaucrats and the local institutions that generate such incentives. The role of the state in directing the economy has been further strengthened in the Xi Jinping era. On the one hand, President Xi pushed for further enhancing the indigenous innovation capacity, and Premier Li Keqiang has been promoting "Made in China 2025."[1] On the other hand, to reduce the anxiety of foreign investors, Premier Li Keqiang has emphasized the continued attraction of FDI in free-trade zones and curbing administrative intervention in market activities.[2] Although most bureaucrats were less bold at expressing their views under the Xi-Li regime, most of them agreed that China has entered a tricky period in which the balance of interests among bureaucrats of different departments could be even more essential for China's performance in nurturing domestic competitiveness.[3]

State incentives are important, but state-led development operates in fundamentally different ways in an economy that is open to FDI compared to economies that are relevantly isolated from the penetration of foreign capital. On the one hand, the local state has the authority to determine the types of foreign firms that are allowed to enter a locality. On the other hand, foreign firms also alter the microfoundation of state policies by generating coalitional as well as structural influences in local policy making and implementation through the local bureaucracy. What has been observed in the Hu–Wen era still remains true in the Xi–Li era, although with new elements added to the economy.

The varieties of local capitalism approaches that have emerged from this study disaggregate the monolithic view among Western observers regarding either the rise or decline of the Chinese economy by investigating the heterogeneous patterns of local development and upgrading. Even with leadership reshuffling, certain elements of local capitalism are highly persistent. At the same time, even when the core elements are kept, there are also sources of institutional evolution and change in the current period and future.

China's Local State: Taking the Incentives of Local Bureaucrats Seriously in the New Era

This study is about the interaction of global capital and local states. The conclusion we eventually come to, however, is that even in a globalized era with rising capitalism the state continues to play a significant role. This is not merely because of the authoritarian nature of China's regime; it also stems from the decentralization of economic policy making and implementation. The ways that local government officials influence the economy and businesses have diverged across localities, depending on the perceptions and policy tools of the bureaucrats. With China's transition to a market economy and with the increasing percentage of private enterprises, the state's role went beyond public ownership by its making of direct instructions to enterprises on production plans, as seen in the initial reform period in some of the centrally monopolized sectors. However, even in manufacturing industries, local bureaucrats, as the agents of the central state, have continued to play important roles by responding to the signals of central policy paradigms, by advocating their own interests, and by forging alliances with business clients. At the most profound level, these bureaucrats shaped the emerging institutional context of the varieties of capitalism in which businesses operated.

Studies on local political economy, especially the role of local states in China, have employed various terms, including local state corporatism (Oi 1999), corporatism Chinese style (Unger and Chan 1995), entrepreneurial state (Duckett 1998), developmental state (Blecher and Shue 1996), local mafia state (Pei 2006), nomenclature capitalism (Saich 1992), bureaucratic capitalism, and capitalism with Chinese characteristics (Huang 2008).[4]

These studies captured the various roles that the Chinese state plays in governing the economy, but they also suggest that further work needs to be done to examine the incentives of local bureaucrats, especially regarding the variation of the incentives that many of the previous studies failed to capture. This aspect is especially important when bureaucrats are found to implement policies selectively (O'Brien and Li 1999). What determines the response of local bureaucrats to central policy signals? What enters into the calculation of local bureaucrats when implementing economic policies and allocating beneficial policies? What goals do local bureaucrats tend to prioritize?

This book suggests that the preferences of local bureaucrats and their perceived interests drove their choice of strategies both before and after the era of globalization and in the period of local upgrading. Yet, at the same time, the consequence that such strategies produce on the economy reinforces bureaucratic preferences, and has instilled a strong path dependence so that bureaucratic interests and behaviors have become embedded in the local forms of capitalism in the long term. When the central government decentralized FDI-approval authority, some local governments asked how to maximize their political achievement by prioritizing large multinationals, whereas, in other localities, they maximized local income and brought in smaller projects through flexible adaptation. On the central state's decision to shift attention to the promotion of domestic competitiveness, some local bureaucrats were immediately threatened and went out of their way to weaken the new policy, whereas others were able to minimize interdepartmental competition and directed their energy toward building resources for localities.

Therefore, despite the fact that bureaucrats across China are governed by the same set of institutions—the cadre evaluation systems, the fiscal-contracting system, and fragmented competition—there have still been different ways of prioritizing and maximizing political or economic interests, shaped by long-established patterns of development strategies. At the same time, the business allies that the state chose—foreign and domestic—have conditioned their future choices of business allies and their ways of adapting to central policy changes.

The emphasis on the importance of local states does not directly deny the role of business-level institutions and networks (Hamilton 2006; Kennedy 2005). Rather, it shows that, in an authoritarian country where businesses do not have a direct role in setting the agenda and implementing policies, the local bureaucrats, by pursuing their own political and economic interests, can influence the incentives, ambitions, and behaviors of local firms. In other words, whether a region has a vibrant business environment that facilitates learning and innovation should not be treated as an external factor in addition to causes studied herein. Rather, such an environment was endogenously determined by the dominant interests of local bureaucrats and the state–business relations arising from such interests.[5] This finding is in stark contrast to the studies of comparative capitalism in more advanced democratic countries, where the government's economic policy making is dependent on firm-level institutional advantages and may be punished by producer groups (Hall and Soskice 2001: 45–54). In an emerging, authoritarian economy, the state is not the rule follower but the rule shaper for the economic and industrial activities of domestic producers.

Going Forward: Local Capitalism, Leadership, and Possibilities of Institutional Change

One caveat is needed about this study. I am not arguing that cases studied in this book are the only patterns of local capitalism in China. There were the typical cases, but there were also cases that fell into the intermediate category with mixed elements of the two typical cases, as Chapter 4 and Chapter 5 suggest. In fact, a study has identified a total of 42 regional development models found in various studies of local political economy in China (Zhang 2001: 88–89). Unpacking the heterogeneous patterns of political economy and industrial upgrading in China helps us to go beyond the monolithic view of the country's economy.

Despite the vast regional heterogeneity, one should also avoid the pitfall of calling each region a distinct model without examining its influence and representativeness. The patterns of state capitalism studied in this book emerged from the two largest manufacturing bases in China, the Yangtze River Delta and the Pearl River Delta. Their upgrading strategies are influential and were implicitly and explicitly copied by other Chinese regions and localities, as governments in the rest of China sponsored various field trips to the two regions. As such, a focus on these two regions, which have similar levels of development but contrasting bureaucratic preferences and development outcomes, can help identify key dimensions for placing other localities in a comparative perspective.[6] Which regional model eventually emerges as the dominant pattern at the national level is crucial for understanding "the rise of China" from an internal perspective rather than an external perspective. Instead of focusing on measures such as total GDP, exports, and high-tech product output—as international observers often do regarding China—the local perspective advanced in this study directly tackles the rise of China in its bureaucratic incentives and the upgrading incentives of the domestic producers.

As has been shown, the regional patterns of state capitalism examined in this study are highly persistent, as the preferences of the bureaucrats, their business allies, and their policy tools mutually complement each other. Does this paint an overly deterministic and stagnant picture without taking into consideration the role of leadership? Research suggests that this is not necessarily the case. For example, interviews indicate that when party secretaries and especially mayors (as mayors often manage the economic and industrial affairs of the city) are technocrats, they tended to put more emphasis on (and also have more experience with) domestic technology upgrades. But such leadership, however, would find it equally difficult to make a difference if placed in a local environment inimical to the issue of domestic development.

As mentioned in Chapter 4, Wang Rong has been party secretary of Wuxi, Suzhou, and Shenzhen during the 2000s, yet the paths of industrial development in these cities differ. An official whom I interviewed in Shenzhen noted that, after Wang Rong and his secretary arrived in Shenzhen, they had a hard time getting used to the bottom-up, flexible work styles of the city, as they came from Suzhou City, where economic policies were always bureaucratic and top-down. In this case, leadership had to yield to the long-established local form of capitalism.[7]

Another possible source of change came from the iterative relations between central policy paradigms and local development outcomes. As Tsai (2006) and Heilmann (2011) found, institutional changes in China often follow a sequence in which formal national policies are adjusted according to the outcomes of regional policy experiments before new policies are issued. Over the past three decades, FDI attraction and indigenous innovation have been key economic policy paradigms that the central government has promoted. The Xi–Li government has certainly continued to push for industrial upgrading and innovation in their plan of "made in China 2025." At the same time, 11 free-trade zones have been set up across coastal and inland areas as experiments. In that regard, the current government has largely kept the previous development paradigms in place while using new labels. During this change, reforms have been certainly taking place (mostly under an initiative led by Premier Li Keqiang) to curb local government procedures and reduce bureaucratic departmental fights in economic affairs. Although this reform certainly reflected the central government's intention to address problems arising from the previous Hu–Wen period, it remains to be seen how many substantial changes the reform can bring to industrial transformation, given that most of the target bureaucratic procedures have been trivial and marginal to national economic development.

Making Economic Policies Work: Old and New Generations

The study of China's local patterns of capitalism not only facilitates the understanding of emerging capitalism in contemporary China but also carries important lessons in a cross-national context. It has almost become a cliché to argue that the more backward a country is economically, the stronger the institutional vehicles it needs to catch up. Following this logic about the gradation of backwardness among late developers, China would require even stronger state institutions than Russia to mobilize an industrial transformation (Gerschenkron 1962). After all, it was recently argued that China and other developers live in an era of "compressed" development, a stage in which the time span for development is even shorter than previous generations of late developers (Whittaker et al. 2010). Yet an examination of China's regional variation defies such an expectation. In localities where the local state was able to pick the winners in a top-down and coherent manner, bureaucrats also failed to mobilize the incentives of local businesses to engage in learning and innovation. The crux of the problem lies in the changing context for the implementation of economic policies and for state–business interactions.

In the preglobalized era before the 1990s, directly picking the winners in a top-down manner through a set of strictly selective state policies was often an effective way of allocating state support. This was the case with the state's support for *keiretsu* in Japan, *chaebols* in South Korea, and the large SOEs in Taiwan. These upper-stream large firms played important roles in driving up local capabilities and generating spillover effects through forward and backward linkages.[8] Although it eventually did not develop into a full-fledged East Asian model, the southern Jiangsu area in the 1980s (as shown in Chapter 4) started on a path of development that relied on the driving role of SOEs and large publicly owned enterprises, which was especially similar to the industrial strategies of Taiwan before the 1970s.

The East Asian developmental economies were certainly integrated into the world economy and combined the ISI strategy with an export-led strategy that limited imports and promoted exports. To promote the competitiveness of domestic enterprises in the world market, the state uses carrot-and-stick policies to discipline businesses and force them to compete internationally. Under such circumstances, a state is viewed as most likely to succeed in its industrial transformation when it has the autonomy and capacity to pick the industrial winners and enforce its decisions. The key has been to build development coalitions with businesses and to ally the interests of the states and businesses (Haggard 1990; Chibber 2003). It is also within such a context that discussions emerged about the advantages of an authoritarian state in "getting things done" and leading economic growth compared with multiclass democratic economies such as India (Onis 1991; Evans 1995; Kohli 2004). One should note that the integration of the world economy was mainly export driven rather than FDI driven. After entering the 1980s, FDI started to penetrate these countries, albeit still in a more restricted and selective manner. The key, however, is that there was a relatively stable period in the 1960s and 1970s when domestic businesses were the major participants of globalization through exports and were shielded from the systematic entrance of foreign firms.

Since the 1990s, however, the rise of global outsourcing and the influx of FDI into the current generation of developers has brought a new era of state–business relations. The surge of exports and FDI often took place at the same time, with the later playing an important role in the former. It is not fair to say that countries like China have not experienced a period of government-sponsored promotion of exports by domestic firms at all in the 1980s, but the period was relatively brief if it occurred at all (Zweig 2002). As the Suzhou case suggests, it was interrupted and washed away by the wave of global outsourcing. Among the top recipients of FDI, such as China, Brazil, India, and Southeast Asia, global firms have become important development partners of the government, especially in industries where the traditional industrial basis is weak. Under such circumstances, how states select business allies and construct developmental coalitions has become crucial for the survival and development of local producers. The Suzhou case suggests that, in the new globalized era, the top-down strategy adopted by previous successful developers may turn out to be counterproductive. The overlap of foreign firms and exporters and the existence of large firms have given rise to cohesive and strong vested interests. Additionally, at the same time, because large global lead firms are closely linked to their long-term global suppliers, attempts to support winners and leverage local linkages would increase the tendency for lead firms to co-outsource foreign suppliers to the same region. Rather than helping local producers to move up the value chain, such policies risk narrowing the developmental coalition, reinforcing the inequality between global firms and local producers and depriving the latter of supportive resources. In contrast, the bottom-up approach, although less prominent in the preglobalized era, provides a more suitable institutional environment for the state to mobilize the incentives for upgrading among domestic firms within the new context.

China is certainly not alone in striving to develop indigenous businesses within the context of an increasing penetration of global capital. A spate of work over the past decade has examined the opportunities and pitfalls for the current generation of developing countries to attract foreign investors (Lall 2000; Scott and Storper 2003; Jordaan 2011; Ivarsson and Alvstam 2005; Salim and Bloch 2009; Zhang 1999; Zhou and Tong 2003; Huchet 1997; Yeung, Liu, and Dicken 2006). Not only does research on other Chinese cities directly resonate with the findings of this study, but studies in Southeast Asia have also suggested the challenges of using MNCs to induce local development (Doner 2009; Ritchie 2005). In Vietnam, the launch of the *Doi Moi* reform and the inability to develop competitive state enterprises have given way to the rise of FDI and private firms, with domestic private firms directly participating in exports but striving to build their competitiveness (Beresford 2008; Anh, Duc, and Chieu 2014). In Singapore, it remains a big concern for the People's Action Party to build the indigenous capacity among the relatively weak local private firms, even though FDI had brought significant success in the earlier years of development (Prime 2012). In Thailand, the influx of FDI brought an export boom in the 1980s, but the incentives to improve competitiveness among domestic private firms remain weak at the same time that the state tried to fight with rent-seeking behavior between the government and businesses, as the government started to show tendencies of being captured by narrow vested interests after the liberalization reforms (Doner, Ritchie, and Slater 2005; Haggard 1998). In Malaysia, the fragmentation of the state and the relatively weak bargaining power of local officials similarly diverted the state's attention away from building a broader coalition of development, even when the state sought to press for offshore processing from FDI (Doner 1992; Haggard 1998).

These countries have certainly experienced diverse trajectories of development under globalization, and making generalizations across national contexts is difficult. One lesson that resonates with the current study, though, is that the emulation of a top-down approach embraced by the previous East Asian developmental states is neither feasible nor desirable. The presence of both domestic and foreign firms has complicated state–business relations. As Doner argues in his various works, building a broad developmental coalition is more helpful than merely emphasizing the strength of the state. Yet, by delving into China's local economies, this study points out that the challenge is not simply whether the state can get businesses on board for the coalition or how much bargaining power the state holds versus a foreign company. Rather, the state itself is often so fragmented that different parts of the state apparatus were competing to advance their interests in the process of implementing industrial and economic policies. If one agrees that a completely insulated and autonomous state almost does not exist in the 21st century (that is, certain degrees of fragmentation always exist) then positive studies on when such fragmented coalitions lead to more effective implementation of policies as opposed to others will go a long way toward understanding the political economy of development. A fragmented government can facilitate or impede the building of local competitiveness, and the crucial explanatory factor lies in how the bureaucrats' long-entrenched way of implementing development policies interacts with global production to produce distinctive forms of local capitalism.

The fast-changing global context influences whether a particular set of political institutions and state–business relations can provide advantages for domestic development. As manufacturing has started to relocate to other countries, and as China begins to make outward investments in Africa, Latin America, and other developing regions, China may be competing with the current generation of developers on other fronts. Nevertheless, the role of the local state remains highly important, as bureaucrats in China are intentionally harming or promoting the interests of domestic businesses. The development outcomes are both heavily influenced by state policies and remain largely out of the control of individual bureaucrats, who see themselves as pursuing their own political and economic interests.

Appendix

TABLE A.1.
List of interviews cited.

Code	Location	Year	Interviewees*
BJ002	Beijing	2008	Scholar, Peking University
BJ004	Beijing	2014	Official, Ministry of Science and Technology
BJ011	Beijing	2017	Official, Ministry of Science and Technology
GD003	Guangdong	2010	Official, Science and Technology Innovation Committee; former official, Economic and Information Committee
GD008	Guangdong	2011	Scholar, Guangdong Academy of Social Sciences
GD009	Guangdong	2010	Manager, optoelectronics company
GD010	Guangdong	2011	Founder, Taiwan electrical and electronics equipment company
GD022	Guangdong	2010	Official, Bureau of Commerce
GD025	Guangdong	2010	Director, computer and mobile phone manufacturer
GD028	Guangdong	2010	Manager, 3D electronics equipment company
GD029	Guangdong	2014	Official, Economic and Information Committee
GD033	Guangdong	2010	Manager, telecommunication equipment company
GD034	Guangdong	2010	Manager, home electronics company
GD044	Guangdong	2010	Vice Director, Bureau of Science and Technology
GD053	Guangdong	2009	Manager, electronics and electrical equipment company
JS003	Jiangsu (a)	2010	Director, Administrative Division, Economic and Technology Development Zone
JS013	Jiangsu (b)	2009	Director, Division of High Technology, Bureau of Science and Technology
JS023	Jiangsu (b)	2010	Official, Economic and Information Committee
JS029	Jiangsu (a)	2010	Director, Office of Policy Research, Economic and Technology Development Zone
JS034	Jiangsu (a)	2010	Official, Bureau of Science and Technology
JS036	Jiangsu (a)	2010	Manager, semiconductor equipment company
JS037	Jiangsu (b)	2008	Official, Economic and Information Committee
JS038	Jiangsu (b)	2010	Official, Bureau of Science and Technology
JS039	Jiangsu (a)	2010	Director, Administrative Division, High-Tech Development Zone
JS043	Jiangsu (b)	2008	Vice director, Division of Foreign Investment, Foreign Economic and Trade Bureau
JS044	Jiangsu (a)	2010	Manager, Taiwan LCD manufacturing firm

JS045	Jiangsu (a)	2010	Manager and chief representative, major electronic equipment and foreign invested company
JS046	Jiangsu (a)	2010	Official, Investment Promotion Bureau
JS056	Jiangsu (a)	2010	Official, Foreign Economic and Trade Bureau
JS057	Jiangsu (a)	2010	Group of officials and directors, Economic and Technology Development Zone
JS062	Jiangsu (a)	2010	Vice president, automobile electronics manufacturing company
JS064	Jiangsu (b)	2010	Manager, camera electronics company
JS066	Jiangsu (b)	2010	Official, Management Committee, High-tech Development Zone
JS067	Jiangsu (b)	2010	Director, Office of Policy Research, New District Zone
JS068	Jiangsu (b)	2010	Official, Office of Policy Research, New District Zone
JS069	Jiangsu (a)	2010	Manager, mobile phone equipment manufacturing company
JS085	Jiangsu (a)	2010	Manager, mobile phone equipment manufacturing company
JS089	Jiangsu (a)	2010	Director, Administration Office, High-tech Development Zone
JS090	Jiangsu (a)	2011	Director, R&D department, computer equipment manufacturing company
SD001	Shandong	2009	Official, Bureau of Science and Technology
SD011	Shandong	2009	Vice director, Bureau of Science and Technology
SD012	Shandong	2009	Secretary, Bureau of Science and Technology
SC002	Sichuan	2014	Official, Provincial Development and Reform Commission
SC004	Sichuan	2017	Official, Bureau of Commerce
SH001	Shanghai	2014	Former official, Development and Reform Commission
ZJ002	Zhejiang	2010	Official, Economic and Information Committee
ZJ012	Zhejiang	2010	Vice director, Bureau of Science and Technology
ZJ013	Zhejiang	2010	Official, Economic and Information Committee
ZJ024	Zhejiang	2010	Official, Industrial Development Division, High-Tech Development Zone
ZJ033	Zhejiang	2010	Group of officials, the Bureau of Science and Technology, Economic and Information Committee, the Bureau of Finance, the Foreign Economic and Trade Bureau
ZJ055	Zhejiang	2010	Vice director, Coordination Division, Economic and Information Committee

* Given that many of the interviews cited involve directors and vice directors, city names are not given to protect the anonymity of the interviewees. The listed interviews include only those cited in the book.

Notes

Chapter 1: Bureaucrats, Businesses, and Economic Policies in a Globalized China

1. For examples explaining challenges of industrial upgrading and transformation in other regions, please see Doner (2009); Cammett (2007); and Schneider (2013).

2. This observation is based on gross industrial values 1990 through 2008 provided by national statistical yearbooks in this period.

3. A business is identified as the client for a government agency if the agency's function mainly involves regulating the business and the business also relies on that agency for preferential policies.

4. The number of employees in the state is provided by the NBS (2011).

5. For state-monopolized industries, such as electric power, oil, telecommunication, and aviation, central state industrial policies have a more direct impact on enterprises.

6. See Evans (1995) and L. Chen (2008). This body of literature also stresses the role of business and industrial associations bridging state and business, but this problem is not the most crucial for the overall context of China, as associations such as those play a much less important role in implementation compared to local governments. Further, even in the context of East Asian developmental states, the role of associations is to help devise better-informed policies, rather than really dealing with the issue of implementation.

7. Another important element of the global supply chains is the labor standard associated with the production. See Berliner at al. (2015).

8. For "second image reversed" literature, see Gourevitch (1978); Rogowski (1989); and Hiscox (2002).

9. One of the exceptions can be found in Malesky, Gueorguiev, and Jensen (2014).

10. For an excellent example of how business attributes affect the formation of coalitions within authoritarian regimes, see Pepinsky (2009).

11. Please also see Rithmire (2014) for analysis of these works in a comparative context with China.

12. For discussion along the Leninist top-down mode of capitalism in China (regardless of whether in a positive or negative light), see White (1988); Yang (2004); Huang (2008); and Pei (2006). For studies on the bottom-up development pattern of capitalism, see Arrighi (2007); Tsai (2007); Hamilton (2006); and Nee and Opper (2012). For a dialectic relationship between the two, see Heilmann (2011) and McNally (2012).

13. For past works that examine the role of the local state in the Chinese economy, especially the relationships among legacies of economic structure, current institutions, and the incentives of local officials, see Oi (1999); Whiting (2001); and Blecher and Shue (1996).

14. Comparative institutional advantages refer to the type of advantages that institutions provide for firms to engage in specific types of activities. See Hall and Soskice (2001).

15. This survey was conducted in collaboration with the Chinese Academy of Social Sciences in 2011 across China's manufacturing cities.

Chapter 2: Chasing Foreign Capital

1. This took place when the president of the China Automotive Industry Corporation suggested to the central government that China would benefit from the transfer of foreign technology through the formation of joint ventures in exchange for the state's permission for foreign-brand cars to enter the domestic market. See Xia (2016).

2. The leaders group is led by Vice Premier Wan Li, and the MOE was led by Jiang Zemin (1983-1985) and Li Tieying (1985-1988); see Pecht (2007: 72).

3. "Yejingshi yu zhongguo yejing de fazhan," unpublished manuscript.

4. "Jishu luohou" 2011. This situation in flat screens started to change in 2009, when a domestic firm Jing Dongfang began to manufacture 8-inch flat screens.

5. Although foreign investors were concerned with profit rates, market shares, and production costs, Chinese managers were usually concerned with the scale of total production, the amount of exports, and employees' welfare (Pearson 1991: 182; Naughton 2007).

6. This is not to mention the fact that some of the JVs were disguised acquisitions, where the Chinese partner was diverted to other products and had nothing to do with the actual production (Huang 2008).

7. Similar situations occurred in other manufacturing industries as well; the automobile industry is a typical example (Lu 2006).

8. Interview SD012.

9. More detailed preferential policies will be given in Table 3.1 later in Chapter 3.

10. Please see Chapter 5 for further discussion of alternative explanations.

11. Interviews JS023.

12. The method was first publicly announced in 2008 but was very similar to the actual method informally used by the province over the past two decades. See Jiangsu Government (2008).

13. This formula was announced by Jiangsu Government in 2009 and acquired by the author through fieldwork in 2010. For full information of the Jiangsu cadre evaluation system, see the appendix to Chapter 4.

14. This was especially so when the one-level-down appointment system was implemented in 1984; see Lieberthal (2004) and Landry (2008).

15. Interview JS029.

16. Interview JS067.

17. For speeches of vice provincial governor and Suzhou CCP Secretary, see Xia and Xuan (2000: 439, 445); "Jiangsu sheng renmin zhengfu guanyu jiakuai kaifaqu jianshe ruogan wenti de tongzhi (The Decision of Jiangsu Government on Several Questions Regarding the Acceleration of Development Zone Building" (85); and "Kunshan shiwei, shi renmingzhengfu guanyu jiakuai jingji jishu kaifaqu jianshe de jueding (The Decision of Kunshan CCP Committee and Kunshan Government on Accelerating the Building of Economic and Technology Development Zone" (101).

18. Interview JS029.

19. Interview JS057.

20. Interviews JS057, JS043, and JS046.

21. Interview JS045.

22. Interview JS046.

23. Also see Kunshan Government (2008).

24. Even within Jiangsu province, the tendency can be illustrated by the fact that the rural areas, which had more practical concerns about attracting small FIEs in the early 1990s, had a 17.25 percent higher rate of disbursement than the average value of the province.

25. Interview GD044.

26. Interview GD053.
27. Interview GD044.
28. Interviews JS023 and JS043.
29. Such fuzzy boundaries existed more often between Hong Kong and mainland investors than between Taiwan and the mainland, as Taiwan's national government tended to have stricter control over outward FDI.

Chapter 3: From FDI Attraction to Domestic Competitiveness

1. See Yu and Zhang (2004).
2. Although many view the paradigm as beginning in 2006, I show here that this paradigm can actually be traced back to a much earlier period and that the year 2006 was when the paradigm reached its zenith.
3. The 863 Plan was largely targeted at supporting basic research in high-tech areas, rather than developing high-tech enterprises, whereas the Torch Plan was aimed at building high-tech industries and commercializing basic research.
4. State Science and Technology Commission, "1999–2000 kexue jishu fazhan shinian guihua he 'ba wu' jihua gangyao" (1999–2000 Ten-Year Plan of Science and Technology and the Eighth Five-Year Plan) 1991; SSTC and State Planning Commission (SPC) "Quanguo keji fazhan 'jiu wu' jihua he dao 2010 nian yuanjing mubiao gangyao" (The ninth five year plan of science and technology development and the long term plan till the year of 2010), 1994 (delayed in publication after a 1998 conference); see Li and Hu (2007).
5. Ibid.
6. There were debates among high-level elites regarding whether to frame national policies in terms of "open innovation" (rather than emphasizing the indigenous part) or "indigenous innovation." Eventually, indigenous innovation won out. Sometimes, the term *zizhu chuangxin* is translated as "independent innovation," but most translations view "indigenous innovation" as more appropriate. This book adopts the translation of "indigenous innovation."
7. Each locality has its own understanding and interpretation of the policy, which will be examined in Chapter 4. The current chapter focuses on how national-level agencies interpreted the speech and indigenous innovation, that is, the signals that were generated nationwide.
8. State Development and Planning Commission and MOST, "Shi wu keji fazhan guihua" (Tenth Five-Year Plan of Science and Technology Development), May 2001 (Li and Hu 2007: 112).
9. Although the State Council announced having cut the number of development zones to 1,568 by the end of 2006, many of them still existed in informal forms. See S. Li (2008).

10. Due to the lack of nationwide statistical data of development zones below the state level, it would be hard to estimate the overall number of zones that belong to each category. How the two forces play out in localities will be examined in Chapters 4 and 5.

Chapter 4: Local Policy Making, Globalized Coalitions, and Resource Allocations

1. Part of this chapter is reprinted from *World Development*, Ling Chen, "Grounded Globalization: Foreign Capital and Local Bureaucrats in China's Economic Transformation," (c) 2017, with permission from Elsevier.

2. The tax rate reflects the legislation known as the Income Taxes for Enterprises Act (2007) enacted by the National People's Congress.

3. Interview JS037.

4. Interview GD029. For other studies that have examined city level variation, see Thun (2006) and Rithmire (2015).

5. Note that the Foreign Economic and Trade Bureau was subsumed by the Bureau of Commerce in 2010 in Chinese localities; this study relies on research that largely covers pre-2010 data.

6. Officials believed that by arguing for their own department's interests, they also advanced their careers within the department. For a similar point, see Shirk (1993: 101).

7. These cities—Suzhou, Wuxi, Ningbo, and Shenzhen—began attracting FDI in 1985, 1981, 1980, and 1980, respectively.

8. For this reason, I did not include in case studies any inland cities in the middle western or western regions for the in-depth case study section; including them would have made it too difficult to control for economic conditions. However, these cities will be briefly discussed in a later section.

9. See Appendix 4.2 for an example. Shih, Adolph, and Liu (2012) found that factional ties, rather than cadre performance, are the main determinant of political promotion. However, their study uses the database of Central Committee members, which is at a much higher political level than this chapter; that is, for their object of study, the cadre evaluation system may not matter as much as it does at the local level. See Landry, Lu, and Duan (2015).

10. For instance, after the decline of township and village enterprises (TVE) in the mid- to late 1990s, the Bureau of TVE was quickly merged with the Bureau of Small and Medium Enterprises, a government agency that subsequently became a subdivision of the Economic and Information Commission (EIC).

11. Interviews BJ002, SD001, and ZJ012. See Appendix 4.2 at the end of this chapter for the list of interviews cited.

12. As far as the enterprises are concerned, a 1982 science and technology plan conceded that they should primarily introduce technology "from abroad"

and should move away from independent research. See State Planning Commission and State Science and Technology Commission 1982. This is in stark contrast to the direction taken by the Chinese government in the 2000s.

13. Interviews JS089, SD011, and ZJ005.

14. For a detailed account of state business relations and relationship building, see Lin (2017).

15. Although the rules allowing ministries to directly benefit from the earnings of enterprises were abolished during the 1990s, patron–client relations between government and businesses (especially with private and foreign firms) are still prevalent in an authoritarian state that lacks rule of law and property rights protection (Shirk 1993: 101–102).

16. Technically, there are two ways to examine the overlap of foreign firms and exporters. First, one can examine the proportion of foreign firms that are exporters as opposed to foreign firms that sell only in domestic markets. Second, one can examine the proportion of exporters that are foreign firms as opposed to domestic firms. The first method is not relevant to our theoretical concern, however. Whether an FIE exports or not, it will be considered international commerce because the investment stems from a foreign business. This method cannot tell us if clients for the international commerce department are foreign businesses only or also have domestic businesses. The second method, that is, to investigate the proportion of exporters that are foreign firms, determines if international commerce officials have only foreign firms as clients.

17. Interview JS043.

18. Interview JS029.

19. Interviews JS038 and JS039. See also the *People's Daily* (2006).

20. Interview JS003.

21. Interviews JS067 and JS068.

22. Interview ZJ002.

23. Interview GD003.

24. Interviews ZJ013 and ZJ024.

25. Author's participant observation, March 22 and March 26, 2010.

26. For more on large industrial firms as vested interests, though related to a different topic, see Lorentzen, Landry, and Yasuda (2014).

27. Interviews JS045, JS029, and ZJ002.

28. In other words, provincial-level bureaucracies—whether in international commerce or domestic technology—usually do not step in under such circumstances, as their relationship with city-level bureaucracies is a professional relationship rather than one of leadership.

29. Since the late 1990s, there have been back-and-forth reform efforts by the central state to strengthen the control of vertical lines or horizontal pieces.

30. Interviews JS038, GD044, and ZJ033.

31. Interviews JS056 and JS057.

32. Interviews JS045 and ZJ055.

33. Vice mayors were put in charge of a particular aspect of the city, such as international business and trade, science and technology, culture, environmental protection, and social organizations.

34. Interviews BJ004, SH001, JS013, and GD003.

35. Interviews JS023 and ZJ012.

36. Interview JS013.

37. Interview JS066.

38. Interview JS067.

39. Interviews ZJ013 and ZJ033.

40. Interview ZJ023.

41. Interviews ZJ023 and ZJ024.

42. Interview ZJ003, which was conducted with a group of officials at Ningbo Bureau of Science and Technology.

43. Wang (2014) would agree regarding the lack of direct political connections among FIEs.

44. Note that the cities of Beijing, Tianjin, and Shanghai are included in the data as single cities, due to lack of data, despite being municipalities.

45. The model ends in 2010 because after that year the state adjusted its standard for what counts as above-scale industrial firms. See Lardy (2014) for further detail. The estimation did not consider panel data for fixed effects across cities because the primary interest of this research is variation among cities. Furthermore, between 2007 and 2010, the independent variable and the dependent variables stayed relatively stable (in spite of their variation across cities), which makes it very hard to conduct panel data analysis.

46. The definition of large firms is based on that used by the National People's Congress (2003).

Chapter 5: The Microfoundation of State Intervention and Policy Effectiveness

1. Part of this chapter appears in Ling Chen, "Varieties of Global Capital and the Paradox of Local Upgrading in China," *Politics & Society* 42(2; 2014): 223–252. Copyright © 2014. Reprinted by permission of Sage Publications.

2. The full name of the industry, according to the China National Statistical Bureau, is telecommunication, IT (computers), and other electronics. It is similar to the information communication technology (ICT) industry. For the convenience of readers, it will be called the electronics industry in this book.

3. This is based on the microlevel data conducted in the economic census in 2008. The data were accessed in person through the Economic Census Center of the National Statistical Bureau of China in Beijing.

4. For the *sunan* model, please refer to Fei and Luo (1988); Whiting (2001); and Oi (1999).

5. Note that in 2012 Suzhou had changed to include six districts and four county-level cities.

6. Peacock was jointly run by the state and the collective, thus had mixed ownership.

7. Large-scale TVEs share many similarities with SOEs; see Huang (2003).

8. There are also triangle debt problems (largely related to SOEs) and subsequently the large nonperforming loans.

9. See Huang (2003: 216) for why the FIEs were most capable of doing so instead of other nonpublic firms. The fact that the Sunan area was dominated by public firms in the late 1980s and lacked large-scale private enterprises at that time also made it hard for nonpublic firms to buy off the large-scale public firms.

10. The case of Peacock was clearly a disguised acquisition, which was not just to exchange the market for technology but to solve the insolvency of the enterprise, whose assets were sold to Philips (Huang 2003: 214).

11. This phenomenon stemmed from the prevalent role of the government in various aspects of the investment process. Local officials not only controlled decisions on which companies were able to come in and the specific tax and finance arrangements but also went so far as to specify the exact proportion of the land to be invested and the pattern in which factories should be built.

12. Interviews JS003 and JS046.

13. Interviews JS044 and JS045.

14. Interview JS036.

15. Interview JS034.

16. Interviews JS062, JS064, and JS069.

17. See Zhang and Zhang (2007: 177).

18. Interviews JS062, JS064, and JS069.

19. This tendency at the higher management level to expand horizontally often created tension with the technicians in the R&D department, who favored moving up vertically. However, the former almost always won the debate, and the upgrading initiatives were largely quashed. Interviews JS085 and JS090.

20. Interviews JS036, JS089, and JS090.

21. Some of them are not shown in the figure due to space limitations.

22. Interviews GD033 and GD034.

23. As Barry Naughton points out, "Crucial in this process was the ability to link up with firms in Hong Kong and Taiwan and benefit from incoming investment from those sources." See Naughton (1997: 29).

24. Interview GD003. See Xu (2009).

25. Interviews GD08 and GD09.

26. Interview GD022.

27. Interviews GD033, GD034, and GD028.

28. Interviews GD044 and GD003.

29. Interview GD025.

30. For another example of taking advantage of domestic markets for upgrading, see Brandt and Thun (2010).

31. Interview GD010.

32. This means that the dataset excludes 59 cities that did not have electronics FIEs, as they were missing the main predictor that this chapter was interested in at the city level. The dataset also does not include three cities that each have one FIE in the electronics industry but do not have any domestic industries.

33. There is certainly much criticism of using patent applications as a measure of upgrading, such as the argument that patent subjects can be trivial and that they are often driven by policy targets. However, the decision to use this measure stems from the fact that it maintains a level of consistency with other literature on the subject, given the limited quantitative measures that one can possibly find for firm upgrading behaviors. Using patent applications also shows the level of effort that a firm is willing to put into upgrading and innovation, which is consistent with R&D expense.

34. Although what matters ultimately might be the outcomes of upgrading and innovation (which often lack reliable measures), at the stage where China is now, simply motivating firms to engage in these kinds of behaviors is difficult and therefore worthwhile to examine. In fact, firms that invest a high proportion of sales in R&D (such as Huawei in Shenzhen) are often observed to have success in upgrading.

35. This means that private firms have to rely on informal finance in most of the cases; see Tsai (2002).

36. Note that this does not imply that foreign firms directly cause the decline of the local developmental state or the decline of TVEs. It means, instead, that the context is so different that what worked with domestic businesses does not necessarily work with foreign firms. For studies on how global firms affect local industrial upgrading in Southeast Asia, see Doner (1992, 2009). For the influence of FDI on domestic politics, see Malesky (2008).

Chapter 6: Varieties of Local Capitalism in Historical Perspective

1. This understanding of bureaucratic interests does not necessarily involve a deeply constructivist approach, but it does entail a thicker understanding of "interests" along the lines of historical institutionalism and norm-based argument in policy implementation. For a good example of norm-based argument, see Herrera (2010).

2. For varieties of capitalism, see Hall and Soskice (2001). For historical institutionalist perspective, see Thelen and Steinmo (1992); Thelen (1999); Mahoney (2010); and Pierson (2004).

3. For the ranking of social classes in imperial China, see Lieberthal (2004: 7–17).

4. Please note that in terms of national background, this "New Leap Forward" is related to Hua Guofeng rather than Deng Xiaoping. Deng did not beat Hua until later.

5. For the cadre evaluation system, also see Chapter 4.

6. Interviews ZJ033 and SC004. Although it is an empirical question whether achievement has led to promotion, and studies have debated this issue, local officials seem to think so.

7. At the provincial level, there is still substantial debate around whether economic performance or other factors such as factional policies determine the promotion of bureaucrats. See Shih, Adolph, and Liu (2012) and Li and Zhou (2005).

8. Oi 1999; Wong 1992; and Qian and Weingast 1997. The introduction of tax-sharing system in 1994 has brought changes to state–business relations, as will be shown. But the decentralization of responsibility for local expenses has continued to push local governments to search for sources of revenue, among which local enterprises remained to be a key contributor.

9. Note that northern Zhejiang, where the city of Hangzhou is located, resembles Suzhou and the southern Jiangsu model and is quite different from Southern Zhejiang, where Wenzhou and Taizhou are located.

10. During the 1980s, they were often called jointly run (*lian ying*) enterprises between state-owned and collective enterprises. But the actual production that these collective firms engaged in was subcontracting.

11. Thus, to the extent that there was a state–business alliance, the relationship remains self-evident, as the state was not separate from the business in publicly run enterprises.

Chapter 7: Making Economic Policies Work

1. For more detailed information on "Made in China 2025," please visit the website of the People's Republic of China (2016).

2. For foreign firms' concerns about the "Made in China 2025" plan, see Hsu (2017) and Bradsher and Mozur (2017).

3. Interviews BJ011, SC002, and SC004.

4. For an earlier review on the study of the Chinese state, see Baum and Shevchenko (1999).

5. Although it is not the major focus of the study, I also found that in the Jiangsu region industrial organizations tended to be co-opted into the local government, whereas the chambers of commerce in Guangdong and southern Zhejiang regions tended to emerge spontaneously among businesses. This corresponds to the top-down and bottom-up natures of the local capitalism under study.

6. For another example of study that compares top-down and bottom-up patterns of developmental strategies across two regions in China (Yunan and Guizhou), see Donaldson (2011).

7. Interview GD022.

8. See Johnson (1982); Amsden (1989); Wade (1990); and Hobday (1995). After the 1970s, Taiwan's small and medium enterprises began to play the major role in high-tech industries. See Wu (2005).

Bibliography

Acemoglu, Daron, Simon Johnson, and James A. Robinson. 2001. "Reversal of Fortune: Geography and Institutions in the Making of the Modern World Income Distribution." *The Quarterly Journal of Economics* 117(4): 1231–1294.

Alt, James, and K. Alec Chrystal. 1983. *Political Economics*. Berkeley: University of California Press.

Amsden, Alice H. 1989. *Asia's Next Giant: South Korea and Late Industrialization*. New York: Oxford University Press.

Andrews, David M. 1994. "Capital Mobility and State Autonomy: Toward a Structural Theory of International Monetary Relations." *International Studies Quarterly* 38(2): 193–218.

Ang, Yuen Yuen. 2016. *How China Escaped the Poverty Trap*. Ithaca, NY: Cornell University Press.

Anh, Nguyen, Luu Duc, and Trinh Duc Chieu. 2014. "The Evolution of Vietnamese Industry." Brookings Institution "Learning to Compete" Working paper no. 19.

Arayama, Yuko, and Panos Mourdoukoutas. 1999. *China against Herself: Innovation or Imitation in Global Business?* Westport, CT: Quorum Books.

Arrighi, Giovanni. 2007. *Adam Smith in Beijing: Lineages of the Twenty-First Century*. New York: Verso.

Bao, Yonghui. 2006. "Zhengfu Zhaoshang zhi lei: yundongshi zhaoshao mang huai lingdao he ganbu" (The investment attraction of the government: campaign-style investment attraction kept leaders and cadres occupied). *Ban yuetan*, July 28.

Bauer, P. T. 1981. *Equality, the Third World and Economic Delusion*. Cambridge, MA: Harvard University Press.

Baum, Richard, and Alexei Shevchenko. 1999. "The 'State of the State.'" In *The Paradox of China's Post-Mao Reforms*, edited by Merle Goldman and Roderick MacFarquhar. Cambridge, MA: Harvard University Press, 1999.

Bell, Lynda. 1999. *One Industry, Two Chinas: Silk Filatures and Peasant-Family Production in Wuxi County, 1865–1937*. Stanford, CA: Stanford University Press.

Beresford, Melanie. 2008. "*Doi Moi* in Review: The Challenges of Building Market Socialism in Vietnam." *Journal of Contemporary Asia* 38(2): 221–243.

Berliner, Daniel, Anne Regan Greenleaf, Milli Lake, Margaret Levi, and Jennifer Noveck. 2015. *Labor Standards in International Supply Chains: Aligning Rights and Incentives*. Cheltenham, UK: Edward Elgar Publishing.

Bhagwati, Jagdish. 2004. *In Defense of Globalization*. New York: Oxford University Press.

Blecher, Marc. 1991. "Developmental State, Entrepreneurial State: The Political Economy of Socialist Reform in Xinji Municipality and Guanghan County." In *The Chinese State in the Era of Economic Reform*, edited by Gordon White, 265–289. London: Macmillan Press.

———. 2010. *China against the Tides: Restructuring through Revolution, Radicalism and Reform*, 3rd ed. New York: Continuum.

Blecher, Marc, and Vivienne Shue. 1996. *Tethered Deer: Government and Economy in a Chinese County*. Stanford, CA: Stanford University Press.

Bradsher, Keith. 2010. "Sitting out the China Trade Battles." *The New York Times*, December 24. Bradsher, Keith, and Paul Mozur. 2017. "China's Plan to Build Its Own High-Tech Industries Worries Western Businesses." *The New York Times*, March 7.

Brandt, Loren, and Eric Thun. 2010. "The Fight for the Middle: Upgrading, Competition, and Industrial Development in China." *World Development* 38(11): 1555–1574.

———. 2016. "Constructing a Ladder for Growth: Policy, Markets, and Industrial Upgrading in China." *World Development* 80: 78–95.

Branstetter, Lee, and Nicholas Lardy. 2006. "China's Embrace of Globalization." National Bureau of Economic Research (NBER) Working Paper 12373.

Breznitz, Dan, and Michael Murphree. 2011. *Run of the Red Queen: Government, Innovation, Globalization, and Economic Growth in China*. New Haven, CT: Yale University Press.

Cammett, Melani. 2007. *Globalization and Business Politics in Arab North Africa: A Comparative Perspective*. New York: Cambridge University Press.

Carroll, Peter J. 2006. *Between Heaven and Modernity: Reconstructing Suzhou, 1895–1937*. Stanford, CA: Stanford University Press.

The Central Committee of the CCP and the State Council of China. 1984. *Yanhai bufen chengshi zuotanhui jiyao* (The record of conferences on part of the coastal cities). Beijing.

———.1985. "Guanyu yanhai kaifang chengshi xingban jingji jishu kaifaqu de huibao tigang" (The synopsis on the establishment of ETDZs among coastal cities). Beijing.

Chan, Anita, Richard Madsen, and Jonathan Unger. 2009. *Chen Village: Revolution to Globalization*. Berkeley: University of California Press.

Chan, Anita, and Robert Ross. 2003. "Racing to the Bottom: International Trade without a Social Clause." *Third World Quarterly* 24(6): 1011–1028.

Chan, Gordon. 2003. "The Communists in Rural Guangdong, 1928–1936." *Journal of the Royal Asiatic Society* 13(1): 77–97.

Chen, Bingan. 2010. *Da tao gang* (The great escape). Guangzhou: Guangdong Renmin chubanshe.

Chen, Jianfen. 2008. "Suzhou: bei wudu de 'waizihua'" (Suzhou: Foreign investment misunderstood). *Zhongguo qiyejia* (China Entrepreneur) 16: 74–77.

Chen, Ling. 2008. "Preferences, Institutions and Politics: Re-interrogating the Theoretical Lessons of Developmental Economies." *New Political Economy* 13(1): 89–102.

———. 2014. "Varieties of Global Capital and the Paradox of Local Upgrading in China." *Politics & Society* 42(2): 223–252.

———. 2017. "Grounded Globalization: Foreign Capital and Local Bureaucrats in China's Economic Transformation." *World Development* 98: 381–399.

Chen, Rong. 2006. "Zhujiang Changjiang sanjiaozhou jingjiqu chanye jiqun bijiao yanjiu" (The comparison of industrial clusters in the Pearl River and the Yangtze River Delta). *Zhujiang jingji* 3: 64–69.

Chibber, Vivek. 2003. *Locked in Place: State Building and Late Industrialization in India* Princeton, NJ: Princeton University Press.

China Economic Census. 2008. Microlevel database accessed in Beijing at the Census Center of the National Bureau of Statistics on January 11, 2010.

Dean, Jason, Andrew Browne, and Shai Oster. 2010. "China's 'State Capitalism' Sparks a Global Backlash." *The Wall Street Journal*, November 16.

Donaldson, John A. 2011. *Small Works: Poverty and Economic Development in Southwestern China*. Ithaca, NY: Cornell University Press.

Doner, Richard. 1992. "Limits of State Strength: Toward an Institutionalist View of Economic Development." *World Politics* 44(3): 398–431. doi:10.2307/2010544.

———. 2009. *The Politics of Uneven Development: Thailand's Economic Growth in Comparative Perspective*. New York: Cambridge University Press.

Doner, Richard, Bryan Ritchie, and Dan Slater. 2005. "Systemic Vulnerability and the Origins of Developmental States: Northeast and Southeast Asia in Comparative Perspective." *International Organization* 59(2): 327–362.

Doner, Richard, and Ben Ross Schneider. 2016. "The Middle-Income Trap: More Politics Than Economics." *World Politics* 68(4): 608–644.

Duckett, Jane. 1998. *The Entrepreneurial State in China: Real Estate and Commerce Departments in Reform Era Tianjin*. New York: Routledge.

Evans, Peter. 1995. *Embedded Autonomy: States and Industrial Transformation*. Princeton, NJ: Princeton University Press.

Fan, Ning. 1996. "Waishang kaihao Suzhou xinqu" (Foreign investors held positive views about suzhou new district). *Huaren shikan* 2: 23.

Faure, David. 2007. *Emperor and Ancestor: State and Lineage in South China*. Stanford, CA: Stanford University Press.

Fei, Xiaotong, and Hanxian Luo. 1988. *The Comparison of Township and Village Economic Models*. Choingqing: Chongqing chubanshe.

Feigenbaum, Evan. 2003. *China's Techno-Warriors: National Security and Strategic Competition from the Nuclear to the Information Age*. Stanford, CA: Stanford University Press.

Feuerwerker, Albert. 1958. *China's Early Industrialization Sheng Hsuan-Huai (1844–1916) and Mandarin Enterprise*. Cambridge, MA: Harvard University Press.

Finnane, Antonia. 2004. *Speaking of Yangzhou: A Chinese City, 1550–1850*. Cambridge, MA: Harvard University Asia Center.

Frieden, Jeffry. 1991. "Invested Interests: The Politics of National Economic Policies in a World of Global Finance." *International Organization* 45(4): 425–451.

Fu, Jun. 2000. *Institutions and Investments: Foreign Direct Investment in China during an Era of Reforms*. Ann Arbor: University of Michigan Press.

Gallagher, Mary Elizabeth. 2005. *Contagious Capitalism: Globalization and the Politics of Labor in China*. Princeton, NJ: Princeton University Press.

Gao, Dezheng. 1993. "Kunshan kaifaqu xingban waishang duzi qiye bada zuoyong" (The eight functions for Kunshan ETDZ to establish wholly foreign owned enterprises). February 5. Unpublished manuscript.

Gao, Gaifang. 2003. "908 gongcheng zhong jie pian (The end of the 908 Project)," *21 shiji jingji baodao*, September 4.

Gao, Jie. 2015. "Pernicious Manipulation of Performance Measures in China's Cadre Evaluation System." *The China Quarterly* 223: 618–637.

Gao, Mobo. 2008. *The Battle for China's Past: Mao and the Cultural Revolution*. Ann Arbor: Pluto Press.

Gates, Hill. 1996. *China's Motor: A Thousand Years of Petty Capitalism*. Ithaca, NY: Cornell University Press.

Gereffi, Gary, John Humphrey, and Timothy Sturgeon. 2005. "The Governance of Global Value Chains." *Review of International Political Economy* 12(1): 78–104.

Gerschenkron, Alexander. 1962. *Economic Backwardness in Historical Perspective.* Cambridge, MA: Harvard University Press.

Gilboy, George J. 2004. "The Myth behind China's Miracle." *Foreign Affairs* 83(4): 33–48.

Gilboy, George, and Eric Heginbotham. 2004. "The Latin Americanization of China?" *Current History* 103(674): 256–261.

Gourevitch, Peter. 1978. "The Second Image Reversed: The International Sources of Domestic Politics." *International Organization* 32(4): 881–912.

Grimm, Tilemann. 1977. "Academies and Urban Systems in Kwangtung." In *The City in Late Imperial China*, edited by George Skinner, 475–498. Stanford, CA: Stanford University Press.

Guangdong Statistical Bureau. 1986. *Guangdong Statistical Yearbook 1985*. Beijing: China Statistics Press.

———. 2011. *Guangdong Statistical Yearbook 2010*. Beijing: China Statistics Press.

Guangming Daily. 2004. "Dui xin shiqi yi jishu huan shichng de sikao" (Reflection on the exchange market for technology policy in the new era). *Guangming Daily*, December 10.

Guangzhou Tianhe District Research Office of Party Committee. 2005. *Shequ xing gufen hezuo jingji fazhan xin silu: Guangzhou shi yangji cun de diaocha* (Stock sharing in communities and the new method of economic development: A study based on Yangji Village in Guangzhou).

Guo, Zhaocai. 2006. "Chang sanjiao zhaoshang xuan zi, kaishi xue tiaofei jianshou." *Xinhua meiri dianxun* (The Yangtze River Delta started to be selective in their investment attraction), November 1.

Haggard, Stephan. 1990. *Pathways from the Periphery: The Politics of Growth in the Newly Industrializing Countries*. Ithaca, NY: Cornell University Press.

Haggard, Stephen. 1998. "Business, Politics and Policy in East and Southeast Asia." In *Behind East Asian Growth: The Political and Social Foundations of Prosperity*, edited by Henry Rowen. London and New York: Routledge.

Hall, Peter A., and David W. Soskice. 2001. *Varieties of Capitalism: The Institutional Foundations of Comparative Advantage*. New York: Oxford University Press.

Hamilton, Gary. 2006. *Commerce and Capitalism in Chinese Societies*. New York: Routledge.

Harwit, Eric. 2007. "Building China's Telecommunications Network: Industrial Policy and the Role of Chinese State-Owned, Foreign and Private Domestic Enterprises." *The China Quarterly* 190: 311–332.

He, Weidong. 2002. "Suzhou: waizi 'tiantang' de mijue" (Suzhou: the secret of being the heaven for foreign investors). *Huadong jingji guanli* (East China Economic Management) 16(1): 17–18.

Heilmann, Sebastian. 2011. "Policy-Making through Experimentation: The Formation of a Distinctive Policy Process." In *Mao's Invisible Hand: The Political Foundations of Adaptive Governance in China*, edited by Sebastian Heilmann and Elizabeth Perry. Cambridge, MA: Harvard University Press.

Heilmann, Sebastian, and Elizabeth Perry, eds. 2011. *Mao's Invisible Hand: The Political Foundations of Adaptive Governance in China*. Cambridge, MA: Harvard University Press.

Herrera, Yoshiko M. 2010. *Mirrors of the Economy: National Accounts and International Norms in Russia and Beyond*. Ithaca, NY: Cornell University Press.

Herrigel, Gary. 1996. *Industrial Constructions: The Sources of German Industrial Power*. Cambridge, UK: Cambridge University Press.

Herrigel, Gary, Volker Wittke, and Ulrich Voskamp. 2013. "The Process of Chinese Manufacturing Upgrading: Transitioning from Unilateral to Recursive Mutual Learning Relations." *Global Strategy Journal* 3(1): 109–125.

Hill, Emily. 2010. *Smokeless Sugar: The Death of a Provincial Bureaucrat and the Construction of China's National Economy*. Vancouver, Canada: UBC Press.

Hiscox, Michael J. 2002. *International Trade and Political Conflict: Commerce, Coalitions, and Mobility*. Princeton, NJ: Princeton University Press.

Ho, Ping-ti. 1964. *The Ladder of Success in Imperial China: Aspects of Social Mobility, 1368–1911*. New York: Science Editions.

Hobday, M. 1995. *Innovation in East Asia: The Challenge to Japan*. Cheltenham, UK: Edward Elgar.

Hsing, You-tien. 1998. *Making Capitalism in China: The Taiwan Connection*. New York: Oxford University Press.

Hsu, Sara. 2017. "Foreign Firms Wary of 'Made in China 2025,' But It May Be China's Best Chance at Innovation." *Forbes*, March 10.

Hsueh, Roselyn. 2011. *China's Regulatory State: A New Strategy for Globalization*. Ithaca, NY: Cornell University Press.

Hu, Jintao. 2006. "Jianchi zou zhongguo tese zizhu chuangxin daolu, wei jianshe chuangxin xing guojia er nuli fendou" (Adhere to the road of indigenous innovation with Chinese characteristics and exert every effort to build an innovation oriented country). The speech on the National Convention of Science and Technology, Beijing, January 9.

Hu, Qili. 2006. *Xinlu licheng: 909 chaoda guimo jicheng dianlu gongcheng jishi* (The history of integrated circuits industry: the super large integrated circuits project report). Beijing: China Electronics Industry Press.

Hu, Zhaoliang, et al. 2006. *Zhongguo wenhua dili gaishu* (Overview of culture and geography in China). Beijing: Beijing University Press.

Huang, Shigen. 1993. "Xunhan huoli de shengzhang dian: Baoan xian nongcun gufen hezuo jingji de fazhan yu wanshan (Dynamic growth point: The development and practice of the rural joint-stock economy in Baoan County)." In *Zhongguo nongcun gufen hezuo jingji: lilun, shijian, zhengce* (The joint-stock economy in rural China: Theory, practice, and policies), edited by Hanjun et al. Beijing: Jingji guanli chubanshe.

Huang, Yasheng. 1996. *Inflation and Investment Controls in China: The Political Economy of Central–Local Relations during the Reform Era*. New York: Cambridge University Press.

———. 2003. *Selling China: Foreign Direct Investment during the Reform Era*. New York: Cambridge University Press.

———. 2008. *Capitalism with Chinese Characteristics: Entrepreneurship and the State*. New York: Cambridge University Press.

Huchet, Jean Francois. 1997. "The China Circle and Technological Development in the Chinese Electronics Industry." In *The China Circle: Economics and Electronics in the PRC, Taiwan, and Hong Kong*, edited by Barry Naughton. Washington, DC: Brookings Institution Press.

Hung, Ho-Fung. 2015. *The China Boom: Why China Will Not Rule the World*. New York: Columbia University Press.

Ivarsson, I., and C. G. Alvstam. 2005. "The Effect of Spatial Proximity on Technology Transfer from TNCs to Local Suppliers in Developing Countries: The Case of AB Volvo in Asia and Latin America." *Economic Geography* 81(1): 83–111.

Jiang, Weiqing. 2009. "Kuangre de da lian gangtie" (The zealous steel making). In *Qinli guoheguo 60 nian: lishi jincheng zhong de zhongda shijian yu juece* (Personal experience of PRC in 60 years: The important events and decisions in history), edited by Yiran Chen. Beijing: Renmin chubanshe.

Jiangsu Government, 2008. "Shengwei, sheng zhengfu guanyu jianli kexue fazhan pingjia kaohe tixi de yijian" (The suggestion from the Provincial CCP Committee and the Provincial Government on the establishment of a scientific evaluation system). July 21.

Jiangsu Statistical Bureau, 2008. *Jiangsu Statistical Yearbook 2007*. Beijing: China Statistics Press.

———. 2011. *Jiangsu Statistical Yearbook 2010*. Beijing: China Statistics Press.

Jin, Xinyi. 2005. "Suzhou dongguanhua de you lv" (Why Suzhou is becoming another Dongguan). *Zhongguo baodao zhoukan*, April 14.

———. 2010. *Shenzhen keji chanye shi* (The history of science and technology industries in Shenzhen]. Unpublished manuscript.

Jing, Yijia, Yangyang Cui, and Danyao Li. 2015. "The Politics of Performance Measurement in China." *Policy and Society* 34(1): 49–61.

"Jishu luohou zhiyue zhongguo jicheng dianlu ye guimo (The Backwardness of Technology Has Constrained China's Integrated Circuits Industry)." Retrieved on July 15, 2011, from http://cn.made-in-china.com/info/article-1343814.html.

Johnson, Chalmers A. 1982. *MITI and the Japanese Miracle: The Growth of Industrial Policy, 1925–1975*. Stanford, CA: Stanford University Press.

Jordaan, Jacob A. 2011. "FDI, Local Sourcing, and Supportive Linkages with Domestic Suppliers: The Case of Monterrey, Mexico." *World Development* 39(4): 620–632.

Keng, Shu. 2010. "Developing into a Developmental State: Explaining the Changing Government-Business Relationships behind the Kunshan Miracle." In *Dynamics of Local Governance in China during the Reform Era*, edited by Leng Tse-Kang Zhu Yunhan, 225–271. Lanham, MD: Lexington Books.

Kennedy, Scott. 2005. *The Business of Lobbying in China*. Cambridge, MA: Harvard University Press.

Kim, Linsu. 1997. *Imitation to Innovation: The Dynamics of Korea's Technological Learning*. Boston: Harvard Business School Press.

Kohli, Atul. 2004. *State-Directed Development: Political Power and Industrialization in the Global Periphery*. New York: Cambridge University Press.

———. 2009. "Nationalist versus Dependent Capitalist Development: Alternate Pathways of Asia and Latin America in a Globalized World." *Studies in Comparative International Development* 44(4): 386–410.

Krueger, Anne, et al. 1983. *Trade and Employment in Developing Countries*. Chicago: University of Chicago Press.

Kunshan ETDZ. 2009. "Kunshan kaifaqu jisuanji ye quan qiu zhizao jidi" (Kuanshan ETDZ has become the global manufacturing base for the computer industry). *China Electronics Daily*, October 20.

Kunshan Government. 2008. "Guanyu jinyibu gaohao dui waishang touzi qiye fuwu de yijian" (The Suggestion on Further Improving the Service for Foreign Invested Firms). Unpublished document.

Lall, Sanjaya. 2000. "The Technological Structure and Performance of Developing Country Manufactured Exports, 1985–98." *Oxford Development Studies* 28(3): 337–368.

Lampton, David. 2013. *Following the Leader: Ruling China, from Deng Xiaoping to Xi Jinping.* Berkeley and Los Angeles: University of California Press.

Landry, Pierre F. 2008. *Decentralized Authoritarianism in China: The Communist Party's Control of Local Elites in the Post-Mao Era.* New York: Cambridge University Press.

Landry, Pierre, Xiaobo Lu, and Haiyuan Duan. 2015. "Does Performance Matter? Evaluating Political Selection along the Chinese Administrative Ladder." Working paper.

Lardy, Nicholas. 2014. *Markets over Mao: The Rise of Private Business in China.* Washington, DC: Institute for International Economics.

Lee, Hong Yung. 1990. *From Revolutionary Cadres to Party Technocrats in Socialist China.* Berkeley: University of California Press.

Leng, Min. 2005. "Cong Taiwan weidianzi chanye de fazhan kan liyong waizi yu tigao zizhu chuangxin nengli de guanxi" (*The relationship between foreign investment and the promotion of indigenous innovation in Taiwan's microelectronics industry*). *Zhongguo keji luntan* (China science and technology forum) 3: 77–81.

Li, Baojin. 2008. "VIA shanzhan zhenying xunsu kuoda, ying lai tiaozhan Intel zuijia shijian" (The *shanzhan* producers for VIA have been rapidly growing; which brought the best time to challenge Intel). *Diyi caijing ribao* (China Business News), December 10.

Li, Haijiang and Juguan Zhao. 2006. "Establishing the Business Friendly Idea and Building a Service-Oriented Government," *Zhongguo Waizi* 10 (2006): 90–91.

Li, Hongbin, and Li-An Zhou. 2005. "Political Turnover and Economic Performance: The Incentive Role of Personnel Control in China." *Journal of Public Economics* 89(9–10): 1743–1762.

Li, Jiaqiu. 1993. *Suzhou Zhuangyuan.* Shanghai: Shanghai shehui kexueyuan chubanshe.

Li, Keqiang. 2015. "Avoid the Legitimization of Departmental Interests." Retrieved on April 15, 2015, from www.gov.cn/xinwen/2015-03/25/content_2838374.htm.

Li, Liang. 2004. "Zhongguo zhengtan chuxian Suzhou xianxiang: di jishi chengwei shengzhang yaolan" (The Suzhou phenomenon emerged in China's political arena: the prefecture city became the cradle for provincial governors). *Nanfang zhoumo* (Southern Weekly), November 18.Li, Sen. 2008. *Kunjing he chulu: zhuangxingqi zhongguo kaifaqu fazhan yanjiu* (Dilemma and solutions: The study of the development zones in transitional period China). Beijing: Zhongguo caizheng jingji chubanshe.

Li, Zhengfeng, and Yue Hu. 2007. *Jianshe chuangxinxing guojia: mianxiang weilai de zhongda jueze* (Building an innovative country: The important decision in the face of the future situation). Beijing: Renmin chubanshe.

Lieberthal, Kenneth. 2004. *Governing China: From Revolution to Reform*, 2nd ed. New York: W. W. Norton & Company.

Lieberthal, Kenneth, and Michel Oksenberg. 1988. *Policy Making in China: Leaders, Structures, and Processes*. Princeton, NJ: Princeton University Press.

Lin, Yi-min. 2017. *Dancing with the Devil: The Political Economy of Privatization in China*. New York: Oxford University Press.

Lipkin, Zwia. 2006. *Useless to the State: "Social Problems" and Social Engineering in Nationalist Nanjing, 1927–1937*. Cambridge, MA: Harvard University Asia Center.

Little, Ian. 1982. *Economic Development: Theory, Policy, and International Relations*. New York: Basic.

Liu, Feng-chao, Denis Fred Simon, Yu-tao Sun, and Cong Cao. 2011. "China's Innovation Policies: Evolution, Institutional Structure, and Trajectory." *Research Policy* 40(7): 917–931.

Liu, Mingxing, and Ran Tao. 2007. "Local Governance, Policy Mandates, and Fiscal Reform in China." In *Paying for Progress in China: Public Finance, Human Welfare, and Changing Patterns of Inequality*, edited by Vivienne Shue and Christine Wong, 166–198. New York: Routledge.

Liu, Shih-chi. 1984. "Some Reflections on Urbanization and the Historical Development of Market Towns in the Lower Yangtze Region, ca. 1500–1900." *The American Asian Review* 2(1): 1–27.

Liu, Yang. 2004. "Duoshao quanqiu 500 qiang zoujin chengshi qun" (How many global fortune 500 entered the urban communities). *Guoji jinrong bao* (International Finance News), September 13.

Locke, Richard. 1995. *Remaking the Italian Economy*. Ithaca, NY: Cornell University Press.

Long, Cheryl, Jin Yang, and Jing Zhang. 2015. "Institutional Impact of Foreign Direct Investment in China." *World Development* 66: 31–48.

Lorentzen, Peter, Pierre Landry, and John Yasuda. 2014. "Undermining Authoritarian Innovation: The Power of China's Industrial Giants." *The Journal of Politics* 76(1): 182–194.

Lu, Feng. 2006. *Zouxiang zizhu chuangxin: xunqiu zhongguo liliang de yuanquan* (Marching toward indigenous innovation: Seeking the sources of China's strength). Guilin, Guangxi: Guangxi Normal University Press

———. 2011. "Zhongguo bu de bu zuo chanye jiu zuo zheyang de chanye." Retrieved on June 1, 2011, from www.chinavalue.net/Article/Archive/2011/3/31/194720_2.html.

Lu, Feng, and Ling Mu, 2003. "Bentu chuangxin, nengli fazhan he jingzheng youshi" (Indigenous innovation, capacity development, and competitive advantage). *Guangli shijie* 12: 68–69.

Lu, Litao, and Yihan Xu, 2009. "Sanlai yibu qiye: cong heihu dao gongmin de shanbian" (Sanlai yibu enterprises: From black immigrants to formal citizens). *Dongguan shibao* (Dongguan Times), August 14.

Lu, Yang. 2003. "Shenshi Sunan" (Relection on the southern Jingsu region). *Shidai chao*, no. 8.

Luo, Huixiang. "Hezi de lu wei shenme yue zou yue zhai" (Why the path of joint ventures has become narrower). Unpublished manuscript.

Mahoney, James. 2000. "Path Dependence in Historical Sociology." *Theory and Society* 29: 507–548.

———. 2010. *Colonialism and Postcolonial Development Spanish America in Comparative Perspective*. New York: Cambridge University Press.

Malesky, Edmund. 2008. "Straight ahead on Red: How Foreign Direct Investment Empowers Subnational Leaders." *Journal of Politics* 70(1): 97–119.

Malesky, Edmund, D. D. Gueorguiev, and N. M. Jensen. 2014. "Monopoly Money: Foreign Investment and Bribery in Vietnam, a Survey Experiment." *American Journal of Political Science* 59(2): 419–439.

Manion, Melanie. 1985. "The Cadre Management System, Post-Mao: The Appointment, Promotion, Transfer and Removal of Party and State Leaders." *The China Quarterly* 102: 203–233.

McGregor, James. 2010. "China's Drive for 'Indigenous Innovation': A Web of Industrial Policies." Report by US Chamber of Commerce. Retrieved on January 26, 2012, from www.uschamber.com/reports/chinas-drive-indigenous-innovation-web-industrial-policies.

McNally, Christopher. 2012. "Sino-Capitalism: China's Reemergence and the International Political Economy." *World Politics* 64(4): 741–776.

Mei, Ciqi. 2009. *Bringing the Politics Back In: Political Incentives and Policy Distortion in China*. Doctoral dissertation, University of Maryland, College Park.

Mei, Yingdi. 2010. "The Notebook Computer Production in Kunshan Has Accounted for Half of the Global Volume." *Xinmin wanbao*, November 3.

Meri, Thomas. 2009. "China Passes the EU in High-Tech Exports." *European Commission Statistics in Focus* 25: 1–7.

Mertha, Andrew. 2006. "Policy Enforcement Markets: How Bureaucratic Redundancy Contributes to Effective Intellectual Property Implementation in China." *Comparative Politics* 38(3): 295–316.

———. 2009. "'Fragmented Authoritarianism 2.0': Political Pluralization in the Chinese Policy Process." *The China Quarterly* 200: 995–1012.

Miles, James. 2011. "China's Future: Rising Power, Anxious State." *The Economist*, June 23.

Miles, Steven B. 2006. *The Sea of Learning: Mobility and Identity in Nineteenth-Century Guangzhou*. Cambridge, MA: Harvard University Asia Center.

Ministry of Commerce. 2008. "Waishang touzi qiye jinchukou qingkuang." March 10. Retrieved on January 22, 2013, from www.fdi.gov.cn/pub/FDI/wzyj/yjbg/zgwstzbg/2007chinainvestmentreport/t20080312_90340.htm.

———. 2011. "The Mobile Phone Production of Shenzhen Has Accounted for a Quarter of the World Total Production." March 28.

Ministry of Science and Technology (MOST). 2001. "Guojia gaoxin jishu yanjiu fazhan guihua (863 jihua) guanli banfa (The national plan for high and new technology research and the measures for managing the 863 plan)." Beijing: MOST.

———. 2008. "2007 nian guojia gaoxin jishu chanye kaifaqu jingji fazhan qingkuang (The overview of the development of state HTDZs in 2007)." *Keji Tongji Baogao* (Science and Technology Statistical Report) 420, July. Retrieved on July 11, 2011, from www.most.gov.cn/kjtj/tjbg/200811/t20081104_64782.htm.

Montinola, Gabriella, Yingyi Qian, and Barry R. Weingast. 1995. "Federalism, Chinese Style: The Political Basis for Economic Success in China." *World Politics* 48(1): 50–81.

Myint, Hla. 1987. "The Neo-Classical Resurgence in Development Economics: Its Strengths and Limitations." In *Pioneers in Development*, edited by Gerald Meier, second series. New York: Oxford University Press.

———. 2002. *China Statistical Yearbook 2002*. Beijing: China Statistics Press.

———. 2007. *China Statistical Yearbook 2007*. Beijing: China Statistics Press.

National Bureau of Statistics (NBS). 2008. *China City Statistical Yearbook 2008*. Beijing: China Statistics Press.

———. 2009. *China City Statistical Yearbook 2009*. Beijing: China Statistics Press.

———. 2010. *China City Statistical Yearbook 2010*. Beijing: China Statistics Press.

———. 2010. *China Statistical Yearbook 2010*. Beijing: China Statistics Press.

———. 2011. *China City Statistical Yearbook 2011*. Beijing: China Statistics Press.

———. 2011. *China Statistical Yearbook 2011*. Beijing: China Statistics Press.

National People's Congress. 1979. *The Joint-Venture Law of People's Republic of China*. Beijing: National People's Congress.

———. 2003. *The Law for Facilitating Medium and Small Entperises*. Beijing: National People's Congress.

Naughton, Barry. 1995. *Growing out of Plan: Chinese Economic Reform, 1978–1933*. New York: Cambridge University Press.

———, ed. 1997. *The China Circle: Economics and Electronics in the PRC, Taiwan, and Hong Kong.* Washington, DC: Brookings Institution Press.

———. 2007. *The Chinese Economy: Transitions and Growth.* Cambridge, MA: MIT Press.

Naughton, Barry, and Kellee Tsai, eds. 2015. *State Capitalism, Institutional Adaptation and the Chinese Miracle.* New York: Cambridge University Press.

Nee, Victor, and Sonja Opper. 2012. *Capitalism from Below: Markets and Institutional Change in China.* Cambridge, MA: Harvard University Press.

Nie, Zhiqi. 2003. "Zhidu bianqian zhong de zhengfu xingwei fenxi: sunan moshi de qishi" (The analysis of government behavior under institutional change: Lessons from the sunan model). *Kaifang Shidai* (Open times) 2: 39–50.

Ningbo Government. 2008. *The Government Report Based on Interviewing and Surveying Enterprises in the Ningbo High-tech Zone.*

Nolan, Peter, and Xiaoqiang Wang. 1999. "Beyond Privatization: Industrial Innovation and Growth in China's Large SOEs." *World Development* 27(1): 169–200.

Nolan, Peter, and Jin Zhang. 2002. "The Challenge of Globalization for Large Chinese Firms." *World Development* 30(12): 2089–2107.

O'Brien, Kevin J., and Lianjiang Li. 1999. "Selective Policy Implementation in Rural China." *Comparative Politics* 31(2): 167–186.

Oi, Jean C. 1999. *Rural China Takes Off: Institutional Foundations of Economic Reform.* Berkeley: University of California Press.

Ong, Lynette. 2012. *Prosper or Perish: Credit and Fiscal Systems in Rural China.* Ithaca, NY: Cornell University Press.

Onis, Ziya. 1991. "The Logic of the Developmental State." *Comparative Politics* 24(1): 109–126.

Pan, Wei. 2003. *Nongmin yu shichang: zhongguo jiceng zhengquan yu xiangzhen qiye* (Peasants and the market: China's grassroots governments and township and village enterprises). Beijing: Shangwu yinshuguan.

Pearson, Margaret. 1991. *Joint Ventures in the People's Republic of China: The Control of Foreign Direct Investment under Socialism.* Princeton, NJ: Princeton University Press.

———. 2005. "The Business of Governing Business in China: Institutions and Norms of the Emerging Regulatory State." *World Politics* 57(2): 296–322.

Pecht, Michael. 2007. *China's Electronics Industry.* Norwich, NY: William Andrew Publishing.

Pei, Minxin. 2006. *China's Trapped Transition: The Limits of Developmental Autocracy.* Cambridge, MA: Harvard University Press.

People's Daily. 1958. "Guoqing xian li man di hong, gang tie sheng chan zheng chu chun" (The red gift everywhere for the National Day and the burgeoning of steel making). *People's Daily*, September 29.

———. 2006. "Quanguo keji dahui you yinglai yige kexue de chuitian" (The national science and technology convention has brought another spring of science). *People's Daily*, January 9.

———. 2011. "Cong tiepai daguo maixiang pinpai daguo" (From a country that makes products for other brands to a country that owns its own brands). *People's Daily*, March 30.

People's Republic of China. 2016. "Made in China 2025." Retrieved on December 7, 2017, from http://english.gov.cn/2016special/madeinchina2025/.

Pekinsky, Thomas. 2009. *Economic Crises and and the Breakdown of Authoritarian Regimes: Indonesia and Malaysia in Comparative Perspective*. New York: Cambridge University Press.

Pi, Qiansheng, and Wang Kai. 2004. *Zou chu gu dao: zhongguo jingji jishu kafaqu gailun* (Walking out of the lonely island: a general theory of China's Economic and Technology Development Zones). Beijing: Sanlian Shudian.

Pierson, Paul. 2004. *Politics in Time: History, Institutions, and Social Analysis*. Princeton, NJ: Princeton University Press.

Pinto, Pablo M. 2013. *Partisan Investment in the Global Economy: Why the Left Loves Foreign Direct Investment and FDI Loves the Left*. New York: Cambridge University Press.

Prime, Penelope. 2012. "Utilizing FDI to Stay Ahead: The Case of Singapore." *Studies in Comparative International Development* 47(2): 139–160.

Qian, Y., and B. R. Weingast. 1997. "Federalism as a Commitment to Preserving Market Incentives." *The Journal of Economic Perspectives* 11(4): 83–92.

Qian, Yingyi, and Joseph Stiglitz. 1996. "Institutional Innovations and the Role of Local Government in Transition Economies: The Case of Guangdong Province of China." In *Reforming Asian Socialism: The Growth of Market Institutions*, edited by John McMillan and Barry Naughton. Ann Arbor: University of Michigan Press.

Rankin, M. Backus. 1994. "Managed by the People: Officials, Gentry, and the Foshan Charitable Granary, 1795–1845." *Late Imperial China* 15(2): 1–52.

Rhoads, Edward, 1974. "Merchant Associations in Canton, 1895–1911." In *The Chinese City between Two Worlds*, edited by Mark Elvin and G. Skinner, 97–117. Stanford, CA: Stanford University Press.

Ritchie, Bryan. 2005. "Coalitional Politics, Economic Reform, and Technological Upgrading in Malaysia." *World Development* 33(5): 745–762.

Rithmire, Meg. 2014. "China's 'New Regionalism': Subnational Analysis in Chinese Political Economy." *World Politics* 66(1): 165–194.

———. 2015. *Land Bargains and Chinese Capitalism: The Politics of Property Rights under Reform*. New York: Cambridge University Press.

Rodrik, Dani. 2007. *One Economics, Many Recipes: Globalization, Institutions, and Economic Growth*. Princeton, NJ: Princeton University Press.

Rogers, Adam, Mac Margolis, Emma Daly, Anna Esaki-Smith, and Christopher Dickey. 2001. "A New Brand of Tech Cities." *Newsweek*, April 30.

Rogowski, Ronald. 1989. *Commerce and Coalitions: How Trade Affects Domestic Political Alignments*. Princeton, NJ: Princeton University Press.

Saich, Tony. 1992. "The Fourteenth Party Congress: A Programme for Authoritarian Rule." *China Quarterly* 132: 1136–1160.

Salim, Ruhul A. and Harry Bloch. 2009. "Does Foreign Direct Investment Lead to Productivity Spillovers? Firm Level Evidence from Indonesia." *World Development* 37(12): 1861–1876.

Sargeson, Sally, and Jian Zhang. 1999. "Reassessing the Role of the Local State: A Case Study of Local Government Interventions in Property Rights Reform in a Hangzhou District." *The China Journal* 42: 77–99.

Schneider, Ben Ross. 2013. *Hierarchical Capitalism in Latin America*. New York: Cambridge University Press.

Scott, A., and M. Storper. 2003. "Regions, Globalization, Development." *Regional Studies* 37(6–7): 579–593.

Segal, Adam. 2003. *Digital Dragon: High-Technology Enterprises in China*. Ithaca, NY: Cornell University Press.

Segal, Adam, and Eric Thun. 2001. "Thinking Globally, Acting Locally: Local Governments, Industrial Sectors, and Development in China." *Politics & Society* 29(4): 557–88.

Shao, Qin. 2004. *Culturing Modernity: The Nantong Model, 1890–1930*. Stanford, CA: Stanford University Press.

Shen, Dengmiao. 1999. "Mingqing quanguo jinshi yu rencai de shikong fenbu jiqi xianghu guanxi" (The temporal and spatial distribution of *jinshi* and *rencai* in the Ming and Qing Dynasty). *Zhongguo wenhua yanjiu* 26(4): 59–66.

Shen, Xiaoxiao, and Kellee Tsai. 2016. "Institutional Adaptability in China: Local Developmental Models under Changing Economic Conditions." *World Development* 87: 107–127.

Shen, Yunfu. 2009. *Yijun xianfeng: zhongguo xiangzhen qiye fayuan di guanlan ji* (The vanguard: A study of the birthplace for China's township and village enterprises). Beijing: Huaxia chubanshe.

Sheng, Yumin. 2010. *Economic Openness and Territorial Politics in China*. New York: Cambridge University Press.

Shenzhen Gazetteer Committee. 2011. *Shenzhen Gazetteer*. Beijing: Fangzhi chubanshe.

Shenzhen Statistics Bureau. 1993. *Shenzhen Statistical Yearbook 1992*. Beijing: China Statistics Press.

———. 2012. *Shenzhen Statistical Yearbook 2011*. Beijing: China Statistics Press.

Shih, Victor, Christopher Adolph, and Mingxing Liu. 2012. "Getting Ahead in the Communist Party: Explaining the Advancement of Central Committee Members in China." *American Political Science Review* 106(1): 166–187.

Shirk, Susan. 1993. *The Political Logic of Economic Reform in China*. Berkeley: University of California Press.

Skinner, George William. 1977. *The City in Late Imperial China*. Stanford, CA: Stanford University Press.

Southern Metropolis Daily, ed. 2007. *Shen-gang guanxi sibai nian* (The four hundred years of history of Shenzhen-Hong Kong relations). Shenzhen: Haitian chubanshe.

State Council. 1986. *The Implementation Codes of the Joint-Venture Law of People's Republic of China*. Beijing: State Council of China.

———. 2006. "The National Medium to Long Term Plan of Science and Technology Development." Retrieved on April 20, 2008, from www.gov.cn/jrzg/2006-02/09/content_183787.htm.

State Planning Commission and State Science and Technology Commission. 1982. "1986–2000 kexue jishu fazhan guihua gangyao" (1986–2000 Science and Technology Development Plan). December 10.

The Statistics Department of the Center for Torch Plan. 2007. "Guojia gaoxin qu dui defang jingji gongxian zhuangkuang" (The contribution of national HTDZs to the local economy). September 19. Available at www.chinatorch.gov.cn/yjbg/yjbg/200709/5356.html.

Steinfeld, Edward. 2004. "China's Shallow Integration: Networked Production and the New Challenges for Late Industrialization." *World Development* 32(11): 1971–1987.

———. 2010. *Playing Our Game: Why China's Economic Rise Doesn't Threaten the West*. New York: Oxford University Press.

Sun, Jinping. 2007. "Exing jingzheng de dixian zai nali" (Where is the bottom line for ruinous competition?). *Zhongguo shehui daokan* (China Society Periodical): 40–42.

Suzhou Bureau of Science and Technology, 2010. "Guanyu gongbu 2009 Suzhou shi gaoxin jishu chanye zhuyao tongji shuju de tongzhi" (The announcement of the major data on Suzhou's high-technology industries in 2009). April 1.

Suzhou Foreign Trade and Economic Relations Commission. 1991. *Suzhou duiwai jingji zhi* (Suzhou Gazetteer of Foreign Economic Relations). Nanjing: Nanjing University Press.

Suzhou Gazetteer Committee. 1995a. *Suzhou Gazetteer*, volume 1. Nanjing, Jiangsu: Jiangsu renmin chubanshe.

———. 1995b. *Suzhou Gazetteer*, volume 14. Nanjing, Jiangsu: Jiangsu renmin chubanshe.

———. 1995c. *Suzhou Gazetteer*, volume 19. Nanjing, Jiangsu: Jiangsu renmin chubanshe.

Suzhou HTDZ Management Committee, 2011. "Zhuanxing shengji pujiu kuayue zhi lu" (Transformation and upgrading laid the path for leaping forward). August 24.

Suzhou Industrial Park, "Suzhou Industrial Park Guidebook for Manufacturing Industries," Retrieved on October 1, 2011, from www.sipac.gov.cn/tzzn/zzy/201107/t20110710_103911.htm.

Suzhou Statistics Bureau. 1993. *Suzhou Statistical Yearbook 1992*. Beijing: China Statistics Press.

———. 2012. *Suzhou Statistical Yearbook 2011*. Beijing: China Statistics Press.

Tao, Ran, and Dali Yang. 2008. "The Revenue Imperative and the Role of Local Government in China's Transition and Growth." Paper presented at the Coase Chicago Conference on China's Reform Transformation, University of Chicago, July 2008.

Tao, Yi-Feng. 2006. "A Catch-up Strategy? China's Policy towards Foreign Investment." In *Japan and China in the World Political Economy*, edited by Saadia Pekkanen and Kellee Tsai. New York: Routledge.

Thelen, Kathleen. 1999. "Historical Institutionalism in Comparative Politics." *Annual Review of Political Science* 2: 369–404.

Thelen, Kathleen, and Sven Steinmo. 1992. "Historical Institutionalism in Comparative Perspective." In *Structuring Politics: Historical Institutionalism in Comparative Analsysis*, edited by Sven Steinmo, Kathleen Thelen, and Frank Longstreth, 1–32. New York: Cambridge University Press.

Thun, Eric. 2006. *Changing Lanes in China Foreign Direct Investment, Local Government, and Auto Sector Development*. New York: Cambridge University Press.

Tong, Sarah Y., and Yi Zheng. 2008. "China's Trade Acceleration and the Deepening of an East Asian Regional Production Network." *China & World Economy* 16(1): 66–81.

Tsai, Kellee. 2002. *Back-Alley Banking: Private Entrepreneurs in China*. Ithaca, NY: Cornell University Press.

———. 2006. "Adaptive Informal Institutions and Endogenous Institutional Change in China." *World Politics* 59(1): 116–141.

———. 2007. *Capitalism without Democracy: The Private Sector in Contemporary China*. Ithaca, NY: Cornell University Press.

Tsai, Kellee, and Saadia Pekkanen. 2006. "Introduction: Late Liberalizers: Comparative Perspectives on Japan and China." In *Japan and China in the World Political Economy*, edited by Saadia Pekkanen and Kellee Tsai, 11–28. London and New York: Routledge.

Unger, Jonathan, and Anita Chan, 1995. "China, Corporatism, and the East Asian Model." *Australia Journal of Chinese Affairs* 33(January): 29–53.

———. 1999. "Inheritors of the Boom: Private Enterprise and the Role of Local Government in a Rural South China Township." *The China Journal* 42(July 1): 45–74.

Vogel, Ezra. 1969. *Canton under Communism: Programs and Politics in a Provincial Capital, 1949–1968.*Cambridge, MA: Harvard University Press.

———. 1989. *One Step ahead in China: Guangdong under Reform*. Cambridge, MA: Harvard University Press.

Vogel, Steven. 2006. *Japan Remodeled: How Government and Industry are Reforming Japanese Capitalism*. Ithaca, NY: Cornell University Press.

Wade, Robert. 1990. *Governing the Market: Economic Theory and the Role of Government in East Asian Industrialization*. Princeton, NJ: Princeton University Press.

Walder, Andrew. 1995. "Local Governments as Industrial Firms: An Organizational Analysis of China's Transitional Economy." *American Journal of Sociology* 101(2): 263–301.

Wang, Congfei, and Xianbiao Chen, 2000. "Guangdong 'san lai yi bu' hai neng zou duo yuan" (How far can *san lai yi bu* Enterprises Go in Guangdong?). *People's Daily*, October 9.

Wang, Huiliang. 2009. "Zhengfu qingshi tuijin, Kunshan zhuda chuangxin pai" (With the strong push from the government, Kunshan is playing the major card on innovation). *Keji ribao*, November 19.

Wang, Weijian. 2006. "Yi wei jiceng zhaoshang ganbu de kunhuo" (A dilemma faced by a grass-root investment-attraction cadre). *China Daily*, May 26.

Wang, Yuhua. 2014. *Tying the Autocrat's Hands: The Rise of The Rule of Law in China*. New York: Cambridge University Press.

Wei, Dazhi, Xianwei Zhang, and Qihua Guo. 2010. *Zhidu bianqian zhong de jiegou yu chuangxin: Shenzhen dianzi xinxi chanye jueqi lujing de dangdai kaocha* (Innovation during institutional change: A contemporary investigation of the rise of electronics and information technology industry in Shenzhen). Beijing: Renmin chubanshe.

Wells, Louis. 1983. *Third World Multinationals: The Rise of Foreign Investment from Developing Countries*. Cambridge, MA: MIT Press.

Wen, Jiabao. 2006. "Renzhen shishi keji fazhan guihua gangyao, kaichuang woguokeji fazhan de xin jumian" (Earnestly implementing the plan for science and technology development, breaking a new situation in the science and technology development of our country). Speech at the National Convention of Science and Technology. Beijing, January 9, 2006.

Wen, Xin, and Xuan Hua. 2006. "Yinjin luohou zai yinjin: hushi chuangxin de houguo zhengzai xianxian" (Import—lag—import again: The consequences of ignoring innovation are emerging). *Dangjian wenhui yuekan* 1: 24–24.

White, Gordon. 1988. "State and Market in China's Socialist Industrialization." In *Developmental States in East Asia*, edited by Gordon White. Houndmills, Basingstoke, Hampshire, UK: Macmillan.

Whiting, Susan. 2001. *Power and Wealth in Rural China: The Political Economy of Institutional Change*. Cambridge Modern China Series. New York: Cambridge University Press.

———. 2004. "The Cadre Evaluation System at the Grass Roots: The Paradox of Party Rule." In *Holding China Together: Diversity and National Integration in the Post-Deng Era*, edited by Barry J. Naughton and Dali L. Yang, 101–119. New York: Cambridge University Press.

Whittaker, D. Hugh, Tianbiao Zhu, Timothy Sturgeon, Mon Han Tsai, and Toshie Okita. 2010. "Compressed Development." *Studies in Comparative International Development* 45(4): 439–467.

Williamson, John. 1989. "What Washington Means by Policy Reform." In *Latin American Readjustment: How Much Has Happened*, edited by John Williamson. Washington, DC: Institute for International Economics.

Wong, Christine. 1992. "Fiscal Reform and Local Industrialization: The Problematic Sequencing of Reform in Post-Mao China." *Modern China* 18(2): 197–227.

Wu, Jianguo, and Yongqing Ji, 2006. *Huawei de shijie* (The world of Huawei). Beijing: China CITIC Press.

Wu, Yongping. 2005. *A Political Explanation of Economic Growth: State Survival, Bureaucratic Politics, and Private Enterprises in the Making of Taiwan's Economy, 1950–1985*. Cambridge, MA: Harvard University Press.

Wuxi Government. 2009. "Zengqiang wuxi zhizaoye jingzhengli" (Enhancing the competitiveness of Wuxi's manufacturing industries). Government document, October 28.

Xia, Liang. 2016. "Yi shichang huan jishu fangzhen de youlai" (The origins of the "exchanging market for technology" policy). *Jingjixue jia chazuo* 2: 132–136.

Xia, Liangxin, and Binglong Xuan, eds. 2000. *Kunshan kaifaqu shiwu nian* (The Fifteen Years of Kunshan Economic and Technology Development Zone). Kunshan: Kuanshan ETDZ.

Xia, Tian 2012. "Ningbo's Patent Applications and Authorized Patents Both Topped the Province." Retrieved in July 2016 from www.cnipr.com/news/gndt/201204/t20120410_142841.html.

Xiao, Jingdong. 2004. "Chang sanjiao chanye shengji bianqian" (Industrial upgrading and transformation in the Yangtze River Delta). *Mei ri jingji xinwen*, December 21.

Xin, Wang. 2005. *Sunan moshi de zhongjie* (The end of the Sunan model). Beijing: Sannian shudian.

Xu, Mingtian, 2008. *Chuntian de gushi: Shenzhen chuangye shi* (The story of spring: The history of starting industries in Shenzhen), vol.1. Beijing: China CITIC Press.

———. 2009. *Chuntian de gushi: Shenzhen chuangye shi* (The story of spring: The history of starting industries in Shenzhen), vol. 2. Beijing: China CITIC Press.

Xu, Zhiqiang. 2007. "SEG-Hitachi tingchan zhi hou." *21 shiji jingji baodao*, August 2.

Xue, Yong. 2006. *Zhongguo buneng yongyuan wei shijie dagong* (China cannot be the permanent workshop for the world). Kunming: Yunan remin chubanshe.

Yang, Dali. 2004. *Remaking the Chinese Leviathan: Market Transition and the Politics of Governance in China*. Stanford, CA: Stanford University Press.

Yang, Xiao. 2006. "Zhongguo kaifaqu 20 nian gongguo fansi" (Reflections on the pros and cons of China's development zones in the past 20 years). *Zhongguo jingying bao*, November 12.

Yang, Yonghua. 1998. "Guangdong liyong waizi jiegou fenxi" (The analysis of the structure of foreign investment in Guangdong). *Huanan shifan daxue xuebao* 3: 35–40.

Ye, Min. 2014. *Diasporas and Foreign Direct Investment in China and India*. New York: Cambridge University Press.

Yeung, Henry. 2009. "The Rise of East Asia: An Emerging Challenge to the Study of International Political Economy." In *Routledge Handbook of International Political Economy (IPE): IPE as a Global Conversation*, edited by Mark Blyth. New York: Routledge.

Yeung, Henry, Weidong Liu, and Peter Dicken. 2006. "Transnational Corporations and Network Effects of a Local Manufacturing Cluster in Mobile Telecommunications Equipment in China." *World Development* 34(3): 520–540.

Yin, Huafang, et al. 2007. "Zhongyang defang zhengfu guanxi he zhengce zhixing li: yi waizi chanye zhengci weili" (Central-local government relations and the capacity of policy implementation). *Guangli shijie* 7: 22–36.

Yuan, Jian. 2006. "Zhongguo zai quanqiuhua jincheng zhong de daijia yu wenti" (The cost and problems for China in the process of globalization). *Zhongguo guancha* (China Observer), September 29.

Yuan, Yongke. 2008. *Di erci kaifa yu jishu chuangxin* (The second undertaking and technological innovation). Beijing: Zhongguo caizheng jingji chubanshe.

Zeng, Fankui. 2004. "Shenzhen dianzi gongye fazhan lishi huigu" (A review of the development history of Shenzhen electronics industry). In *Shenzhen dianzi xinxi chanye nianjian* (Shenzhen Electronic and Information Industry Yearbook), edited by Yimu Cheng, 15–22.

Zhan, Xunwei. 2007. "San lai yi bu qiye falv diwei yanjiu" (A study on the legal nature of san lai yi bu enterprises). *Dongguan falu* (Dongguan Law Journal), July 13.

Zhang, Dunfu. 2001. *Quyu fazhan moshi de shehui xue fenxi* (A sociological analysis of regional development models). Tianjin: Tianjin renmin chubanshe.

Zhang, Gongpu. 1997. "Kuobu mai xiang xinshiji: laizi kunshan jingji jishu kaifaqu de baogao" (Entering the new century: A report from Kunshan ETDZ). *Xinhua Ribao*, September 24.

Zhang, Guohua, and Erzhen Zhang. 2007. *Kaifang tiaojian xia de kunshan zizhu chuangxin zhi lu* (The path of Kunshan's indigenous innovation within economic openness). Beijing: Renmin chubanshe.

Zhang, Kevin. 1999. "Impact of FDI on the Foreign Trade of China." *Journal of the Asia Pacific Economy* 4(2): 317–339.

Zhang, Xuebo. 2012. "Zhongguo xian xing jianmianshui zhidu zhi fansi (Reflections on the current tax reduction and exemption regime in China)." *Xibu faxue pinglun* (Western Law Review) 96(02): 60–70.

Zhang, Yugui. 2008. "Qiu jie 'shichang huan jishu' zhizao ye kunju (Finding solution for the 'exchanging market for technology' dilemma)," *Zhengquan shibao*, August 28.

Zhao, Dingxin. 2009. "The Mandate of Heaven and Performance Legitimation in Historical and Contemporary China." *American Behavioral Scientist* 53: 416-433.

Zheng, Yu. 2014. *Governance and Foreign Investment in China, India, and Taiwan*. Ann Arbor: University of Michigan Press.

Zhi, Qiang, and Margaret Pearson. 2017. "China's Hybrid Adaptive Bureaucracy: The Case of the 863 Program for Science and Technology." *Governance* 30(3): 407–424.

Zhong, Yongyi, and Shucheng Zhang, ed. 2009. *Jiangzheng zhongguo di yige zifei kaifaqu* (Witnessing the first self-funded development zone in China). Nanjing: Jiangsu renmin chubanshe.

Zhou, Maoqing. 1995. "90 niandai yilai Jiangsu liyong waizi de xianzhuang fenxi" (The analysis of the utilization of foreign investment in Jiangsu since the 1990s). *Xiandai jingji tantao* (Contemporary Economic Discussion) 4: 27–29.

Zhou, Yan. 2005. "Shi lun 'san lai yi bu' qiye de hezuo shizhi: dui Guangdong zhusanjiao diqu qiye de yi xiang diaocha fenxi" (The corporative nature of the *san lai yi bu* enterprises: A study of enterprises in the Guangdong Pearl River Delta). *Xiandai guanli kexue* (Modern Management Science) 4: 48–49.

Zhou, Yu, and Tong Xin. 2003. "An Innovative Region in China: Interaction between Multinational Corporations and Local Firms in a High-tech Cluster in Beijing." *Economic Geography* 79(2): 129–152.

Zhu, Boliang. 2017. "MNCs, Rents, and Corruption: Evidence from China." *American Journal of Political Science* 61(1): 84–99.

Zhu, Rongji. 1984. "Guanyu gaijin jishu yinjin gongzuo de jige wenti (Several problems regarding the work of introducing technology)." *Gongye jishu* 2: 21–22.

Zong, Wenwen. 2008. "Gaoxin jishu chanpin jinchukou shou po qian yi meiyuan" (The import and export of high-tech products first time exceeded 100 billion US dollars). *Suzhou Daily*, January 26.

Zuo, Cai. 2015. "Promoting City Leaders: The Structure of Political Incentives in China." *The China Quarterly* 224: 955–984.

Zweig, David. 2002. *Internationalizing China: Domestic Interests and Global Linkages*. Ithaca, NY: Cornell University Press.

Index

Note: Page numbers followed by *f* or *t* indicate figures and tables, respectively.

ALSO PUBLISHED IN THE
SHORENSTEIN ASIA-PACIFIC RESEARCH CENTER SERIES

Zouping Revisited: Adaptive Governance in a Chinese Society
Edited by Jean C. Oi and Steven M. Goldstein (2018)

Poisonous Pandas: Chinese Cigarette Manufacturing in Critical Historical Perspectives
Edited by Matthew Kohrman, Gan Quan, Liu Wennan, and Robert N. Proctor (2017)

Uneasy Partnerships: China's Engagement with Japan, the Koreas, and Russia in the Era of Reform
Edited by Thomas Fingar (2017)

Divergent Memories: Opinion Leaders and the Sino-Japanese War
Gi-Wook Shin and Daniel Sneider (2016)

Contested Embrace: Transborder Membership Politics in Twentieth-Century Korea
Jaeeun Kim (2016)

The New Great Game: China and South and Central Asia in the Era of Reform
Edited by Thomas Fingar (2016)

The Colonial Origins of Ethnic Violence in India
Ajay Verghese (2016)

Rebranding Islam: Piety, Prosperity, and a Self-Help Guru
James Bourk Hoesterey (2015)

Global Talent: Skilled Labor as Social Capital in Korea
Gi-Wook Shin and Joon Nak Choi (2015)

Failed Democratization in Prewar Japan: Breakdown of a Hybrid Regime
Harukata Takenaka (2014)

New Challenges for Maturing Democracies in Korea and Taiwan
Edited by Larry Diamond and Gi-Wook Shin (2014)

Spending Without Taxation: FILP and the Politics of Public Finance in Japan
Gene Park (2011)

The Institutional Imperative: The Politics of Equitable Development in Southeast Asia
Erik Martinez Kuhonta (2011)

One Alliance, Two Lenses: U.S.-Korea Relations in a New Era
Gi-Wook Shin (2010)

Collective Resistance in China: Why Popular Protests Succeed or Fail
Yongshun Cai (2010)

The Chinese Cultural Revolution as History
Edited by Joseph W. Esherick, Paul G. Pickowicz, and Andrew G. Walder (2006)

Ethnic Nationalism in Korea: Genealogy, Politics, and Legacy
Gi-Wook Shin (2006)

Prospects for Peace in South Asia
Edited by Rafiq Dossani and Henry S. Rowen (2005)

Printed and bound by CPI Group (UK) Ltd, Croydon, CR0 4YY
13/04/2025
14656448-0001